The Human Capital Edge

21 People Management Practices Your Company Must Implement (or Avoid) to Maximize Shareholder Value

**Bruce N. Pfau, Ph.D., and
Ira T. Kay, Ph.D.**

McGraw-Hill

New York   Chicago   San Francisco   Lisbon   London   Madrid
Mexico City   Milan   New Delhi   San Juan   Seoul
Singapore   Sydney   Toronto

Library of Congress Cataloging-in-Publication Data

Pfau, Bruce N.
    The human capital edge : 21 people management practices your company must
implement (or avoid) to maximize shareholder value / Bruce N. Pfau and Ira T. Kay
        p.   cm.
    Includes bibliographical references.
    ISBN 0-07-137883-9 (hc.)
    1. Personnel management.   I. Kay, Ira T.   II. Title.

    HF5549.P4555   2002
    658.3—dc21   2001055791

McGraw-Hill

A Division of The **McGraw·Hill** Companies

1 2 3 4 5 6 7 8 9 0 AGM/AGM 0 7 6 5 4 3 2 1

ISBN 0-07-137883-9

*This book was set in Times by the McGraw-Hill Professional's Hightstown, N.J.,
composition unit.*

Printed and bound by Quebecor/Martinsburg.

How to Contact the Publisher

To order multiple copies of this book at a discount, please contact the McGraw-Hill
Special Sales Department at 800-842-3075, or 212-904-5427 (2 Penn Plaza, New York,
NY 10121-2298).

To ask a question about the book, contact the author, or report a mistake in the text,
please write to Richard Narramore, Senior Editor, at *richard_narramore@mcgraw-
hill.com.*

CONTENTS

Foreword

Will Companies Ever Learn?

You would think that we would get it by now—what with the "war for talent" metaphor, the many writings by pundits talking about the importance of intellectual capital rather than physical assets in today's economy, the fact that CEOs and even strategy consulting firms have come to realize that having a great strategy without great people to implement it won't do much. With all these forces in play, one might expect that companies would have done the things required to attract and retain people. One might expect companies to be developing and unleashing the talent and motivation of their people. But they haven't done these things, at least not as much as one might expect. Sometimes I think not much has changed at all.

In the midst of the dot-com craze and the high-tech labor shortage, I was interviewed for *Fast Company* on the topic of "toxic companies." The premise of my argument was that there was not a talent shortage for those places that knew how to treat people. But there was (and ought to be) a shortage of people at places that had created toxic work environments. The e-mails I received after the article appeared were both numerous and depressing. Professional people, managers, engineers, software programmers—the very people that many companies were supposedly struggling to find and keep—wrote me describing bosses who screamed at and threatened them, companies that did not let them make decisions or fully use their abilities, leaders who did not listen, and work environments where what was required to get ahead was mostly the ability to win in some zero-sum competition for status.

Who cares, you might think. The war for talent is over, isn't it? There are now thousands of high-technology workers being laid off, and the job market for MBAs has completely reversed so that people who at one point treated recruiters from consulting firms rudely have rediscovered their manners and are praying for callbacks in a labor market that has gone from feast to famine very quickly.

You should care. It turns out that, as many, many studies have demonstrated, how you manage people affects numerous organizational outcomes, ranging from quality and productivity to the survival rate of initial public offerings and the time to initial public offering for small, high-technology companies. Now, Bruce Pfau and Ira Kay from Watson Wyatt Worldwide, a human resources consulting firm, have done some studies that should help to convince companies, once and for all, that people *do* matter and that there are some straightforward things those companies should do if they are interested in enhancing their performance. These data form the foundation for this book, *The Human Capital Edge*. Some of the data come from a large survey of employees. Some come from an annual survey of compensation practices. And perhaps the most important data come from a study of the connection between shareholder returns earned by 750 publicly traded companies and their people management practices.

I have to make a confession—I believe that shareholder returns should only be one of several measures of corporate performance, and maybe not even the primary one. In a world in which labor is a lot scarcer than capital, it has never been clear to me why returns to capital should be *the* measure of a company's value. Moreover, as Dennis Bakke, the CEO of AES, an independent power producer that operates all around the world, has pointed out, capital is nothing more than the result of past labor. When you work, you earn income. Some you spend and some you save. Those savings, for an individual or a country, become capital. In that sense, capital is the residue of past labor. Why should past labor get a higher priority than current labor? Nonetheless, most CEOs seem to be enamored with shareholder value—stock price—in no small measure because of how their compensation packages have been structured. So who am I to argue?

What the Watson Wyatt study shows is that a) there is a significant correlation between how companies manage their people—assessed by the Human Capital Index (HCI)—and shareholder returns; and b) using panel (longitudinal) data, the evidence is that the HCI predicts shareholder returns much better than shareholder returns predict the HCI. These results help to address the question of causality and the comment, frequently made, that companies that are doing better financially can "afford" to use high-performance management practices. These data show that no company can afford not to use such practices because they lead to vastly superior financial performance. Although some other studies have attempted to statistically assess causality, this study is one of the few to be able to use panel data to resolve the issue.

The Human Capital Edge not only presents a lot of data showing how and to what extent various management practices affect shareholder return; the book also provides concrete examples of what these management practices look like in practice. Executives who read the book should be both convinced by the data and inspired by the examples. This study also covers some of the voluminous evidence, previously gathered, that makes the same point—there is an advantage to be gained by how companies manage their human capital, their people.

By the way, many, although certainly not all, of the findings from this study will strike most readers as common sense. This is because many of the results conform to our intuitions about human psychology and to our own experiences in organizations. For instance, the study found that people want leaders who are in touch, who communicate, who don't just have meetings for the sake of meetings, who don't surround themselves with people who tell them just what they want to hear, who communicate clearly what the company's strategy is and what the business model entails, and who tell the truth. As another example, there are data that indicate that peer recruiting is desirable, first of all because a group is likely to make a better decision than an individual, and second, because people who are involved in hiring others for their team will be more committed to those people and to helping them to ensure they succeed.

I am not troubled by this at all. When people ask me "what's new," I often respond by saying, "you should be asking what's true." Our search for new management fads and the pursuit of novelty for its own sake hasn't gotten companies very far, nor will it. Common sense isn't very common in its implementation in the business world, so companies that are anchored in a few empirically proven, enduring practices will outperform those that institute and then cancel programs depending on the latest seminar that they have attended. I have often commented that if we practiced medicine like we practice management, based on hunch, intuition, and ideology, we would have much more malpractice and a lot of mortality and morbidity. One of the things that Pfau, Kay, and others have accomplished is to bring data and facts to the analysis of human capital management, a very worthy undertaking.

At the end, of course, even though this book offers a lot of ideas, a lot of data, and a lot of wisdom, buying, reading, and even discussing the book will not do much to enhance your company's performance. That's because there is no knowledge advantage without action. Knowing what to do and not doing it doesn't get you very far. One can hope that *The Human Capital Edge* will add enough data and inspiring examples to motivate companies to take those actions that have been recommended in so many writings on how to achieve competitive advantage through people. One can hope that with the demonstration of the connection between people management and shareholder value, finally senior leadership will focus sufficient time and attention—and resources—on this critical dimension of managing the business. We can hope that finally we will begin to close the gap between knowing and doing in the domain of how we manage people.

But changing the management of human capital will not necessarily be easy. Many companies and their leaders have developed bad habits—for instance, layoffs at the first sign of economic distress—that will be hard to change. And most importantly, even though much of what Pfau and Kay have uncovered is "common sense," it is rare in its implementation. Too many businesses try to excel through benchmarking and looking at what everyone else does. One cannot earn extraordinary returns by copying everyone else. If you do what everyone else does, you will probably get about the same results. What *The Human Capital Edge* shows is how to achieve exceptional results. Courage is required to put that knowledge to use.

Jeffrey Pfeffer
Thomas D. Dee II Professor of Organizational Behavior, Graduate School of Business, Stanford University, and author of *The Human Equation: Building Profits by Putting People First* and co-author of *The Knowing-Doing Gap: How Smart Companies Turn Knowledge Into Action*

ACKNOWLEDGMENTS

This book is the result of the collective inspiration and dedication of a variety of individuals. We are especially grateful to Kathryn Callahan, our chief editor, whose ideas, clarity of expression, and enthusiasm made it a reality. We are also indebted to Lisa Swatland, Watson Wyatt's director of marketing communications, who lent her guidance, client focus, and business savvy throughout; Jennifer Arapoff for her editorial assistance and coordination of a diverse team; and Blaire Cahn, our project coordinator, for her invaluable research and organizational efforts to keep us on track and on schedule.

In a book like this, there is also considerable work done by the people behind the numbers. In our case, Richard Luss's immeasurable help and vital expertise with the Human Capital Index™ (HCI) statistical analyses was the foundation for building credible, valuable data.

We are also grateful to Michael Warech and Lily Hui for their help managing the North American HCI study; Diane McKiernan, Jennifer Kohnen, Hugh Mullenbach, and Dan Carpenter for assistance with the WorkUSA2000® research; and Paul Platten and Rick Beal for their leadership in our Strategic Rewards® efforts. Also Diane Lerner and Tamra Lair for assistance in launching the original HCI study in 1999; and Doug

Ross, Steven Dicker, and Richard Stephen for their part in implementing the European HCI study.

We would also like to thank Stanford University professor Jeffrey Pfeffer—a true leader in the area of linking HR practices and business outcomes—for his advice on the original HCI research and analysis.

This book would never have come to light if it weren't for the support and direction of Richard Narramore and the editorial team at McGraw-Hill.

A long list of other colleagues who shared their work and encouragement with us deserve special acknowledgement for their ideas and insights in providing and reviewing material in the book, including Gretchen Ace, Brian Anderson, Janie Brill, Brian Brown, Nancy Campbell, M.J. Carino, Brad Carter, John Finney, Gretchen Heller, Kathy Kibbe, Steve McCormick, Bob McKee, Sam Modoono, Jane Paradiso, John Parkington, Lyle Spencer, Jr., Jim Stewart, Pamela Stout, Steve Vernon, Deborah Wallace, and Valerie Wise.

We'd also like to thank Jeff Hanna, Ralph Schmoldt, and their colleagues at Watson Wyatt's People Management Resources for their research on many of the case studies appearing in the book. Our gratitude is also extended to our clients and other case study participants for their time and willingness to share those best practices.

In addition, a special appreciation goes to Watson Wyatt senior management for their support and encouragement, including John Haley, CEO; John Caldarella, VP Growth and Development; Eric Lofgren, Global Practice Director, Benefits; David Marini, Global Practice Director, HR Technologies; JP Orbeta, Global Practice Director, Human Capital Group; and Sylvester Schieber, VP Research and Information.

Finally, and most importantly, thanks to our wives and children for their patience and support during the year spent writing this book: Amy, Daniel, and Jeremy Pfau; Carol, Sarah, Ben, Jon, Sam, William, and Jacob Kay.

Introduction

It pays—literally—to manage people right.

Companies have long focused huge amounts of resources on many other aspects of their companies, including financial structure, product development, globalization, advertising, and outsourcing, just to name a few. All of this was done to increase shareholder value creation in measurable ways. Some—but certainly not all—tried to use their *human* capital to increase returns to shareholders. But even these companies were shooting in the dark because no one could quantify which human capital programs were linked to the best returns.

The business case for human capital management has been building, and Watson Wyatt's Human Capital Index research has made it airtight. The linkage between superior human capital management and superior shareholder returns—a principal contention of leading management thinkers such as Jeffrey Pfeffer, Dave Ulrich, James Heskett, and Mark Huselid, just to name a few—has been proven.

Our research has identified the specific human resource practices that, when combined and implemented in a superior way, are associated with a 47 percent jump in shareholder value. **Further, our data show that superior HR practices drive financial results more than superior financial results drive HR practices.** (*See Appendix.*)

The statements above are sure to inspire a healthy skepticism—and the challenge presented should not be underestimated. In the chapters that follow, we look at 21 practices to avoid or implement in order to create more value for your organization. In the course of explanation and analysis, we think that skepticism will give way in the face of the numbers.

The Research Behind Our Case

Three key Watson Wyatt studies[1] form the basis for this book. The first is the Human Capital Index (HCI). This research shows—for the first time—a clear relationship between the effectiveness of a company's human capital management and shareholder value creation.

We surveyed more than 750 publicly traded companies in the United States, Canada, and Europe with at least three years of shareholder returns and a minimum of $100 million in revenues or market value. Among the participants: Microsoft, Shell Oil, American Express, Archer-Daniels-Midland, Bank-One Corporation, Ericcson, Gap Inc., Hallmark, IBM, Nokia, Cisco Systems, General Motors, Merrill Lynch, Sara Lee Corporation, Kmart, Rolls Royce, and Textron. We asked respondents (usually the senior-ranking HR executive) how they carry out their human capital practices, particularly in the areas of recruiting, rewards, benefits, culture, HR service technology, and communications.

The results are quantifiable and conclusive: Companies with a high HCI composite score (i.e., very effective human capital management practices) have high shareholder value creation.

Companies with a low HCI composite score (i.e., poor human capital management practices) have low shareholder value creation. Over a five-year period (April 1996–April 2001), the results are striking: a 21 percent total return to shareholders (TRS) for low HCI companies versus a 64 percent TRS for high HCI firms.[2] (See Figure I-1.)

Our research went further to determine exactly which human capital practices, out of the ever-increasing portfolio available to companies, had a positive impact on the bottom line. We discovered that a significant improvement in specific practices in five key areas is associated with a 47 percent increase in market value. (See Figure I-2.)

To put this in perspective, picture two $1 billion companies that have very different human capital strategies (for example, broad versus narrow stock option coverage; flexible versus rigid work arrangements), but are otherwise highly similar (R&D levels; industry; and capital structure).

These two companies could differ in market value four or five hundred million dollars—or more. As discussed in our methodology section (See Appendix), we explicitly tried to measure the impact of market value on *varying human capital practices* while holding all other company attributes constant.

At the other end of the scale, we found that certain practices applauded by conventional wisdom—360-degree review,

Figure I-1. *5-Year Total Return to Shareholders*

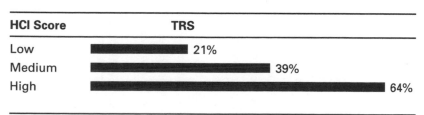

HCI Score	TRS
Low	21%
Medium	39%
High	64%

Watson Wyatt's Human Capital Index®

Figure I-2. *Links Between Human Capital Practices and Value Creations*

Practice	Impact on Market Value	Find details in chapter
RECRUITING & RETENTION EXCELLENCE	**7.9%**	
Company has low voluntary turnover of managers/professionals	1.7%	1
Company has low voluntary turnover of employees in general	1.5%	1
Company emphasizes job security	1.4%	1, 16
Formal recruiting strategy exists for critical-skill employees	0.6%	1
Recruiting efforts are aligned with the business plan	0.5%	1
Employees have input on hiring decisions	0.5%	4
Company has established reputation as a desirable place to work	0.5%	3
Systematic new-hire orientation exists	0.4%	2
Hourly/clerical new hires are well equipped to perform duties	0.4%	2
Professional new hires are well equipped to perform duties	0.4%	2
TOTAL REWARDS AND ACCOUNTABILITY	**16.5%**	
Health benefits are important for recruiting and retention	2.8%	10
High percentage of company stock owned by employees	1.3%	6, 8
Defined contribution and defined benefits plans, combined, important for recruiting & retention	1.3%	10
High percentage of company stock owned by senior managers	1.2%	6, 7, 8

Figure I-2. (*Continued*)

Pay is linked to company's business strategy	1.1%	6
High percentage of employees eligible for stock options	1.0%	6, 8
Company promotes most competent employees	0.9%	6
High percentage of employees participate in incentive/profit-sharing plans	0.9%	6, 8
Defined benefit plan important for recruiting and retention	0.9%	10
Employees have choice regarding benefits	0.8%	10
Defined contribution plan important for recruiting and retention	0.8%	10
Top performers receive better pay than average performers	0.8%	6, 9
Company positions benefits above the market	0.7%	6
Company helps poor performers improve	0.7%	6
Company positions pay above the market	0.7%	6, 9
Company terminates employees who continue to perform poorly	0.6%	6
COLLEGIAL, FLEXIBLE WORKPLACE	**9.0%**	
Company shows flexibility in work arrangements	3.5%	13
Company has high employee satisfaction	1.3%	11
Trust in senior leadership is actively engendered	1.2%	14
Managers demonstrate company's values	1.1%	14
Company culture encourages teamwork and cooperation	0.5%	12
Company avoids using titles to designate status and authority	0.5%	12
Company avoids varying perquisites by position	0.5%	12
Company avoids varying office space by position	0.4%	12

xix

Figure I-2. (*Continued*)

COMMUNICATIONS INTEGRITY	**7.1%**	
Employees have easy access to technologies for communication	4.2 %	19
Employees at all levels give ideas and suggestions to senior management	0.7%	19, 4
Company shares business plans and goals with employee	0.6%	18
High percentage of workforce participates in opinion surveys	0.6%	4
Company shares financial information with employees	0.5%	18
Company takes action on employee survey feedback	0.5%	4
FOCUSED HR SERVICE TECHNOLOGIES	**6.5%**	
Improving service to employees/managers is a key goal in implementing HR service technology	2.3%	Afterward
Reducing cost is a key goal in implementing HR service technology	2.3%	Afterward
Increasing transaction accuracy/integrity is a key goal in implementing HR service technology	1.9%	Afterward

Expected change associated with a significant (1SD) improvement in practice

Watson Wyatt's Human Capital Index®

developmental training, and implementing HR technologies with "softer" goals in mind—did not always add economic value and in fact were often associated with a decrease in market value. (See Figure I-3.) Our hypothesis is that, while there is nothing inherently wrong with these practices, many organizations implement them in misguided ways. Companies must pay special attention to appropriate execution, and for that reason we have categorized these practices into those that require "prudent use of resources."

While the Human Capital Index research provides the structure and framework for our work, we also draw heavily from two other Watson Wyatt studies for a more complete picture. HCI provides the employer viewpoint, while our WorkUSA® 2000 research responds with the employee perspective. WorkUSA® 2000 surveyed 7500 U.S. workers at all job levels and in all major industry sectors. This is the largest, statistically representative and most up-to-date study in existence on the attitudes of American workers. This survey, the sixth conducted since 1987, shows a clear linkage between employee satisfaction and shareholder returns. Companies with high employee commitment have dramatically higher three-year (1996–1998) TRS—112 percent versus 76 percent.[3] (See Figure I-4.) The Employee Commitment Index (ECI) cited below is a single score that reveals whether companies are an employer of choice. It is based on employee responses measuring the degree to which they are satisfied with their job, are satisfied with the company, are proud to work for their company, would recommend it to others, would remain with the company even if offered a comparable job elsewhere, and would rate their company generally superior to others.

A third study, Watson Wyatt's annual Strategic Rewards® survey, shows that organizations that view their people strategy as a source of competitive advantage are outperforming those that do

Figure I-3. *Links Between Human Capital Practices and Impact on Value Creations*

		Chapter
PRUDENT USE OF RESOURCES	**-33.9%**	
Enhancing communication is a key goal in implementing HR service technology	-7.7%	Afterword
Culture change is a key goal in implementing HR service technology	-6.6%	Afterword
Employees have opportunity to evaluate superiors	-5.7%	20
Employees have opportunity to evaluate peers	-4.9%	20
Employees have access to training needed for career advancement	-5.6%	17
Training programs maintained even in difficult economic circumstances	-3.4%	17

Expected change associated with a significant (1SD) improvement in practice

Watson Wyatt's Human Capital Index®

Figure I-4. *Relationship Between Employee Commitment and Shareholder Value*

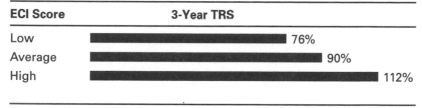

ECI Score	3-Year TRS	
Low		76%
Average		90%
High		112%

WorkUSA® 2000

not by a margin of more than two to one. These companies delivered a median TRS of 109 percent between 1996 and 1998,[4] versus 52 percent for other employers. In addition, the Strategic Rewards® research provides key insights for organizations aiming to recruit and hold onto top-performing employees. It delivers specific details on which compensation and noncompensation programs are most effective at attracting and retaining top performers and compares their viewpoints with those of their employers.[5]

A Summary: What to Do, What Not to Do

As we worked our way through this research, something very complicated began to seem, if not simple, then at least focused. We looked at the various linkages between human capital practices and high shareholder value, and four themes began to emerge. It became clear to us that companies seeking to maximize shareholder value must focus on the following:

1. Achieving recruiting and retention excellence
2. Creating a total reward and accountability orientation
3. Establishing a collegial, flexible workplace
4. Opening up communication between management and employees
5. Implementing focused HR technology

The first four areas form the four main sections of our book; the fifth is the subject of our afterword. In each section we focus on a handful of key practices, each of which is covered in its own chapter. In those chapters, readers will find research (ours and others'), analysis, examples, and case studies all designed to show why and how these practices impact the bottom line. Not only will we present the case for implementing various programs and policies, but we will also present the case for being cautious in implementing others that have less chance of success.

Achieve Recruiting and Retention Excellence

How does a company "achieve recruiting and retention excellence?" First, by committing to it. As the title of our first chapter suggests, organizations must **"approach recruiting and retention as mission-critical."** It takes a daunting amount of two scarce resources—time and money—to get and keep the right talent in place. But missing the mark on people costs even more. Doing the extraordinary amount of work required in developing an easily grasped business plan—and identifying the specific competencies needed to carry it out—is the key.

Our second rule when it comes to recruiting is to **"hire people who can hit the ground running."** Companies like to hire people with potential. They like to hire people who will grow into the job. They like to hire people they think may turn out to be stars. While those are good intentions, the hard economic truth is that they need to hire people who are already stars at doing the same kind of work in a similar environment. No company has the time for any other approach.

The only organizations that will be able to capture those stars will be the ones who understand the following: **"It's not enough to *be a great place to work. Make sure your company is* known as a great place to work."** Only 11 percent of the market is out seeking a job. The brightest stars are most likely in the 89 percent of the workforce that is not actively looking. Companies that focus on refining and then communicating their employer identity will not only net a higher percentage of the people they seek to hire, but they also will have access to that much larger talent pool that is not working with recruiters or reading employment listings.

Having improved the applicant pool with employer branding, companies need to improve their odds of making the right final picks. Where should they seek help? Their own employees. They know the job. They know the environment. They know the culture. **"Involve employees in the hiring process,"** and the percentage of great hires will improve significantly.

Our final thought on excellent recruiting: **"Focus on the basics. People are more alike than different."** It seems counter-intuitive when researchers use detailed data to identify the unique factors that make people tick, but we suggest that companies stop looking so hard for differentiating factors. Over and over again we have seen organizations spending phenomenal amounts of money figuring out what their target employees (say, female Generation Xers) want, and then putting special programs in place to attract them. In our view, this is a serious misallocation of resources. Because what those female GenXers want the *most* from the workplace is exactly what everyone else wants the *most:* pay for performance, opportunity, strong leadership, fairness. It is very difficult for companies to get those big things right, so they should place their resources where they can do the most good.

Create a Total Reward and Accountability Orientation

One of the most important things a company can do to increase shareholder value is to create a true pay for performance environment. That means, **"link rewards to performance."** Put systems in place that will provide significant rewards and great contributions. Use rewards and penalties to improve the performance of subpar players. Remove those who don't improve. Not only will that aim all energy squarely at what the company values, but it will work powerfully in the attraction and retention of top performers. Furthermore, when employees see pay for performance fairly executed, their faith in senior leadership will skyrocket, along with their satisfaction.

Underlying the practice of paying for performance is a philosophy of true accountability, where actions have consequences. If it is to transform the workplace, accountability must begin at the top, which is why companies must **"demand that CEOs hold a significant stake in the company."** A CEO's compensation package should combine stock option grants with stock ownership so that the leader's fortunes will rise and fall with the value he or she creates for shareholders.

Employees, too, will focus on shareholder value if companies make it worth their while. The obvious way to do that is to link compensation to stock price through stock options. The concern has been whether using too many stock options—and the resulting dilution—could hurt total return to shareholders. Our research says that, used wisely, stock options work. Companies should **"offer significant stock-based incentives across the board."**

Just as we believe stock options should be offered at all levels of the company, we believe compensation packages at all levels of the company should have a similar structure. For example, if the CEO has a salary, the opportunity for a bonus, and stock options, so should his division managers, his salespeople, and his assistant. They share risk, they share opportunity, they share reward. **"Synchronize pay, creating opportunities for all employees to soar."**

Benefits may not get as much media attention as stock options, but great benefits go hand in hand with high shareholder value. A competitive benefits package can function as a powerful weapon in the war for talent, as long as its value is conveyed to employees and recruits via an effective communication strategy. Too many organizations neglect to educate their employees about their benefits. **"Don't treat benefits as 'fringe.'"**

Establish a Collegial, Flexible Workplace

"Understand that employee satisfaction is critical to any business goal." Employee satisfaction has come of age. No longer a secondary corporate goal, it has become one of the key factors examined by leading companies when shareholder returns are not what they should be. The link has never been clearer: Satisfied employees result in a better bottom line.

It may have been popularized by the dot-coms, but **"minimizing status distinctions"** has crept even into the most traditional parts of the old economy. When employees marched lockstep from one rung of the ladder to the next, it made sense to emphasize the hierarchy within a company. But the world has turned, and saving special treatment, respect, and rewards for top executives is bad for business.

Flexible work arrangements are no longer outside the mainstream—no longer a perk offered quietly to one or two workers. Flextime is an official program at 89 of *Fortune*'s list of the 100 best places to work. The issue is no longer whether an organization should offer some kind of flexible work arrangement, whether it is flexible hours, job sharing, telecommuting, sabbaticals, or phased retirement. The issue is exactly how to create the flexible programs and policies that are most mutually beneficial to employees and employers. To attract the best people, companies must **"make work arrangements flexible."**

Conventional wisdom says that when it comes to employee commitment, what counts is that employee's direct supervisor. But current research reveals that senior leadership is a fast-growing key component in employee satisfaction. And it is *senior* leadership—not individual managers—that can make or break a transformation effort. Trust in senior leadership is statistically linked to higher shareholder value. The message: **"Don't underestimate the crucial importance of senior leadership."**

Two-thirds of all organizations have experienced some type of "trauma" in the past year, whether it is a merger, acquisition, management restructuring, or downsizing initiative. Learning how to manage change effectively has never been more important, but less than half of employees say that change is implemented well. When change is handled well, commitment levels are almost four times higher, and three-year total returns to shareholders are a whopping 35 percentage points higher. **"Learn how to manage change."**

"Don't assume workers no longer care about job security"—regardless of all the talk about a new deal between employers and employees. Companies whose employees feel secure in their jobs have both a higher total return to shareholders and higher employee commitment than companies whose workers are worried about losing their jobs. While it may not be possible in this environment to guarantee job security, the best companies show employees that they are doing everything they can to avoid layoffs.

Part of a collegial, flexible workplace might be to demonstrate commitment to an employee's development by providing training. But this is a place to tread carefully. Our research shows that depending on how it's handled, training can actually decrease shareholder value—perhaps by training people into jobs that are not available, and therefore sending them into the arms of the competition. Our rule: **"Be cautious about developmental training."**

Open up Communication between Management and Employees

An increase in the "integrity of communications" is also associated with an increase in value. Communications integrity implies more than information flow. **"Make communication open and candid,"** reflecting a trust and respect among and between managers and employees at all levels of the organization. Companies that still approach employee communications with an eye to control rather than candor will not only fail in their objective, but also will keep the organization from achieving higher shareholder value.

In this era of the knowledge worker, nothing differentiates a company more sharply than the extent to which employees can and will share their expertise. Information flow itself has never been easier, thanks to e-mail, voice mail, intranet, and Web access. Companies should "enable employees to share knowledge by capitalizing on technology."

On the other hand, the wrong kind of communication can be a bad thing. Now that it is so easy to ask for employee feedback, more companies are doing it—and then ignoring the results. That spells disaster. Nothing kills employees' commitment faster than the certainty that their opinions are not valued. The best approach: Ask employees for input and then respond directly. **"Ask for employee feedback only if you intend to act on it."**

Another cautionary flag in the area of communications involves 360-degree feedback. If it is not handled correctly, asking employees to evaluate their managers can decrease shareholder value. Similarly, asking employees to evaluate their peers can interfere with teamwork and, again, hurt shareholder value. **"Be careful in implementing 360-degree feedback."**

Our Afterword looks at the evolving—and increasing—expectations for HR's function in an organization—**"Physi-**

cian, Heal Thyself: The Role of HR." Part of successful HR service delivery is understanding the delicate balance between day-to-day operations and big-picture initiatives. It's an important sequence—HR departments have to establish credibility through seamless performance of their basic operations before moving into more strategic areas. In other words, they need to get the house in order first. That means streamlining the payroll process and getting new hires seamlessly integrated before concentrating on defining the organization's strategies and building programs to attract, retain, and support the right workforce. To ensure success throughout the process, HR needs to link the human capital strategies to the right technology solutions.

Our Human Capital Index research showed that if new technology is used for the fundamentals—improving accuracy, service, and cost-effectiveness—it pays off in higher shareholder value. But when HR groups use HR service technology with less clear, less quantifiable goals in mind—"enhancing communication" and "promoting culture"—the technology is actually linked to a large decrease in market value.

Why People Have Such an Impact: The Creative Economy

The numbers we cite in this book will impress true believers and skeptics alike. So what is behind the dramatic results? How can people practices have become so crucial to the bottom line?

The answer is the Knowledge Economy, the Information Age, or, in a term coined by *Business Week* magazine, the Creative Economy. Whatever it is called, the point is that human creativity—ranging from breakthrough Web applications to simple ideas on how to improve productivity—has become the key driver of growth in today's economy.

Perhaps surprisingly, technology has only increased the importance of the human contribution. Far from diminishing the role of people at work, technology has become a great enabler of human creativity.

We all know that it takes far fewer workers today to produce a car than it did 10 years ago. But the numbers from a macroeconomic perspective are stunning: The top 100 U.S. companies in 1999 employed 3 percent fewer workers than did the top 100 companies a decade ago. But the collective market capitalization of these companies in 1999 was a full 500 percent higher than the top 100 a decade ago.

That is the value of human ideas, leveraged by technology.

A War for Talent

The central role of talent in our economy raises a key problem. As articulated by Watson Wyatt's own CEO, John Haley: "The cruel twist in this is that just when we need human capital the most, it is in short supply."

If you look back to the 1980s, employers dominated. Labor was in abundant supply, and there really was nothing like our modern-day shareholder activism. Employers were in the driver's seat. But as we moved into the 1990s, power started to shift. Financial capital became much more important, and Wall Street exerted its influence.

But human capital is now replacing financial capital as the dominant force in business today. It has become the most important source of growth and wealth in the economy.

The Demographics

But just at this crucial juncture, the demographics have begun working against employers. The workforce is aging. Beginning in 1998, baby boomers began turning 50 at a rate of 11,000 per day. As *The Atlantic* describes it, "By 2025, the proportion of all Americans who are elderly will be the same as the proportion in Florida today.... America, in effect, will become a nation of Floridas."[6]

Why is this important? Because the generations behind the baby boomers aren't big enough to replace them. Generation X, ages 22 to 33, is aptly called the baby bust because its fertility rate fell below the rate for zero population growth. Generation Y, ages 6 to 21, is a bit bigger in size—call it a baby boomlet—but it's a smaller wave than the baby boom itself and not big enough to replace the boomers. So, despite the boomlet, the growth rate of the labor force will steadily decline. See Figure I-5.

Finally, here is a surprising demographic data point: The workforce is becoming much *less* mobile. By 2005, the average age of the workforce will be 40.5—and rising. Despite the conventional wisdom—that baby boomers are different, or that high technology has made everyone more mobile—America has been mobile for one reason only: more workers have been in younger, more mobile age brackets. But as the age of the average worker rises, the average tenure on the job for men and women alike will increase dramatically.

The implications for organizations? Going forward, the number of employees in prime management ages will be larger

Figure I-5. *A Shortfall of Young Workers*

Change in Numbers of U.S. Workers

Age of Worker	1970–1980	1980–1990	1990–2000
20–24	50%	-8%	-5%
25–34	72%	23%	-14%

Source: Bureau of Labor Statistics

than ever before. Despite continual downsizing and retirement, older workers will be competing for too few jobs at the top of the pyramid—and the jobs available will likely require a continually evolving set of skills. At the other end of the spectrum, a shortage of younger workers means they can sell themselves to the highest bidder. Despite the recent economic correction in the United States, that creates havoc for recruitment and retention strategies, driving up costs and threatening future competitiveness and profitability. As wage and benefit costs rise, shareholder returns may fall.

The Power Shift: Welcome to the Decade of the Employee

As the environment becomes more precarious for employers, it becomes more rewarding for employees. The boom has inverted the traditional employee-employer relationship: Workers now hire companies. An article in *American Demographics* compares hunting for a job to shopping for stereos. "More of us have begun to 'comparison shop' for employment the same we do for home electronics," writes Rebecca Gardyn.[7]

On the surface, this "Decade of the Employee" poses a cost nightmare for employers: higher pay, more expensive benefits, reduced leverage on most job issues.

But the same economic conditions that are spawning the labor cost problems are also creating the solution. The financial return on people and their ideas can be astronomical. Ultimately, an empowered workforce doesn't cost—it pays—by strengthening an organization and its bottom line. The talent shortage and demands of the New Economy will finally force companies to back up their claims of viewing their people as assets rather than costs. That means doing what's necessary to attract, retain, and motivate this all-important creative workforce: pay for performance, stock options, flexible work arrangements, employee involvement, great leadership.

Investment in people is expensive, but the returns easily justify the expense. Just look at our numbers.

PART

Achieve Recruiting and Retention Excellence

CHAPTER

Approach Recruiting and Retention as Mission-Critical

"Take our twenty best people away, and I can tell you that Microsoft would become an unimportant company."
—Bill Gates, Chairman and CEO,
Microsoft Corporation

In today's business environment, the pace is lightning fast. The competition is tough, smart, and coming from every direction. Those who succeed, in the end, will do so because of the talent they put on the field. Companies without creativity, performance, and problem solving at every level of the organization will never even get into the game.

The problem: that critical talent is in short supply. As a result, recruiting has never had a more significant upside—or a more devastating downside. When companies get the right people in place, there is no telling how high the profits will go. But when they miss the mark on human capital, they will be unceremoniously left in the dust.

As if those stakes are not high enough, you also need to consider the hard costs of a hiring mistake. In his book *Topgrading,* Bradford Smart quantifies the expense of a mishire. He includes the obvious (the executive recruiting fee, the signing bonus, the compensation for someone who does not make a contribution, a severance package) and the less obvious (the costs of disruption and lost time). The result? A mistake at the $100,000–$250,000 salary level costs an average of $4.7 million.[1]

The cost of passing over someone who may have contributed the company's next big idea is untold.

That is the downside. The upside is that having a few of the right people in exactly the right positions will dwarf even a $4.7 million mistake. And having the majority of a company's jobs filled with great fits will create a virtuous cycle that ensures profitability, success, and a continuing stream of top-notch job candidates. The right talent can catapult a company into the kind of financial success that creates a buzz—which attracts more star performers. Increasing numbers of top performers building on each other's talents will take the company to new heights. The resulting profitability and growth will allow for top-notch compensation programs and great opportunity. Attraction and retention will begin to happen naturally.

So how does a company get there? The answer is hardly mysterious: Simply put, the answer is commitment. The tools are out there—using them to achieve excellent recruiting just takes time and focus.

It may at first seem impossible to squeeze more time out of the day for recruiting. Then again, a bad hire drains away more time than any of us would like to admit. It takes weeks to hire even the wrong person. What follows is lost productivity, lost credibility for management, and a wasted investment in getting an employee on board. The legal aspects of dismissal take time.

Finally there is the investment in another search. All the while, the actual work is still on hold. Whatever results the employee was hired to achieve are no closer to completion than they were the day he was hired.

Viewed from this perspective, organizations can't afford *not* to invest the additional time and focus required for recruiting excellence.

What the Numbers Say

Excellent Recruiting and Retention is Valuable, Rare

Watson Wyatt's Human Capital Index research showed that, all else being equal, companies that have better recruiting/retention are worth 7.6 percent more in the market. There were ten specific recruiting/retention practices that were revealed as having the most impact on a company's market value. (See Figure 1-1.) A short discussion of each follows, and more information is found in the later chapters.

Low Turnover Rates

Turnover is the single most important recruiting/retention issue when it comes to affecting financial performance. The best companies do what they need to do to hold onto their talent, and find themselves in a virtuous cycle as a result: it becomes easier to retain people as the company builds on its success. Many companies make the mistake of focusing solely on recruiting new faces, forgetting that the gold mine is in the tested talent that is already up and running. (A full discussion of employee commitment and satisfaction can be found in Chapter 11.)

Emphasis on Job Security

Companies that emphasize job security perform better on the stock market.[2] Of course even successful firms sometimes lay

Figure 1-1. *Links Between Recruiting/Retention Excellence and Value Creation*

Practice	Impact on Market Value
Company has low voluntary turnover of managers/professionals	1.7%
Company has low voluntary turnover of employees in general	1.5%
Company emphasizes job security	1.4%
Formal recruiting strategy exists for critical-skill employees	0.6%
Recruiting efforts are aligned with the business plan	0.5%
Employees have input on hiring decisions	0.5%
Company has established reputation as a desirable place to work	0.5%
Systematic new-hire orientation exists	0.4%
Hourly/clerical new hires are well equipped to perform, with little need for training	0.4%
Professional new hires are well equipped to perform, with little need for training	0.4%

Expected change associated with a significant (1SD) improvement in practice

Watson Wyatt's Human Capital Index®

employees off, but they appear to do so only as a last resort. Seeing that attitude in play increases employee commitment, decreases turnover, and helps turn potential recruits into new hires. (See Chapter 16 for details.)

Recruiting Efforts Support the Business Plan, Company Has Formal Strategy

It seems that recruiting efforts would naturally support a business plan, but that is not necessarily true. There may be a business plan in development in one end of the office, and new people being hired in the other end, but nobody thinks to call a meeting. Even if the thought of it does cross a manager's mind, it is often dismissed, as it is hard enough just finding the candidate with the right mix of skills to get the work done—never mind what lies ahead. But our research suggests that failing to link these efforts is a mistake. Companies that have a formal recruiting strategy for key positions enjoy a financial advantage.[3]

Take, for example, the utility sector. Before deregulation, a typical utility's business plan would have been based on "cost-plus." Pricing and margins were regulated. Companies had to be reasonably reliable and moderately efficient—but no more than that. There was less need to have the best and the brightest workers in their corner. But in this new era, a utility's business plan calls for competing—which must affect its recruiting effort. Utilities were previously engineering- and operations-focused, but now must be marketing- and customer-focused as well. That means hiring for an entirely new set of skills and competencics.

A similar scenario has unfolded at U.S. car companies. When the Big Three owned the market, they could dictate quality standards. They had a proven product with a captured market. The smart staffing philosophy under those circumstances is to hire people who will maintain the status quo, the goal being a few key decision-makers surrounded by good, loyal implementers who adhere strictly to established rules and specifications. But the rise of Toyota and Honda dramatically changed the business environment for the Big Three, demanding new strategies focused on competing. Recruiting efforts were turned around to focus on exactly the opposite type of employee: creative, risk-taking, flexible innovators.

Failing to link recruiting efforts to a business plan can spell disaster.

Employees Have Input on Hiring

Even though team-based approaches have made a splash on the corporate field, few companies truly seek and use the input of current employees when hiring. That is a mistake. Workers know what it takes to succeed in their areas. Plus, team-based decisions are usually of a higher quality than those made by individuals, if

only because they reflect multiple points of view. And any decision arrived at by a team will be supported more strongly by the
team—thus increasing the likelihood that the decision will be
"proven" right. Additionally, team-based interviewing gives candidates a deeper look into the potential work environment,
encouraging poor fits to self-select out of the process. (See Chapter 4 for details.)

Company Known as Great Place to Work

The reason this "practice" is not followed is that executives fail
to make a distinction between being a great place to work and
being *known* as a great place to work. They focus all their efforts
on the former—an approach sure to be appreciated by current
employees and completely unnoticed by the candidates companies would like to attract. (See Chapter 3 for details on how to do
it right.)

New Hires Are Well Equipped and Programmatically Oriented

Choosing candidates who can hit the ground running and making new-hire orientation a priority combine to increase shareholder value by more than a percentage point. Why would a
company choose anyone other than a candidate who is well
equipped for the job? Most likely because another one who
seems very promising can be hired at 75 percent of the cost. Or
because someone seems like a good fit for the company in general, even though she will need some training to handle this particular job. They are bad ideas, both. Sure, hiring someone
based on perceived potential sometimes produces a star. But
that's a risky proposition. Our research shows that hiring anyone but the one best able to actually do the job on day one is a
mistake. (See Chapter 2 for details.)

This principle should be applied even when hiring entry-
level employees who require orientation and training to do their
jobs. A company's best bet is to choose candidates who most

closely demonstrate the skill and competencies needed to succeed. Internships can play a helpful role here.

The specifics provided above by the Human Capital Index are illuminating. But having the corporate house in order when it comes to recruiting—with all of these key programs in place—affects the bottom line and that overall idea will not surprise executives. In fact, the explosive growth of the executive recruiting industry is proof that top management recognizes the importance—and difficulty—of getting the right talent in place. Hunt-Scanlon expects executive recruiting revenues to double to $15 billion by 2005.[4]

And yet, even with all of this professional help, the right people often do not land in the right jobs.

Our research shows that close to 40 percent of companies are reporting that turnover is on the upswing. (See Figure 1-3.)

That is an important indicator. The same study showed a difference of almost 20 percent in the average annual shareholder return between companies with decreasing turnover versus those with increasing turnover. (See Figure 1-4.)

Figure 1-2. *Growth of Executive Recruiting Industry*

| 2000 Revenues | $7.5 billion |
| 2005 Revenues (projected) | $15 billion |

Source: Hunt-Scanlon

Figure 1-3. *Companies Reporting Change in Turnover Compared to Last Year*

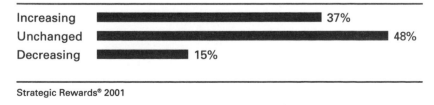

Increasing	37%
Unchanged	48%
Decreasing	15%

Strategic Rewards® 2001

Figure 1-4. *Annual Shareholder Return, Averaged Over Five Years*

Companies with
decreasing turnover   26%

Companies with
unchanged turnover   9%

Companies with
increasing turnover   7%

Strategic Rewards® 2001

How to Do It Right

Know Your Company, Know the Job, Know the Candidate

By and large, increasing turnover is not news to executives. Companies know that it is increasing, and they know it impacts their bottom line. They know a major part of the problem is poor hiring. What they do not know is what to do about it.

The first task for a company is knowing what the organization needs. We had a yellow pages directory company as a client. Historically, their salespeople had gone back and forth between a client and the their own art department, creating and refining the ad that would close the sale. It was typically a lengthy process involving several calls. But as competition increased, the company invested in technology that would enable the salesperson to design the ad on site, working directly with the client to perfect it. But instead of helping the company to compete, sales slipped. Why? The salespeoples' skills matched the old job description rather than the new one, and the company continued to hire the skills and competencies that had succeeded in the old environment, rather than taking the time to identify the new model: people with one-call close ability, and some art skills.

After coming to an understanding of its true needs, the second task for a company is assessing actual candidates against that ideal. Very often, rather than working painstakingly through those two challenges, people would rather believe they can simply "trust their gut." Their mantra: "I'll know it when I see it."

The truth is that spot-on recruiting is almost the opposite of the gut impression. It involves a great deal of preparation both before and after meeting the candidate.

The components of a successful recruitment strategy include:

- A carefully articulated and well-understood business strategy.
- Current and comprehensive turnover data, recruitment cost data and retention "hit rate" data.
- Competency models that directly support the business strategy.
- A thorough "inventory" of current competency demographics (e.g., where in the organization and with whom do necessary competencies reside? What gap does this recruit fill?)
- Accurate and relevant position descriptions, including a description of career/development tracks.
- Intimate knowledge of market/competitor opportunities along with pay and incentive packages.
- A sound candidate evaluation process (e.g., systematic, rigorous evaluation criteria vis-a-vis skills and competencies, culture, fit, background check).

The work involved has to take place at three levels: the organization, the job and the individual.

Establish Organizational Knowledge First

It is critical that HR or the hiring manager be able to articulate the organization's (or business unit's) top strategic goals. If key people in the organization cannot articulate these goals, a clarification process is clearly in order. An ill-defined strategy or one that is not shared by senior management too often results in a poor recruiting and retention record.

For example, a consulting firm decided to enter into the change management business. At great expense, the organization hired people who had a track record of selling change management.

These "stars" failed miserably. Why? Because the consulting firm's strategy was flawed. When working for the competition, these employees had almost always sold change management *after* the firm had sold the client a $100 million system redesign. They could simply walk in and convince management that a mere $700,000 in change management assistance was a small price to pay for a worry-free implementation. But at the new firm, these consultants were trying to sell change management by itself. They were making cold calls. A flawed strategy had resulted in hiring the wrong employees.

A flawed strategy can also wreak havoc on retention. We worked with a credit card company that was incredibly successful at something that is very hard to do: finding people who would carry a balance but pay a portion of their bill every month. Their financial performance was impressive. But a new COO inexplicably got the company into various side businesses that had nothing to do with their strengths. The traditional side of the business was continually called on to support failing start-ups. The talented, knowledgeable talent at the "cash cow" became frustrated, and left in droves. As a result, the core business began to fail. Eventually, the COO had to sell the company.

(Incidentally, turnover and retention data are another important element of organizational knowledge. Knowing what kind of people leave, and why, helps a company identify the critical success factors of the position being filled.)

Detailed Job Information Comes Next

A competency model should outline the knowledge, skills, behavioral style, and personal characteristics that spell success for this position. Accurate and current position descriptions, including development opportunities, are critical to successfully recruiting professional new hires. Well-written position descriptions serve to set and manage expectations at the outset for both the candidate and the hiring manager. Explicit articulation of expectations is key to successful performance and retention.

Current knowledge of internal and external pay and reward practices is another critical element in successfully recruiting job-ready candidates.

Finally, Assessment of the Individual

Once the relevant organizational and job information is clearly articulated, assessment of the individual candidate begins. The old-fashioned interview is still important, but these days a great deal can happen before and after that. Detailed questionnaires—sometimes completed via the Internet—can save everyone time by eliminating obvious mismatches. Carefully developed interview guidelines bring less obvious factors to the surface, such as tenacity, tolerance for ambiguity, customer service orientation, or leadership style. Interview guidelines can also be helpful in ascertaining the extent of an employee's knowledge in key areas—computer skills, financial products, jewelry, or whatever is required. Furthermore, psychological testing can play a role in providing an extra level of reassurance.

Fortune Magazine's "World's Most Admired Companies" research (see appendix for details) demonstrated that leading firms use numerous methods to minimize risk when hiring. Pre-employment screening and testing is much more pervasive and rigorous in these organizations than in companies in general. Nucor, Bertlesmann, and Disney all rely heavily on assessment centers, psychological tests, and structured interviews that have been designed to identify ideal candidates. Procter & Gamble combines these methods with prehire internships that provide "trial runs," yielding a more telling indication of how well employees and employer will match over the long run.[5]

Competency-Based Selection

Companies are increasingly relying on formally stated "competencies" throughout the process outlined above. Individual competencies are the applied skills, knowledge, behaviors, and personal attributes of the organization's workers that are critical to its success.

1. Skill: A proficiency or ability to perform a specific physical or mental task. A skill is mastered through appropriate learning and verified through demonstration. Examples are machine operation, budgeting, word processing, problem solving, negotiating, listening.
2. Knowledge: A detailed understanding of a specific content area typically acquired through formal education, professional training, or work experience. Examples are accounting, marketing, engineering.
3. Behavior: Actions and expressions that can be observed. Examples are cooperativeness, empathy, risk-taking, team work, fleet-footedness.
4. Personal Attribute: A characteristic, trait, or consistent response that is typically innate and causes things to occur. It cannot be directly observed. Typically, attributes are not of a nature that enables training and are not scalable—they tend to be present or not present in a person, rather than by degree. Examples are integrity, honesty, and self-confidence.

An organization might identify a handful of "organizational" or "core" competencies that it expects to see in all employees. There might be additional competencies important to different business units, and still more, of course, for an individual job.

What is the point of this kind of formalized approach? Identifying and communicating competencies helps to define and communicate an organization's strategy. It helps employees to understand the strategy and achieve its goals. The many roles that competencies can play in an organization include:

- Articulating what the organization values
- Providing a common language for employees and managers to describe value creation
- Linking pay, promotions, and growth directly to what the organization values

- Guiding employees and managers regarding what is expected and how value is defined even in times of dramatic change and restructuring

Competencies serve as a powerful communication vehicle to focus all members of the organization on the skills and activities that will create both value and wealth.

Defining the Culture

Identifying competencies begins with a knowledge of the organization's culture. That allows organizations to look beyond skills requirements and select for personality as well. For example, *Fortune*'s "World's Most Admired Companies" research showed that Disney recruits people with an "up personality," and Federal Express searches for people who have "the courage of their convictions to think outside the box."[6]

Competency Modeling

One way to uncover the competencies that are most valued by a corporation is to "model" the star performers. Rather than trying to pull characteristics and skills out of the air, and arguing about whether they are the right ones, executives can simply point to an employee and say, "We need more of those." This is the essence of *criterion-based* competency modeling.

There are various methods of gathering competency information (including focus groups, observation, and questionnaires), but the most widely used is the structured interview. The approach typically begins with interviews with both the star performers and their managers. Using behavioral statements, interviewers work with the employees to get an idea of what the success profile looks like for each job. The organization then creates a draft model (group of competencies) by combining the results of the interviews with biographical information and test and performance data.

To further refine the model, a questionnaire based on the draft is usually created. It would ask those who were initially interviewed questions like: How often do you perform behavior A? How important is behavior A to the job? To what extent does behavior A differentiate a star performer from an average performer? The scores from the questionnaire can be used to create an index, which is used to eliminate behaviors with low scores from the model. The idea is to isolate the most significant competencies.

Once the model is finalized, the company can use it as a foundation for recruiting, selection, testing, training, and development.

This strategy is often employed by the best firms, as revealed by *Fortune's* "World's Most Admired Companies" research. These organizations continually develop and refine competency models for all of the jobs, roles, and functions that form the foundation of their culture. Their models tend to go beyond desired experience, skills, and educational levels, moving into softer areas like attitudes, character, personality, and intellectual style. During the course of that research, Peter Baback-Letmathe, the CEO of Nestle, said his company's selection process not only "looks into candidates' files, but also into their character."[7]

At many successful firms, judging character is neither arbitrary nor intuitive. Formally defined competencies and behavioral traits—deemed compatible with the organization's mission and culture, as well as with the demands of a specific role—provide the guidelines. The end result: a great balance between impressive on-paper accomplishments and key personal characteristics.

Sealing the Deal

Getting the Top Candidate to Accept

Finally, the hiring team knows which candidate it wants. Its members have used all of the tools at their disposal, and they feel confident that they have discovered exactly the right match for the position. Suddenly a new concern surfaces: What if the candidate says no?

To keep that from happening, companies should heed the following:

- The obvious: offer good opportunity.
- Be prepared to pay top dollar to attract top talent—even if it means incurring some dissatisfaction from existing executives who are paid less. It may be necessary to cut unprecedented equity deals with some hires, particularly if they hold significant option positions with their present employer.
- Emphasize the nonmonetary rewards, for example the opportunity to impact on the organization, work/life flexibility, or the chance to work on cutting-edge projects.
- Permit great flexibility in packages relative to individual situations. Negotiate, and do not assume that any fixed package will work.

Finally, it is important to develop a sales pitch that describes the opportunities for top talent in a way that fits with the kind of people the company is trying to recruit. The intent is to present the candidate with an employment situation and a work challenge uniquely suited for him. This increases the chances that a great candidate will accept an offer, and be motivated enough to do a terrific job for a long time. Further, it lessens the dependence on compensation alone to attract people, and thus may reduce costs somewhat.

How does a company refine its sales pitch? By treating it as a marketing issue, with the product being the company and the customer being the recruits. Using a traditional market research approach works well. Focus groups with existing and potential "customers" can determine desirable and perceived "product features" that will help establish "brand identity."

A final tip: start selling potential employees on the company long before they are candidates for a specific job. How? By making sure that the company is known as a great place to work. (See Chapter 3 for details.)

E-Recruiting Takes the Lead

A commitment to excellent recruiting now means a move to the Web.

Web Is #1 Source for Exempt Employees

The Employment Management Association's most recent survey shows that traditional sourcing strategies have given way to the Internet as the primary source of recruitment for non-hourly employees.[8] (See Figure 1-5.)

Figure 1-5. *Source of Exempt Hires*

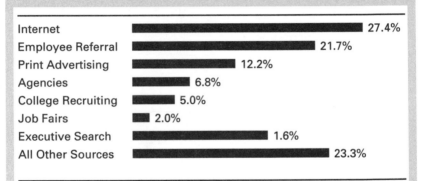

Internet	27.4%
Employee Referral	21.7%
Print Advertising	12.2%
Agencies	6.8%
College Recruiting	5.0%
Job Fairs	2.0%
Executive Search	1.6%
All Other Sources	23.3%

Source: SHRM/EMA 2000 Cost Per Hire and Staffing Metrics Survey

And professional recruiters have already found fertile ground in the Internet. Revenues in this new segment of the recruiting industry are forecast to grow from $250 million in 1999 to almost $8 billion in 2005, according to Hunt-Scanlon Advisors' market intelligence unit.[9]

A growing number of companies themselves are searching the Internet in pursuit of top candidates: 35 percent of companies with over 10,000 employees had at least one recruiter dedicated strictly to Internet recruiting, according to the Association for Internet Recruiting.[10]

It's Cheaper...and Faster

Part of the Internet's attraction is its low cost. Averaging less than $500 per hire, it is significantly cheaper than the $10,000 to $30,000 involved in an agency or executive search.[11] (See Figure 1-6.)

Figure 1-6. *Cost Per Hire by Source*

Source of Hire	Cost
Job Fairs	$99
Employee Referral	$320
Internet	$444
Print Advertising	$943
Other Sources	$1,734
College Recruiting	$2,510
Agencies	$9,187
Executive Search	$30,655

Source: SHRM/EMA 2000 Cost Per Hire and Staffing Metrics Survey

A Well-Designed Web Site Can Be Very Effective

Corporations are finding that their external Web sites are powerful recruiting tools:

- Forty-two percent of all candidates have been directly influenced to pursue employment at a company by a company Web site.[12]
- Ninety-four percent of undergraduate and MBA job seekers are visiting corporate Web sites to obtain company information and decide where and whether to apply, making the company Web site the primary online source of information for student job seekers.[13]
- Student job seekers spent close to three hours per day on online job search activities.[14]

But not all Web sites work as hard as they could to pull in top candidates. To make the most of all of that valuable traffic, organizations should make sure to:

- Update current openings and the campus recruiting schedules regularly.
- Use tags (like "jobs," "career," "work," or "employment") on the home page and employment page to make the site easier to find.
- Briefly describe the resume/hiring process for candidates.
- Allow anonymous submission of resumes, which will help attract passive candidates.

Handling the Increased Volume

While an increased applicant pool is mainly a blessing, the added volume to process can be a curse. Some companies are using on-line assessment tools to do generic prescreening ("Are you willing to relocate?") to cut down on the number of resumes. Others are even doing some position-specific prescreening on-line—testing, for example. But because that can become tricky to handle legally, most are opting for a more advanced Applicant Tracking System (ATS) to cope with ever-increasing numbers of applicants.

How It Plays Out

Commitment to Recruiting Takes Semiconductor Stock to the Top

Company:	LSI Logic Corporation
Revenues:	$2.09 billion
Number of Employees:	7,000
Industry:	Semiconductors
Location of Headquarters:	Milpitas, California

For more than 18 years, LSI Logic has been a top global supplier of custom, high-performance semiconductors, designed and manufactured for communications applications including broadband, data networking, wireless base stations, cell phones and digital set-boxes. In 1999 LSI Logic's stock price jumped 319 percent, making it the fourth-highest-performing S&P 500 stock.

LSI Logic is a company that does, in fact, "approach recruiting as mission-critical." Its philosophy is to attract the most qualified and talented engineers in an ethical and respectful manner. Recruiters' emphasis on training and teamwork has helped LSI Logic attract a strong workforce that has propelled the company to the top of the semiconductor industry.

There are four keys to the successful recruiting work at LSI:

1. *Comprehensive Recruiters Meeting*
   Twice a year, LSI Logic holds two-and-a-half-day meetings for recruiting staff that bring employee and contract recruiters together for training, networking, and sharing of internal best practices. One or two vendors are usually invited to provide training on the vendor's tools and products. The meetings have helped integrate practices and cultures following LSI Logic's acquisition activity by forming common goals and a knowledge base.

2. *Excellent Communication with Executive Management*
   The Corporate Staffing Director meets with LSI Logic's executive vice presidents at least once a year to align recruiting efforts with corporate goals. The team reviews business plans, predicts hiring needs, sets goals, and plans a budget. These meetings open direct lines of communication between functions to ensure that the company's needs and expectations are met. Once the strategy for staffing is linked to corporate goals, staffing managers develop their goals and action plans.

3. *Innovative "Internal Agency" Recruiting Model*
   Under the leadership of the Corporate Staffing Director, the recruiting function has taken on an agency

model in its support of attracting and hiring employees for the majority of LSI Logic's U.S. and Canada locations. Rather than waiting for applicants to come to them, this model teaches staffers how to find potential employees. Recruiters market the company to potential employees, and production numbers drive their success.

4. *Attractive Corporate Culture*

One way LSI Logic attracts talent is by presenting itself as a desirable place to work. The fact that the company is the world's number one ASIC provider attracts engineers. In addition, employees in this high-tech environment are not expected to work 80 hours a week. Executive Vice President and CFO Doug Norby said recently, "We're like a 20-year-old start-up company." This statement suggests that while LSI Logic has history, its strong financial base supports an entrepreneurial spirit. People can be creative, take risks, and make an impact. The company is small enough that individuals are recognized for outstanding performance.

The History: Acquisitions Force New Approach

In 1998 LSI Logic acquired Symbios as well as several other smaller companies. These acquisitions nearly doubled the size of the organization overnight. The desire to integrate staffing practices after the acquisitions was one factor that drove implementation of the corporate recruiters' meetings.

The paradigm shift to view recruiting as an internal agency came from the Corporate Staffing Director's observations of current market conditions. She recognized that the intense challenge to attract talent, especially high-tech talent, extended beyond Silicon Valley to everywhere LSI Logic operates. Two years ago when companies needed to fill a position, recruiters would call a local employment agency, put an ad in the newspaper, post the job on the Internet, and wait for applicants to pour in. Recruiters would then sort through the flood of applicants for a skill set match. When the employment market changed, LSI Logic implemented a recruiting style that emphasizes searching out passive job seekers. By providing information about LSI Logic and developing relationships with passive job seekers, the company believes that when passive job seekers want to change companies, they will check out LSI Logic.

Twice-Annual Recruiters Meeting

LSI Logic thoroughly researched whether the acquired companies had corporate cultures and philosophies that would fit with its own. For example, in the staffing area, all companies shared the same philosophy: hire the right people in an ethical manner, not just to fill positions. After the acquisitions, LSI Logic and the acquired staffing managers met and communicated concerns and ideas regarding the integration of their practices. They discussed and combined their best practices and began to develop recruitment practice standards.

One by-product of integrating practices was the creation of the biannual recruiters meeting. In 1998, LSI Logic began to bring employees and contractors from around the world together twice a year for training and networking.

Input from employees and contractors on designing the training meeting's format and training topics is critical to the training meeting's success. The Director of Corporate Staffing is responsible and accountable for coordinating the event. She creates a tentative agenda that supports corporate goals and passes it along to employees who supply ideas for accomplishing the goals. Directors and managers also coordinate the agenda with other functions that interact with staffing.

Typical sessions on the agenda include these from the July 2000 meeting:

■ Interviewing/Closing Workshop: This workshop provided concrete examples and solutions to the training meeting's theme that an organization helps create its own turnover by hiring the wrong people. An outside consultant helped the Director of Corporate Staffing design a class that marries the skills of behavioral interviewing with the finer points of "closing" an offer. Selling candidates on the company is as important as exploring their technical skills and approach to work. This workshop was presented at the training meeting to solicit feedback from recruiters. The workshop has since been included in hiring managers' training.

- Sourcing Training: A section of the four-hour sourcing training session included an exercise where participants broke into seven groups. Each group leader gave group members names of people to contact and a general script of what to say. The goal of the cold-call exercise was to gain some experience sourcing passive job seekers. The leader made the first call, modeling the skills for others in the group and creating a safe environment to learn and/or practice these skills. Recruiters attempted to acquire as many referral names as possible from the person they called. Making the exercise a contest to see who could gather the most referrals energized the training, which was one of the most effective activities of the meeting.

- Hire.com Update and Training: LSI Logic uses Hire.com's front-end hiring tool on its company Web site to solicit resumes and build relationships with passive job seekers. A recruiter spoke about the advantages of the tool and trained colleagues to use it. Because one of LSI Logic's strategies is to form relationships with passive job seekers, the company maintains a full pipeline of potential candidates. LSI Logic uses noninvasive methods, such as sending corporate articles or news releases, to keep interested people informed about LSI Logic. About 80 percent of its recruiting efforts are targeted toward passive job seekers.

In addition to training and energizing staffing recruiters, this meeting also serves as a great opportunity to connect recruiting efforts to other company functions. Good communications between staffing and other departments (e.g., compensation, relocation services, and hiring managers) is essential for finding the right candidates.

Measurable Goals and Results

LSI Logic measures the percentage of positions it fills within 75 days of an opening. It also tracks the number of offers accepted, its goal being a 75 percent acceptance rate. It aims to keep cost-per-hire below $20,000. In addition, the company also tracks the number of new hires that stay with the company for at least one year, as well as the number of employees hired with H-1 visas.

In fiscal year 2000, LSI Logic made 710 professional new hires in North America, doubling the original target. College and intern programs exceeded goals as well.

The strong internal recruiting environment and effective use of the Internet, which accounts for 60 percent of new hires, have helped decrease external agency utilization by 40 percent.

LSI Logic's internal agency model is attractive to recruiters who formerly worked at traditional external agencies and did not feel a strong connection with the organizations for which they were recruiting. The company's approach enables contractors to attend training meetings and share expertise. Contractors are often excellent sources, and making them a part of the recruiting team creates the opportunity for sharing knowledge. The sales-like attitude of former external agency employees has revived positive competition among recruiters due to the focus on teaching, encouragement, and teamwork.

The biannual recruiters' meeting is one of the most effective means of improving recruiting outcomes at LSI Logic. Its success is reflected in the enthusiasm of attendees, whose numbers doubled over the last year and continue to grow. In addition to serving as a great training vehicle, the recruiters' meetings help foster a strong team environment—and serve as an obvious symbol of the company's ongoing commitment to approach recruiting as mission-critical.

CHAPTER

Hire People Who Can Hit the Ground Running

"They say you can teach a squirrel to fly.
But it's easier to hire the eagle."
—David McClelland, noted personality and
organizational psychologist

A stack of resumes is the most popular place to look for the right hire. Unfortunately, it is not the best place. A better bet: the halls of the competition. Because the best candidate for any job is already doing it—someplace else—and is not out looking for work.

The pace of business is such that it now presents a significant financial advantage to hire people who are already as close as possible to being able to do the job—whether at the highest ranks of the company or over where the employees are paid by the hour. A learning curve is now a luxury. There is a negative ripple effect to hiring people who are not up to the task—every employee who has to deal with them is rendered less efficient. Companies cannot afford to hire people who will not hit the ground running.

This, of course, presents a few problems. If the people who can do the job are already employed and not looking for a job, how will the company find them? What's more, how can they be enticed to leave? Finally, what about the fact that even a well-equipped new hire can flounder for months attempting to navigate an organization's idiosyncrasies?

Finding a way over those hurdles is imperative because making sure an employee can step in and make an immediate contribution is worth a significant increase in market value.

What the Numbers Say

Increase Company's Value by Making Sure People Can Do Their Job on Day One

The days of calmly accepting that a new employee means lost time, lost productivity, and lost revenue are over. The alternative? Companies can fight back against the negative financial effects of turnover by hiring well-equipped candidates and following up with comprehensive new-hire orientation. (See Figure 2-1.)

Figure 2-1. *Links between Hitting the Ground Running and Value Creation*

Practice	Impact on Market Value
Systematic new-hire orientation exists	0.4%
Hourly/clerical new hires are well equipped to perform duties	0.4%
Professional new hires are well equipped to perform duties	0.4%

Expected change associated with a significant (1SD) improvement in practice

Watson Wyatt's Human Capital Index®

Why It Works

The Best Predictor of Future Behavior Is Past Behavior

Because of the nature of the effort, there is simply a great deal of error involved in trying to predict a candidate's future performance. It is impossible to be certain that a candidate will excel in this company, at this time, with these challenges. The best a company can do is to reduce the unknowns by hiring as closely as possible to the actual situation. Ideally, an organization will hire someone doing this exact job, in this exact industry, in this particular business climate, from a company with a very similar culture. The further a company moves away from that in concentric circles, the further it gets from the likelihood of a good hire.

Why is that the case? Because past behavior is the best predictor of future behavior. There may be someone in that stack of resumes who could be a great sales manager. He says he can do the job. The hiring team believes he can do the job. Should they hire him? No. They should go out and find the person who already *is* a great sales manager. Because what someone has already done is a better predictor of future performance than verbal skills and interview behavior ever could be.

Of course, hiring the sure thing means missing the diamond in the rough. The company will miss discovering a star. But it will also miss hiring a complete disaster. It hurts to reject people who might have been great. But it is devastating to hire someone who cannot perform—and the higher the level, the more painful it is. The best strategy is to increase the likelihood that the ultimate hire will be a winner.

Watch the Performance in the Environment

Baseball teams do not interview a player—they give him a tryout. Nobody interviews a Broadway performer—they give her an audition. So why would anyone depend solely on an interview to select an engineer? Or a manager?

Verbal skills have a lot to do with some jobs, and absolutely nothing with others, and yet people still place so much stock in the interview process that they are amazed when it fails them. The truth is, it is a very misleading selection methodology. When people are in interviews, they exhibit interview behavior. On the job, they do job behavior. The two may have nothing to do with each other.

Fortune's "World's Most Admired Companies" research is filled with examples of leading firms who do everything they can to ascertain exactly how the candidate will perform in the job environment. (See Chapter 1.)[1] Internships, three-month trial periods, assessment centers, and simulations are not unusual at top companies, and that is because they have learned that nothing is as predictive as on-the-job performance.

Skills versus Competencies

Current best-practice thinking these days is that organizations have made a mistake in emphasizing skills over personal characteristics. The concept is that a better approach is to select for factors like style, personality, drive, and initiative. A company can always train an employee to make a sales pitch, they say, but not to be outgoing and personable.

For example, a large (but quiet) financial services firm that specializes in selling to high-net-worth individuals was having trouble finding enough recruits from traditional sources on Wall Street. Consultants advised them to hire people with the right style and selling experience from other fields, and then teach them financial services. The results were a disaster. The training time was much longer, the turnover was higher and—most importantly—the new-style hires were not producing the financial results the company needed.

A consulting firm had a similar experience. After numerous problems with hiring corporate executives into senior consulting positions, it instituted a hard-and-fast rule: All senior hires must have consulting experience. The result: A radical reduction in senior consultant washout.

Our advice is somewhat counter to the current trend. We agree with David McClelland: "I suppose you could train a squirrel to fly, but it's easier to hire an eagle." The best answer: Hire somebody who is already capable of doing the job from both a skills *and* a personality standpoint.

Good sales skills and a persuasive personal style were necessary—but not sufficient—for success at the financial services firm mentioned above. Knowledge of personal finance, tax law, and trusts were necessary as well. Of course, this knowledge could be trained, but only at great expense, time, and moderate risk of failure.

Likewise, domain knowledge and experience with "internal selling" did not prepare the corporate executive for success in the consulting world where the pace, level of ambiguity, and requirements to close business in the face of stiff external competition were critical.

Finding Someone Who Isn't Looking

What are the odds of finding that "eagle" who is soaring beautifully somewhere else? Not good for a company limiting its search to active job seekers. Active seekers make up a remarkably small percent of the market. That means most of the market is not out there looking for a new job. Companies that want to tap into the pool of people who are capable of getting down to work on the first day must have a strategy for connecting with passive job seekers. A key component in that strategy is creating a corporate brand. Candidates need to know about the company and have a strong, positive image of it. A highly visible

Web presence is crucial. (Chapter 3 deals with employment branding in detail.)

Luring the Candidate Away from Another Job

A company that wants to entice a happy top performer away from her current job will need to be an employer of choice. It will need to be special. It will need to offer something that is valuable enough to make her want to make the change.

Watson Wyatt asked top performers what would most attract them to a new situation. And we asked employers what they thought top performers were looking for. We found a problem: There are significant gaps between the answers from these two groups. For example, employers far underrate the importance to employees of such things as flexible work schedules or opportunities for advancement in their decision to join or leave a company. That means many companies are working very hard (and using scarce resources) on the wrong tools.

Looking at the compensation reward plans that employers currently use, we can draw two conclusions. One, there are

Figure 2-2. *Effectiveness of Compensation-Based Reward Plans in Attraction*

Reward Plan	% Responding "Very Effective" Employees/Employers	% of Companies with Plan
Paying above market	72% / 33%	43%
Stock grant programs	53% / 30%	40%
Sign-on bonuses	51% / 31%	70%
Group incentives	47% / 15%	31%
Technical pay premiums	44% / 21%	31%
Project incentives	40% / 13%	24%
Exempt overtime (time off)	35% / 6%	15%
Exempt overtime (cash)	31% / 6%	17%

Strategic Rewards® 2001

Figure 2-3. *Effectiveness of Noncompensation-Based Reward Plans in Attraction and Retention*

Reward Plan	% Responding "Very Effective" Employees/Employers	% of Companies with Plan
Opportunities for advancement	79% / 30%	60%
Job redesign	69% / 18%	21%
Learning new skills in current job	65% / 26%	62%
Career development	57% / 20%	48%
Flexible work schedules	56% / 29%	64%
Increased sharing of rationale behind decisions	56% / 23%	34%
Use of competencies for career path/development	53% / 16%	24%
Increased investments toward business literacy	50% / 12%	15%
Clear articulation of employer/employee relationship	38% / 23%	22%
Reduced work week	36% / 30%	19%
Work at home	36% / 28%	33%
Sabbaticals	29% / 26%	6%

Strategic Rewards® 2001

serious gaps in employers' and top employees' opinions of what works. And, two, employers are investing in some plans that are not highly valued by employees and neglecting some plans that are.

While the gap regarding "paying above market" is the largest, that may reflect top-performing employees' sense that as company stars, they are entitled to higher pay. (It might be a bad idea, by the way. The Human Capital Index research found that paying top performers significantly more than average performers correlates with a .8 percentage increase in a firm's market value.)

While signing bonuses are widespread, other plans that are valued nearly as much by employees—group and project incentives and technical pay premiums—are used much more rarely. Employers may want to consider shifting resources within reward budgets. In fact, group incentives and project incentives are considered far more important by employees than companies think they are.

Pay is clearly not the only way to create different deals with different employees. Opportunities for advancement, the opportunity to learn new skills, and having a job redesigned to fit their skills are very important to employees, yet employers consistently underestimate the value of these softer rewards.

Another element to consider: Retention starts before the hiring process is even complete. New employees are immersed in cultural issues, historical education, benefits explanations, and a throng of other confusing bits of information in their first few months on the job. Offering a systematic new-hire orientation conveys a sense of sincerity from the organization and provides much-needed structure during this time. In fact, turnover is greatest in the first one to three years of tenure. Mentoring new hires through a well-designed program helps to combat those odds by personalizing the relationship with the employee and providing a smooth transition into the company.

Look Close to Home

A final word on how to hire people who hit the ground running: look within the company. Most organizations fail to tap into their own talent reserves enough. No one could be as up to speed on a company as its own employees, and watching a worker perform within the company is more revealing than any "work simulation" effort could be. Companies should make every effort to move great employees around within the organization, rather than watching talent walk out the door.

How It Plays Out

Firm Makes the Most of the Web to Attract Passive Seekers and Speed Hiring Process

Company:	KLA-Tencor Corporation
Revenues:	$1.6 billion
Number of Employees:	5500
Industry:	Computer Products
Location of Headquarters:	San Jose, California

Formed in 1997 as a result of a merger between 20-year-old KLA Instruments and Tencor, KLA-Tencor is the leading producer of tools used to identify semiconductor defects during manufacturing. Sixty percent of its revenues come from sales outside the United States, and every major semiconductor manufacturer around the world uses KLA-Tencor technology.

At KLA-Tencor, new employees hit the ground running. And most of the time, they hit that ground in 60 days or less from the time the company starts the hiring process. What does that mean for KLA-Tencor? Higher productivity. Higher morale. Higher shareholder value.

How does the company do it? KLA-Tencor's approach to its current objective—to get to a 60-day-or-less time-to-hire—is typical in that it showcases KLA-Tencor's emphasis on netting the passive seeker via the Web. Here's the outline of the current program:

- Develop and implement a new Web strategy: Updated and improved efficiencies in the Web staffing portal, including new tools and a new look and feel, will enable employees to effectively participate in workforce management issues.
- Formalize a sourcing strategy that utilizes Web presence: Innovative methods using the company's Web site to attract passive job seekers are underway. For example, competitors visiting KLA-Tencor's Web site will see job

opportunities scrolling in a banner window on screen.

- Develop and implement a new advertising campaign: KLA-Tencor aims to brand itself as the employer of choice. Historically, the company's branding has focused on product lines rather than employment. For instance, inviting people to be a part of producing or selling a KLA-Tencor product. The new advertising effort will present KLA-Tencor as a financially sound company with stimulating and challenging opportunities, and invite potential employees to share the excitement.

- Improve offer acceptance time: KLA-Tencor is launching new products offered by its Web solutions vendors that will improve efficiencies in HR's hiring practices, allowing the company to shave off valuable time during the offer-to-acceptance cycle for new hires.

- Implement improvements to increase efficiency and effectiveness of hiring process: KLA-Tencor developed and is testing a job profiling process that streamlines the hiring process and can also be used to assess employee development after hiring. Beyond just determining whether the employee has the necessary skills to do the job at the time of hire, the job profiling process can also be used in workforce planning, performance assessment, compensation decisions, and leadership development opportunities.

Job Profiling Process Ensures New Hires Are Ready to Perform

KLA-Tencor's director of corporate staffing recently introduced the Job Profiling Process, a pilot program for nonexempt positions in the manufacturing group. Job Profiling is one method the company uses to ensure that it hires individuals ready to perform their job.

The first step is creating job profiles for the different positions within a function. Unlike job descriptions, job profiles define four levels of proficiency based on 10 to 15 job elements. The profile acts as a leveling device to differentiate and define skills and experience for each position and grade level within a job function. For example, Exhibit 1 shows a job profile for a test technician/engineer, clearly defining the role/purpose and primary responsibilities. The leveling requirements outline four job levels, minimum experience qualifications, and seven job elements with core competencies that apply to all four levels (See Exhibit 2). A description of computers/software skills, as shown in Exhibit 3, is one of the seven job elements. The description defines computers/software competencies and the required skills for each level within that job function.

Once job profiles are defined, applicants can be sourced and screened based on the skills and experience required in a position. In addition to creating profiles and recruiting based on job profiles, the staffing department has designed behavioral interviewing questions that assess the skill sets for each profile. These tools make hiring much easier for managers and recruiters alike.

Critical to the success of this effort is the quality of information provided by the hiring managers within each function. Hiring managers are responsible for providing job characteristics and responsibilities for the different roles incorporated within the job profiles. Accuracy of the job profile directly impacts how effective sourcers and recruiters can be in finding appropriate candidates for interviews.

In addition to supporting efficient recruiting and hiring efforts, job profiles can be used to determine the following:

- Career Development: The job profile provides promotional criteria for each position as employees develop skills at different levels of their positions.
- Performance Management: Job criteria can easily be translated into measurable performance goals and

objectives used to assess employee performance on an
ongoing basis.

- Improvement: If an employee is not performing a crite-
  rion adequately, training and development opportunities
  can be identified to help improve performance.

- Cross-Functional Redeployment: Creating job profiles in
  other functions will make redeployment of employees
  between groups easier if one product line is experiencing
  a slowdown and another a boom.

Competition for Talent Drives Well-Integrated Approach

From a company philosophical standpoint, staffing is an integral
part of the human resources function. KLA-Tencor's human
resources function does not view recruiting and staffing activities
as isolated events, but rather as part of a larger process. The cycle
of employment at KLA-Tencor begins with attracting and orien-
tating employees, but the ultimate goal is retaining top performers.

Another reason for the well-integrated staffing approach is
that KLA-Tencor faces the same challenges as other high-tech
companies in Silicon Valley: attracting and retaining the best talent in a very competitive marketplace. Manufacturing-level
employees typically come from schools with an electronics focus,
while professional-level employees have software, mechanical, or
electrical engineering degrees. Many of KLA-Tencor's professional-
level employees have doctorate degrees. The organization wants
to continue to employ very bright and well-educated people.

One way KLA-Tencor is trying to attract talented people is
by building an expansive new office an hour northeast of San Jose
in an area called Livermore. Within the next three-to-four years,
this complex will accommodate 2400 employees. By providing a
job site away from the Valley with less-expensive housing and
shorter commutes, KLA-Tencor hopes to appeal to more potential employees via its attractive location. It will be one of the first
large companies to locate in the area.

Annual Strategy Creation Starts the Process

With involvement from the director of staffing, KLA-Tencor's human resources function goes through an annual strategy creation process. At the start of every fiscal year, leaders examine changes in the environment from both an internal and external perspective, so as to either confirm that the right programs and activities are currently in place or identify a need to reset their objectives.

Resetting HR and staffing objectives begins with soliciting strategic information from the executive team regarding corporate-level objectives. HR then identifies how it can do its part to meet those objectives by crafting questions for the senior executive management team that focus on areas where HR's expertise can contribute to KLA-Tencor's success. Using feedback from these questions, HR directors hold an off-site planning meeting to formulate HR's strategic objectives, which are then broken down into specific tactics tied to each objective.

Obtaining executive support is the critical element contributing to the successful implementation of the different staffing programs. HR solicits support during the annual needs assessment with the executive team. Additionally, HR meets every quarter with the senior executive group to summarize existing programs. If more funding is needed for new programs, HR provides justification using a Return On Investment (ROI) model.

Staffing Structure

KLA-Tencor's U.S. staffing department could essentially be considered its own division. It utilizes both functional and divisional recruiting models to employ nearly 70 contractors and employees. Recruiters actually work for and report to the director of staffing, but are aligned and deployed by division. Utilizing contractors in this model allows KLA-Tencor to scale the recruiting function based on the needs of the organization.

The staffing department applies a functional recruiting model to fill positions within the corporate group, which encompasses all the basic components of the organization, such as marketing, customer support (field engineers, telephone response people, etc.), sales, human resources, finance, legal, facilities and information technology. Because these positions are not categorized by product or technical skill sets, recruiters for the corporate group focus on job type, rather than division. As a result, the functional recruiting model seems to be most effective in this environment.

A divisional recruiting model is used to fill positions within the rest of the organization. Recruiters are assigned to a division, primarily divided by product group, utilizing a shared resource model. They work in teams with a lead recruiter acting as the contact point for HR and the vice president of that division. The lead recruiter builds a team of seasoned recruiters and staffing coordinators based on the product group or division's current requisition load. These working relationships help align the recruiter's activities with managers' needs.

Delivery of 1600 Quality Hires in 2000

KLA-Tencor is experiencing phenomenal growth. In just one year its revenues jumped from about $700 million to $1.6 billion. A strong indicator of the quality staffing organization at KLA-Tencor is the delivery of 1600 new hires in fiscal year 2000. Original projections were to hire about 700 employees. The function was able to continue building the staffing group, delivering new hires at a pace that far exceeded original expectations. The size of the staffing department, nearly 70 employees and contractors, demonstrates strong senior management commitment and willingness to provide the resources necessary to attract and retain qualified employees.

Overall, KLA-Tencor's staffing function is providing the company with strong applicants, tools that managers need to make good hiring decisions, processes for encouraging employee retention and satisfaction, and guidelines by which to gauge performance.

Exhibit 1

KLA- Tencor Division Job Profile
Production Test Technician (PTT)/Associate Test Engineer (ATE)

Role/Purpose:
Performs a variety of routine and nonroutine tasks that ensure production quality standards are met. Builds equipment and systems to meet customer expectations and against equipment specifications.

Primary Responsibilities:
- Performs the set-up, calibration, testing, and troubleshooting of circuits, components, system integration and mechanical assemblies.
- Determines and may develop test specifications, methods and procedures from blueprints, drawings and diagrams.
- Tests and troubleshoots assemblies and/or final systems.
- Completes rework on assemblies and/or final systems.
- Prepares technical reports summarizing findings and recommending solutions to technical problems, as required.
- Assists in the selection and set-up of specialized test equipment, as needed.
- Performs a variety of routine and nonroutine tasks to ensure that production quality standards are met.
- Builds systems that meet customer expectation/specifications.

Leveling Requirements:
Leveling requirements build as the level of job increases. For example, if PTT Level 2 includes a set of requirements, ATE Level 1 requirements include the PTT2 requirements in addition to the additional specific requirements listed for ATE2. Definitions for requirements are listed on Exhibit 2. Please refer to grid on next page.

Core Competencies:
Core Competencies are equally applicable to and expected of all positions.

Dealing with Ambiguity • Composure • Priority Setting • Organizing • Timely Decision Making • Patience • Perseverance • Time Management • Quality • Problem Solving • Technical Learning • Written Communications • Teamwork • Safety

Exhibit 2

Job Level	Minimum Qualifications	Assembly/Test/ Troubleshoot	Knowledge of the Prod. Control Process	ECR/ECO Generation	Technical Support	Computer/ Software	Test/Meas. Equipment	Mtg. Process Document
PTT2	AA in electronics or equivalent experience							
ATE1	AA in electronics and 3 years exp. or equivalent; BSEET preferred							
ATE2	AA in electronics and 5 years exp. or equivalent; BSEET preferred							
ATE3	AA in electronics and 7 years exp. or equivalent; BSEET preferred							

Exhibit 3

Computer/Software

Definition:
Performs assembly/test and troubleshooting of computers (materials)/peripherals and related software using procedures and drawings.

1.0 PTT and ATE1
- Duplicates software from all media types.
- Demonstrates a basic knowledge of computer peripherals and their internal components.
- Shows a working knowledge of computers.
- Fully assembles/tests and troubleshoots computers using procedures and assembly drawings.
- Trains others.

2.0 ATE 2
- Knowledgeable with computer hardware and software.
- Demonstrates ability to assemble/test and troubleshoot to pcb level.
- Installs nonproduction/prereleased hardware/software and modify setup/configure files.

3.0 ATE 3
- Demonstrates full understanding of a computer and its internal components as well as the functionality of these components.
- Demonstrates extensive troubleshooting skills.
- Works with engineer to identify and evaluate replacement components/peripherals and to develop qualification tests.

CHAPTER

It's Not Enough to *Be* a Great Place to Work— You Have to Be *Known* as a Great Place to Work

"Recruiting is marketing, without the budget."
—Unattributed

Most companies miss out on 89 percent of the potential candidates for a job opening.[1] Why? Because most of the workforce is not actively seeking employment. Winning the war for talent means finding a way to tap into that rich but elusive segment of the market.

Becoming a desirable place to work is obviously a primary component of a successful recruiting strategy. But it is only by being *known* as a great place to work that will give a company access to a dramatically larger applicant pool.

One approach to increasing awareness and boosting a company's image is adding several popular programs (e.g., flextime, stock options, and "flat" organizational style) and publicizing them in every manner possible. While that won't hurt the recruiting effort, it's not likely to help a company tap very far into the passive market, either.

The companies that recruit most successfully have very strong corporate identities. They know who they are, they know where they are going, and they know how they want to get there. They have a unique corporate culture and a style that permeates everything they do. When that kind of identity has been the driving force behind adding programs like flextime and stock options, potential candidates begin to feel a gravitational pull toward the organization.

What the Numbers Say

Bring Passive Seekers into the Pool

Companies that successfully establish a reputation as a desirable place to work are worth 0.5 percent more in the market, according to our Human Capital Index research.

We believe that is because they have access to the best talent, including workers who are happily employed elsewhere—perhaps by the competition. According to "Building an Employer Brand That Attracts Talent," a 2000 study by WetFeet.com, only 11 percent of the market is actively seeking a new job.[2] (See Figure 3-1.) It is that small fraction of the market from which unknown companies must draw their human capital.

There is even more bad news for those companies that are not top-of-mind for potential employees: The best players get in and out of the job market quickly. (See Figure 3-2.) They receive offers from two-thirds of the companies with whom they interview.

Companies not on these candidates' radar screens will certainly miss out on them. To lure this kind of catch, a company must be on the short list of employers of choice.

Figure 3-1. *Size of Passive Seeker Market*

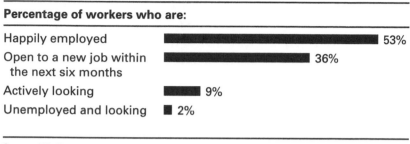

Percentage of workers who are:	
Happily employed	53%
Open to a new job within the next six months	36%
Actively looking	9%
Unemployed and looking	2%

Source: WetFeet.com

Figure 3-2. *Experienced Professional Candidates' Typical Search*

Average number of applications:	8 companies
Average number of interviews:	3.2
Average number of offers:	2.1

Source: WetFeet.com

Establishing an Employer Brand

The most traditional way to earn a spot on that short list is through business success. *Fortune's* "The World's Most Admired Companies" study showed a strong link between a corporation's financial success and the ability to attract and retain the best people.[3] Good people want to work for winners. Having those key players on board, in turn, creates a cycle of success: continually improving performance and an unending stream of top talent.

While financial success plays a helpful role in establishing a company's reputation as a great place to work, it is not enough by itself. The best organizations go a step further and build an "employer brand." Employer branding is essentially the identification and communication of the unique identity that encompasses a firm's values, systems, policies, and behaviors. It conveys the company's style and future direction to potential employees.

A company's external brand sends promises to the market, which includes customers, shareholders, competitors, and potential candidates. In order to leverage that brand internally and turn it into an employer brand, companies need to understand where employees fit into the delivery of those promises. What is expected of them? What can they expect in return? Companies need to align values, systems, policies, and behaviors, externally and internally.

For example, if a company's external brand claims it is more innovative than its competitors, it needs a workforce that delivers innovation. In turn, that workforce will expect innovation to be rewarded and celebrated.

Following that external promise through to its logical conclusions, in terms of both employer and employee expectations and behavior, is what employer branding is all about. Consistently delivering on those promises over time is what will make an employer brand take hold—and make a company known as a great place to work.

So, it is no surprise that employer branding is on the upswing. According to a study by The Conference Board called "Engaging Employees Through Your Brand," of HR executives whose companies have focused on their employer brand, 85 percent said they had begun the process in 1996 or later, and 25 percent had done so in 2000.[4] Why the sudden interest? Many organizations are going through identity crises of sorts, thanks to the proliferation of mergers, acquisitions and spin-offs. To head off confusion, they are working hard to pinpoint—this time for employees, in addition to consumers and shareholders—exactly what differentiates them from the competition.

In fact, it appears that many companies may be rushing to manufacture the image of an appealing brand—an approach that is sure to fail. Branding only works if the image builds on a company's true strengths. For example, one of our clients was trying to position itself as a nimble start-up in an industry of old monoliths. But many members of the senior team were from the old-line companies, and they managed their organizations based on that experience. The day-to-day reality for employees—how processes were executed, how decisions were made—was not consistent with the external brand.

As the authors write in *The Expressive Organization,* "It is not enough to insist on employee behavior that fits whatever management deems a desirable image. Setting up systems to control behavior with rewards simply gets businesses superficial compliance. The behavior that supports a corporate reputation or brand needs to be more deeply rooted, it needs to rest in the organization's identity."[5]

How are Brands Communicated?

Once a company determines its employer brand—identifying the employee message as it translates from the external brand—what does it do next? How exactly should a company use an employer brand to attract and retain talent?

The first step is to get a sense of how the organization is currently perceived by the target audience. (Even companies that have not yet embarked on an official branding effort may have a reputation of some kind.) Organizations must survey those who have accepted and declined their job offers to get a sense of the company's perceived positives and negatives. They must contact professional recruiters and college placement officers to gain an understanding of the image that has been projected about employment with the corporation. And they should talk to existing employees, too, as they refer candidates and conduct interviews. Only after gathering a sense of what its audience is currently thinking can an organization begin to address misalignment between their employer brand messages and the audience's perceptions. Once gaps are identified and addressed, the company is ready to bring together and communicate a more comprehensive brand.

By Employees

When it comes to communicating the brand, often the most powerful step is the personal example of the CEO, business unit heads, and leadership throughout the organization. This is the cornerstone of making an employer brand stick. When it succeeds, current employees become walking recruiters. They can communicate the vision, and they embody the values.

One reason employees' viewpoints are so important is that experienced candidates find out about new jobs primarily through their own networks. According to WetFeet.com, 71 percent of candidates rely heavily on their colleagues and professional contacts as an information source in their job searches.[6]

Good employer branding will help employees bring passive seekers under the tent. Companies need to create strong employee-referral programs to reinforce and make the most of that natural behavior.

A client of ours improved recruiting success dramatically by using references from its far-flung alumni group. In fact, the company turned the usually negative reality of turnover into an enormous positive by utilizing past employees as an excellent source of referrals. (That is obviously another good reason to keep employees satisfied at work.)

By Consumer Advertising

Whether intentionally or not, consumer advertising plays a role in employer branding. Candidates are more likely to pursue employment at companies with which they are familiar. WetFeet.com found that 63 percent of job candidates were aware of their employer before accepting a job. It also found that commercial advertisements are just as likely as employment-specific ads to attract or drive away candidates for employment.[7] A company's consumer advertising can work against its recruiting efforts. For example, a well-known, diversified financial services company was finding it hard to attract and retain energetic, entrepreneurial salespeople, traders, and managers. An employer branding study of the perceptions of potential recruits revealed that the company was viewed as reliable, solid, conservative, and traditional—the precise objectives of their consumer and corporate image advertising. Unfortunately, that image turned off energetic and entrepreneurial recruits.

In this world of instant communication, it is nearly impossible to successfully maintain separate external and internal messages. It is imperative for companies to align their messages. For example, say a toy manufacturer faces the same dilemma as the financial services company above. It wants to communicate "safety first" to consumers, but needs to hire innovators (who might be turned off by that message alone) to stay competitive. The manufacturer simply needs to refine its message. To appeal to both safety-minded consumers and creative workers, the brand should communicate that the company delivers a safe product by hiring the smartest, most innovative engineers. The next step for the company: hire, attract, and retain smart, creative engineers who design safe toys.

By Marketing Materials

To be successful, an employer brand should be incorporated into everything a company produces, and anything it does. According to WetFeet.com's research, a wide variety of outlets pull candidates into the applicant pool. That includes the obvious—employment advertising—but also corporate Web sites, general Web sites, media coverage, and networking.[8] (See Figure 3-3.) Many companies are now including employee profiles on their Web sites as a way of displaying their brand. By describing "a day in the life," companies can convey a sense of what it is like to work there—giving potential candidates a taste of the brand. All of these efforts should work together to convey a single, cohesive corporate brand that appeals to the target employee.

In reviewing its plan to communicate the employer brand, organizations should not underestimate the reach of job listings. While it is true that only 11 percent of the market is actively seeking a job, a much larger portion of the market reads those listings. WetFeet.com found that 47 percent of passive seekers regularly

Figure 3-3. *Influences in Decision to Pursue Employment at Specific Company*

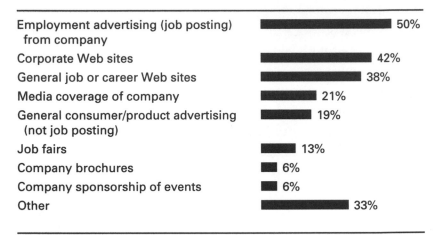

Source: WetFeet.com

scan just to see what the market is offering.[9] Smart companies view their job postings as an ideal place to disseminate messages about their brand.

Does Branding Work?

A strong brand may convince someone skimming the ads to take the time to read further, having already heard the company is a great place to work. Or a candidate may be willing to listen to a headhunter because of the strength of the company name. The Conference Board surveyed HR executives, who reported employer branding to be useful in four key ways.[10] (See Figure 3-4.)

Making sure a company becomes known as a great place to work is an expensive undertaking. And when the competition ups the stakes by embarking on the same effort, it costs even more. But the payoff is worth it. Branding raises awareness and promotes positive impressions among target candidates, in turn increasing the candidate pool, the acceptance rate, and finally the quality of eventual hires.

Figure 3-4. *What Employer Brands Are Most Useful for*

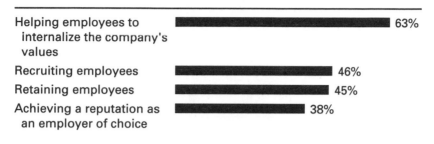

Helping employees to internalize the company's values	63%
Recruiting employees	46%
Retaining employees	45%
Achieving a reputation as an employer of choice	38%

Source: Engaging Employees Through Your Brand, 2001, The Conference Board

How It Plays Out

Utility Becomes the Best; Broadcasts the Message

Company:	CP&L Energy, Inc.
Revenues:	$3.36 billion
Number of Employees:	7119
Industry:	Utilities
Location of Headquarters:	Raleigh, North Carolina

CP&L Energy, Inc., formerly Carolina Power & Light Company, provides electricity and energy-related services to 1.2 million customers in North and South Carolina. In addition to approximately 166,000 natural gas customers, it has diversified nonutility operations including power marketing and trading, telecommunications services, and energy services and management.

The following two statistics go hand in hand:

- CP&L Energy was judged one of the top five places to work in North Carolina in 1999.
- CP&L Energy outperformed the S&P Electric Index for six of the eight years before 2000.

CP&L Energy made no bones about it. They were out to "create a talent pool with a depth and breadth that is the envy of the industry." Their first step was to become a great place to work. Their second step: Make sure the world knew about it.

Generous Packages, Great Environment

The company invested significant resources in their commitment, offering employees the best in pay and benefits, employee involvement and opportunity, job security, work/family concerns, and workplace environment.

At CP&L Energy, Corporate Employment works closely with the company's Compensation and Benefits Section to ensure that job offers are highly competitive. This often means adjusting wage scales frequently to respond to changing market conditions. In addition to benefits like comprehensive health benefits, a generous 401(k) plan, and a savings program with up to a 100 percent employer match when the company meets certain performance goals, CP&L Energy also offers intriguing "extras." For instance, security-conscious employees at the company's headquarters can catch CP&L Energy's parking lot shuttle, which runs until 10 p.m. to a variety of parking lots in the downtown Raleigh area. Workers can opt to work an extra hour a day and take every other Friday or Monday off. New parents are eligible for up to four months off and get paid time off for school events and family obligations. The company also offers employees up to $5250 a year in tuition reimbursement.

Employees as Recruiters

The result? Current employees can't stop boasting about what a nice place CP&L is to work. The statistics are impressive: Of the 2000+ resumes CP&L Energy receives each month, approximately 14 percent are referred by current employees. Even better, those referrals account for more than 28 percent of the company's actual hires. CP&L Energy essentially has 7000 effective, low-cost recruiters among the loyal staff. Since current employees are such a solid resource for recruiting new workers,

CP&L Energy offers referral bonuses for successful job matches in selected areas and often features successful referral stories in its employee publications.

Using Publicity

Also working to pull great candidates into the pool is the media coverage that the CP&L has gotten for being such a great place to work. As mentioned above, *Business North Carolina Magazine* selected the company as one of the top five places to work in North Carolina, based on five objective measures: pay and benefits, employee involvement and opportunity, job security, work/family concerns, and workplace environment. The company was also honored with a Platinum Rule Award, sponsored by the *Triangle Business Journal,* which is awarded to companies with an exceptional track record in the areas of family-friendliness, culture, work environment, incentives, and people development. In 1999, CP&L Energy won the competition's top overall award, the Crown Award. It won the family-friendly and people development categories of the competition for the year 2000.

Communicating to Specific Targets

In addition to working on general publicity, CP&L works hard to develop relationships with certain groups it has targeted as effective sources for future employees. Competing against high-tech employers and well-known national companies, CP&L Energy works hard to educate potential applicants about exciting opportunities in its rapidly changing industry.

CP&L Energy offers hands-on cooperative and internship programs through select colleges and universities. Students get practical job experience before graduating from college, and CP&L Energy gets the opportunity to "road test" highly motivated students. The company's goal is to attract 10 percent of new employees from college-related programs.

CP&L Energy has also targeted the military, with a goal of 6 percent of annual new hires from this sector. A Corporate Employment staff member serves as a liaison to the military bases and helps coordinate job interviews among military personnel who are preparing to transition or retire from the service. In general, CP&L Energy has found that military candidates tend to possess the core skills the company values and that they have historically been a good cultural fit for the company.

The company also targets traditional African-American colleges, associations for professional women, and the Hispanic community to ensure diversity in its employment pool. Bilingual (English-Spanish) employees are in particular demand for the company's customer call center.

Intranet/Internet Outreach

CP&L is also successfully using technology to reach candidates. Approximately 18 percent of new hires come from the company's Web site. Resumes from Internet job boards increased by more than 50 percent from 1999 to 2000. Automated job openings on the company's intranet site provide opportunities for employees to learn about and apply for vacancies two weeks prior to public posting. Current employees have first opportunity to apply, and their bios are sent automatically to the hiring manager when the employees choose an on-line option to submit their resume. Jobs that aren't filled internally are posted on the public Web site and on various Internet job boards. Employees are encouraged, sometimes via incentives, to provide referrals, particularly for hard-to-fill positions.

Systematic Selection Guide

Part of the brand message sent via the Web and all outreach efforts is that there's a clear corporate culture at work: The people at CP&L are smart, profit- and results-oriented people who know how to get things done and embrace change. To make sure that branding stays accurate, the company has developed a systematic selection guide that helps interviewers assess each candidate against a set of five core skills deemed essential for CP&L success:

- Thinking style—Possesses intellectual and problem-solving abilities.
- Business orientation—Understands importance of profitability and shareholder value.
- Change orientation—Anticipates and responds to need for change.
- Performance orientation—Focuses on measurable results.
- Intensity and urgency—Shows responsibility for commitments and deadlines.

The selection guide gives hiring managers a clear road map to assist them in selecting employees who can successfully perform the job at hand as well as develop and contribute to the company's success over time. An on-line/CD-ROM hiring guide is available to managers as well.

Interview Participation by a Variety of Team Members

CP&L is a perfect example of a company that understands the importance of corporate branding. But it's also a bit of a segue into our next chapter, which is on the importance of involving employees in the hiring process. Most CP&L candidates are interviewed by a variety of team members, which may include a diverse mix of peers, subordinates, and/or customers. By exposing the candidate to a number of stakeholders, who all use the Systematic Selection Guide as their basis for evaluation, a comprehensive assessment can be made regarding the candidate's abilities in each of the core skills.

Diversity among interviewers highlights different views, thinking styles, and expectations and helps ensure that candidates will perform successfully in a culture that appreciates and rewards differences. This further strengthens the selection process.

Overall, CP&L Energy feels that its recruitment strategy is an important cornerstone of the company's success. "Drawing the right talent into our organization helps us succeed as a corporation, as well as helping employees exceed their career goals, build solid leadership skills, and attain professional success. Recruiting is a challenge, but we're winning—one person at a time," says one of CP&L's key HR managers.

CHAPTER

Involve Employees in the Hiring Process

Everyone is empowered and responsible for recruiting at Microsoft—whether you're a receptionist, a janitor, a cook, a software design engineer, or a shuttle driver…It's been our culture and our philosophy that if you work at Microsoft—and you typically have an ownership stake in the company—it's in your best interest to make sure the best and the brightest people are hired."
—David Pritchard, HR director, strategic recruiting

"It's like working a crossword puzzle. If you get four people together, their chances of solving the puzzle are greater than if the four work separately."
—HR director using a hiring team

Employees want to know that their coworkers are pulling their own weight. Compensation is increasingly tied to group performance.

Self-directed work teams are common. In this atmosphere, employees experience the damage from a weak link immediately, and personally. And the reverse is also true: Terrific colleagues can translate into a stronger company and a more satisfying work environment for everyone.

That means there is a lot at stake when a position is open, and employees want to have a say in how it is filled. Our research indicates that companies would do well to listen to them.[1] Organizations that make an effort to give employees a voice in hiring decisions have higher shareholder value. While most firms give a nod to the concept—asking employees to help draft job descriptions, or competency profiles—the more successful companies are taking it a step further, including employees in interviewing, analyzing the candidates, and making the final selection. The results: higher quality hires who can hit the ground running, improved teamwork, higher employee satisfaction, and a better bottom line.

What the Numbers Say

Ask Employees Which Candidates Are Best

It hardly takes a stack of research to let executives know that hierarchy is out and the team concept is in. But until now, there has been no research supporting the idea that this swing in philosophy applies to hiring practices as well. But the Human Capital Index has finally provided compelling evidence: Companies that seek employee input more often in making selection decisions have greater market value than companies that do not. In fact, companies in the Human Capital Index study that did a good job on employee involvement enjoyed 0.5 percent more market value compared with companies that placed less emphasis on employee input.

Although it may be difficult to find precise figures that tie team hiring into the bottom line, there is research showing that team decisions are better and that companies using more input from employees in general have higher shareholder value. "Studies of employee involvement...document average productivity growth in the range of 18 to 25 percent, with self-directed work teams setting record levels in the 50 to 100 percent range," according to the Employment Policy Foundation's paper on "Estimating the Potential Productivity and Real Wage Effects of Employee Involvement." The Foundation estimates that employee involvement was directly responsible for 70 percent of the annual increase in the productivity growth rate of the U.S. economy in the late 1990s.[2]

Our own research further confirms the importance of employee involvement, with the Human Capital Index showing that companies who have created a culture of employee input are worth close to two percent more in market value. (See Figure 4-1.)

WorkUSA® 2000 research supports the HCI findings. According to that study, companies with high employee commitment have much higher shareholder returns than those with low employee commitment: 112 percent three-year (1996-1998) total returns to stockholders versus 76 percent. One of the two most important factors in generating that commitment is trust in senior leadership, and two of the major factors driving that trust are: 1) acting on employee suggestions, and 2) encouraging employee involvement. Clearly, asking employees to play a role in selecting their colleagues hits these key hot buttons.

Figure 4-1. *Links Between Employee Input and Value Creation*

Practice	Impact on Market Value
Employees at all levels give ideas and suggestions to senior management	0.7%
High percentage of workforce participates in opinion surveys	0.6%
Company takes action on employee survey feedback	0.5%

Expected change associated with a significant (1SD) improvement in practice

Watson Wyatt's Human Capital Index®

Not every company using an employee hiring team has official "self-directed work teams," but the concepts are similar. Self-directed teams are fully responsible for a well-defined segment of work. The members—as opposed to a manager—take responsibility for planning, setting priorities, coordinating, and problem solving.

Hiring teams share a fundamental philosophy with self-directed work teams, and the same type of corporate culture fosters both. Therefore, it buttresses the argument for using hiring teams to examine the impressive impact of self-directed work teams in general on shareholder value and employee commitment. (See Figures 4-2 and 4-3.)

Figure 4-2. *Self-Directed Work Teams and Shareholder Value*

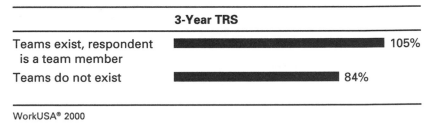

WorkUSA® 2000

Figure 4-3. *Self-Directed Work Teams and Employee Commitment*

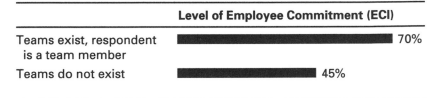

WorkUSA® 2000

Ask for Employee Input Only if You Intend To Act On It

As noted above, our numbers generally show that high levels of employee input across the board (not just in hiring decisions) contribute to financial success. But we do offer a warning:

companies who survey their employees must take some action based on the results, or risk a *decrease* in value.

Our *WorkUSA®* research shows that companies who implement a survey but fail to take subsequent action deliver significantly lower shareholder returns than those who never take the survey in the first place. (See Figure 4-4.)

There are two possible explanations. The first is the theory that the survey builds up the hopes of the workforce, and the inaction dashes them. The resulting drop in faith in senior leadership contributes to a decrease in productivity and overall company performance. However, the *WorkUSA®* research does

Figure 4-4. *Employee Surveys and Shareholder Value*

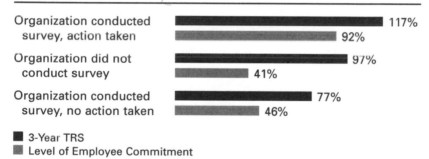

Organization conducted
survey, action taken — 117% / 92%

Organization did not
conduct survey — 97% / 41%

Organization conducted
survey, no action taken — 77% / 46%

■ 3-Year TRS
▨ Level of Employee Commitment

WorkUSA® 2000

not show the dramatic drop in employee commitment that should go along with that explanation. Instead, we believe that companies who survey but then fail to act are demonstrating a pattern of behavior that contributes to poor financial performance: indecision, lack of commitment, poor follow-through, and the squandering of resources.

The bottom line: companies absolutely should survey their employees. And then, as with any other business initiative, they should follow up their investment in the results with an action plan. The next step: watch for a significant increase in shareholder value.

Why It Works

Teams Make Better Decisions, Members Get Invested

A quick analysis shows it is no mystery why companies that give employees a say in new hires have better results:

Quality of New Hires

Team decisions are often better than decisions made by individuals, particularly when the decisions are based on ambiguous and incomplete information—like hiring decisions.[3] Getting multiple points of view about candidates simply provides a richer set of data, enhancing the quality of the choice. Making the right choice on talent, over and over again, is arguably the most important thing a company can do to create value.

Realistic Job Previews

Who better to give job candidates a realistic preview of work life than the people who already work there? Giving job candidates realistic job previews enables them to self-select into or out of a particular employment situation without decreasing job acceptance rates. In addition, giving candidates an early glimpse of the work situation is associated with greater levels of job satisfaction and retention, both of which contribute to value creation.[4]

Satisfaction with the Workplace

Today, people at all levels expect to be involved in decisions that affect them. The greater their involvement, the greater their satisfaction with the workplace. For better or worse, selection decisions very directly affect an employee's work life. Satisfaction with the workplace correlates with retention, thus minimizing the cost of turnover and enhancing the value of the enterprise.

Stake in the Candidate's Success

When a hiring decision is made unilaterally (by the boss), the consequences (good or bad) of that hire's success are attributed to the person who made the decision. When a team makes the decision (even if not all votes are equal), everyone has some "skin in the game" regarding the candidate's success, and people in the organization tend to be more receptive, more welcoming, and more helpful in getting the new hire up to speed and productive.

Hitting the Ground Running

New hires should hit the ground running. But it is human nature to feel timid in new situations—(it takes time to forge friendships and productive alliances with others). The faster new hires can overcome their personal inhibitions about being "the new kid on the block," the faster they can contribute to value creation. Employee involvement in the hiring process helps new hires establish early rapport with their work associates.

They Know the Job

Team members know better than anyone else what qualities and skills are best suited to a position. They are closer to the actual work and deal with the personalities and processes involved on a daily basis. In short, they have a more thorough understanding of the job and its requirements. That is particularly true for technical hires, where those not having much expertise are truly unable to assess a candidate's skills.

Support of the Team Concept

Particularly in organizations that emphasize the team concept— whether officially moving to "self-directed" teams or not—it is critical to use a team approach to hiring. If a new team member is thrust upon an existing group, it clearly communicates that management's commitment to the team concept is shallow. If the employees are to work as a team, they should choose their members as a team.

An Understanding of the Difficulty of Hiring

Finally, a little-known advantage of letting employees have a hand in hiring: Once people have the experience, they understand how hard it is. It is easy enough to roll your eyes at "another bad hire." It is another thing entirely to work through a stack of resumes, interview candidates, and feel the frustration of not being able to find (or maybe lure) the right people. Going through that process even once has the effect of making employees more understanding and more willing to help make any new hire work out.

How to Do It Right

Prepare, Enable Team Members

As everyone knows, hiring is a legal minefield that must be navigated carefully. A haphazard approach to team hiring can endanger a company.

Assembling the Team

The first step is to assemble the team. Seven is a typical number—perhaps an HR facilitator, employees who will work with the individual, the hiring manager, a peer of the hiring manger, subordinates of the position, and experts in the position's field. There are two things to consider when choosing team members: 1) Can they do the job well? and 2) Do they represent the company well?

Companies can (and must) train employees on interviewing skills, but some remain better at it than others. Organizations should make sure all team members know how to get the most out of their time with the candidate. Employee interviewers must be articulate and feel comfortable forming opinions and making decisions.

In terms of representing the company, it is best to include different levels and varying backgrounds on the team. Not only does that offer the employee a more complete view of the company, it also increases the odds that the hiring team will discover different facets of the candidate's personality and skill set.

Finally, companies should look for employees with a positive approach who will represent the company well. While it profits no one to give candidates an overly rosy view, there is no need to let chronically cynical employees destroy the company's chances of hiring the best talent either.

Training the Members

If a company doesn't have time to truly train employees in hiring, it is better not to include them at all. The risks are just too high. But the best option is to develop a quick training program to make sure workers approach the hiring process with confidence.

The program will need to cover, first and foremost, the law. It is entirely natural for novice interviewers to engage a nervous candidate with small talk. But innocently asking, "How many children do you have?" could land the company with a lawsuit. All hiring team members need to know what questions are off limits.

Employees also need to be trained in company policy. Answers they give off the cuff about things like maternity leave or bonuses will be accepted as gospel by candidates, and so had better be right.

Training should also cover interview skills. Even workers with great people skills can realize belatedly that they got nothing substantial out of an interview. Good interview behavior is usually not natural. People need to be trained to ask the right questions and listen well. Selection tools and rating systems make for a much more successful effort. Training employees in their use beforehand is imperative.

Create a Clear Process

A clearly defined process helps group hiring go more smoothly. Typical steps include:

- Develop the job description and competency profile for the target job (with or without help from the team).
- Decide if the company is hiring solely for the target job or also for potential in other roles.
- Give those involved an understanding of their role in the hiring process.
- Develop selection tools that are behaviorally specific to the job's competency profile.
- Give those involved the paperwork on each candidate.
- Prepare for job candidate interviews.
- Conduct interviews.
- Hold formal debrief meetings on the candidate or candidate pool.

What Not to Do

In addition to ensuring that uneducated employees don't get the company into legal trouble, there are two more important "don'ts" when it comes to team hiring:

- Don't make the process too long, overwhelming the candidate.
- Don't override a group's decision, which would be demoralizing. If you cannot agree, start over.

Without these practices, the selection process tends to be ad hoc, compromising decision quality. A hiring process that feels awkward and disorganized can actually turn off viable candidates. In an era in which qualified people are scarce, an effective hiring process could be the difference between the company that wins the applicant and the one that doesn't. In today's war for talent, can anyone afford to have a shoddy selection process?

Employee Referrals

Low Cost, High Return

One of the best ways of involving employees in hiring is to encourage employee referrals. A recent study shows that employee referrals are one of the most effective means of landing, and retaining, the right talent.[5] The study focused on understanding relationships between the hiring source and an employee's job satisfaction, retention, and the likelihood to refer others to the company. Nearly 300 professionals from large and small companies within a variety of industries were surveyed.

One of the study's basic findings was that employee referral systems create the best and longest-lasting results of any recruiting method. Other survey highlights included:

1. Employees who were hired through employee referral tend to successfully refer winning candidates more often than those hired through any other method. Further, when translated into hiring productivity, hires made through referrals tended to account for two to five times the number of hires delivered through other sources.
2. Eighty-eight percent of respondents hired through referral reported their experience with this recruiting method as "good" or "very good," which was higher than for other methods.
3. Referrals tended to be more positively correlated with desired workplace attributes, including job satisfaction, retention, job tenure, and rapid assimilation of new hires. They also tended to be even more effective than expected for management positions.

How do you bump up referrals? Create an official program. But be careful: Employee referral programs that are on the books but not actively promoted tend to produce minimal results. Programs that are promoted periodically, highlighting the needs of the company and the benefits of participating are most productive. Fees run anywhere from $100 to $5000 in the fields where talent is hardest to find.

How It Plays Out

Team Hiring an Extension of Teamwork

Standard Motor Products, one of the largest auto aftermarket manufacturers in the world, has made the move to team hiring. The Edwardsville, Kansas, factory (one of the company's 20+ facilities) has just under 400 employees, who for the most part are divided into teams ranging from 8 to 20 employees. The move into team hiring was a logical extension of the switch to an overall team orientation.

"It's part of the growth pattern of a team," says Steve Simmons, manager of human resources at the company. "As it matures, it makes its own decisions regarding things like overtime and hiring."

Team hiring is used for every opening at Standard Motor Products—including salaried positions. The initial recruiting is done by human resources, which also prescreens the candidates. After that, a list of qualified people is forwarded to the teams. "We provide names to the work area, then they make the choices," says Simmons.

The team winnows the list down to those candidates it feels are most qualified. At that point, the members begin interviewing individuals, discussing both general skills and the ones that relate to the specific opening.

Standard Motor Products provides training on how to conduct interviews. Along with standard information concerning legalities, team members receive general guidelines and an explanation of the company's rules and regulations.

The process is both popular and successful within the company. "It shows employees that they are truly part of the running of this place," says Simmons.

CHAPTER

Focus on the Basics— People Are More Alike Than Different

"We are all kneaded from the same dough; we are just baked in different ovens."
—Yiddish Proverb

As they scramble to attract and retain talent in this market, companies are working hard to identify the hot buttons of their target employees. They are conducting focus groups and analyzing reams of data—all in search of the clues that will show them how to attract the people they most want on board, whether it is women, Generation Xers, minorities, or some other group.

In our opinion, they are working too hard—and perhaps wasting precious resources. In their zeal to appeal to smaller, particular groups of employees, many companies are losing sight of the big picture. While aggressive, targeted recruiting is a solid strategy—changing the *message* for each targeted group is not. Because our research shows that it is just not necessary.

People tend to emphasize differences rather than similarities when looking at research. It is the differences that are interesting, after all. But in stepping back from that impulse, the following becomes clear: When it comes to work, people are more alike than different. It is perhaps not headline-making news, but it is true nonetheless. Men and women, Generation Xers and baby boomers, blacks, whites, and Hispanics all want very similar things from the workplace. When these different segments of the employee population are asked what makes them feel committed to their companies, the things at the top of their lists are the same. When they are asked what they like most (or least) about work, again most answers are the same across the various groups. The depth of feeling may vary, but in general, the ranking order is almost identical.

After moving down lists like this, past the top 3 or 5 or sometimes even 10 answers, differences begin to emerge. But that is just our point: It is only after getting beyond the responses that the employees themselves said were most important that we find things that set workers apart.

For companies, their immediate task is likely much simpler than they thought. Ample evidence exists that companies are not getting the top priorities right. If an organization wants to attract the Generation Xers, it could spend a lot of time and money chasing down the offbeat qualities that are important only to these young workers. Or it could allocate those resources to successfully achieving the three workplace characteristics those Xers said were actually the most crucial to them—which happen to be the same three characteristics most important to the rest of the workforce as well. And then aggressively target those audiences. Great companies have learned to focus on what people have in common. They get the big things right.

What the Numbers Say

Employees Agree on What They Want from the Workplace

In Watson Wyatt's *WorkUSA® 2000* research, we asked 7500 workers at all job levels and in all major industry sectors to respond to roughly 130 statements about the workplace. We broke down the answers so that we could look at the differences in the attitudes of men versus women, whites versus minorities, and those under 30 years of age versus those over 30.

Employees Agree on What Inspires Their Commitment

We asked workers which factors play a role in their level of commitment to their company. There was a great deal of agreement across different employee groups. (See Figure 5-1.) Workers of all ages, races, and both genders say they need to support the company's business direction to feel committed to their employer. Four out of the six groups said that getting the chance to use their skills on the job and the company acting on employee suggestions inspire their commitment. Four out of the six groups rated the company's ability to retain highly qualified employees and the competitiveness of the reward package as determinative factors.

If companies want to increase employee commitment, they need to start here. They must look at these five factors that are almost universally important to all their employees. Only when they are quite certain they have succeeded in these areas should they move beyond them to try to appeal specifically to targeted groups.

A 2001 study by Korn Ferry and the Center for Effective Leadership at USC confirms that there are almost no differences between men and women, young and old, managers and non-managers, or Europeans and Americans regarding self-reported critical factors driving commitment.[1] Even a regression analysis that looks beyond what employees say to actual predictors of commitment shows more similarity than difference.

Figure 5-1. *Top Five Drivers of Employee Commitment by Group*

Men	Women
Support of the company's business direction	Support of the company's business direction
Chance to use skills on the job	Chance to use skills on the job
Acting on suggestions of employees	Acting on suggestions of employees
Retaining highly qualified employees	Retaining highly qualified employees
Competitiveness of total reward package	Competitiveness of total reward package

Whites	Minorities
Support of the company's business direction	Support of the company's business direction
Chance to use skills on the job	Chance to use skills on the job
Acting on suggestions of employees	Retaining highly qualified employees
Retaining highly qualified employees	Personal growth and development
Competitiveness of total reward package	Climate of mutual respect among employees

Under 30 years old	Over 30 years old
Support of the company's business direction	Support of the company's business direction
Acting on suggestions of employees	Chance to use skills on the job
Sr. mgmt behaving consistently with core values	Acting on suggestions of employees
Kind of work done in job	Competitiveness of total reward package
Better performance, better pay	Job security to employees who perform well

WorkUSA® 2000

Employees Agree on What Companies Do Right

As for how companies in general are actually doing in the eyes of their employees, we again turn to *WorkUSA®*. We made "Top 10" lists for each of the six groups consisting of workplace attributes the employees rated most positively. We found that the attitudes of the different employee groups were so similar that—out of 130 possibilities—five of the statements made it onto every single list (see Figure 5-2.) That "Top 5" list reveals that most companies are doing an excellent job of communicating to employees exactly what role their position plays in the business. Employees of all types, at all levels, reported that they understand how their job affects customers, fellow workers, and the company's goals. Employees also universally report that companies are putting out quality products and services, and keeping the workplace safe.

Employees Agree on What Needs to Be Improved

We then set out to discover whether these groups of employees also had the same ideas about what was wrong at the workplace. As it turns out, they do. (See Figure 5-3.)

We think two particularly important messages emerge from these lists of complaints:

Figure 5-2. *What People Rate Must Positively About Work*

Factors cited by men, women, whites, minorities, those under 30 and those over 30:
Understanding of how own job affects external customers
Understanding of how own job affects internal customers
Rating of company's products/services
Understanding of how job contributes to company business goals
Rating of safety

WorkUSA® 2000

Figure 5-3. *What People Rated Least Positively About Work*

Men

Company helps employees to manage job-related stress

Fairness in promoting the most qualified employees

Involvement of employees in decisions that affect them

Company's management of poor performers so that their performance improves

Company acts on suggestions of employees

Women

Company helps employees to manage job-related stress

Fairness in promoting the most qualified employees

Opportunity to provide meaningful input in hiring decisions

Involvement of employees in decisions that affect them

Company's management of poor performers so that their performance improves

Whites

Company helps employees to manage job-related stress

Fairness in promoting the most qualified employees

Opportunity to provide meaningful input in hiring decisions

Involvement of employees in decisions that affect them

Company's management of poor performers so that their performance improves

Minorities

Company helps employees to manage job-related stress

Fairness in promoting the most qualified employees

Opportunity to provide meaningful input in hiring decisions

Link of pay and performance

Competitiveness of total reward package

Under 30 years old

Company helps employees to manage job-related stress

Opportunity to provide meaningful input in hiring decisions

Involvement of employees in decisions that affect them

Company's management of poor performers so that their performance improves

Link of pay and performance

Over 30 years old

Company helps employees to manage job-related stress

Fairness in promoting the most qualified employees

Opportunity to provide meaningful input in hiring decisions

Involvement of employees in decisions that affect them

Company's management of poor performers so that their performance improves

WorkUSA® 2000

First, employees of all types are unhappy with the level of input they have at the workplace. Employees say they do not they have a voice in hiring decisions, and their companies do not involve them in other decisions that affect them either. Considering that "acting on the decisions of employees" is one of the top five factors driving employee commitment across all groups, this is obviously a place where companies need to focus.

Second, employees think their companies neither promote the best performers nor help the worst performers to improve.

Combining these findings with the key drivers of employee commitment, it is very clear where companies should focus their efforts:

- Create trust in organizational effectiveness. People want to know their leaders are capable, and they want to understand where the business is headed.
- Give employees a chance to contribute. People want a chance to use their skills, and they want to be involved in decision making.
- Fix "pay for performance." People want a competitive package, they want to see the right people rewarded, and they want to see poor performers either shaped up or shipped out.

A company that successfully addresses these three areas will have solved the most pressing issues for every employee group in its workforce.

Attracting the Best and the Brightest

It's important to know how to attract all talent, but it's particularly important to know how to attract top performers. So we checked our findings above against Watson Wyatt's Survey of Top-Performing Employees. We asked the best and brightest workers which reward strategies truly factored into their decision-making when it came to taking a new job. (See Figure 5-4.) Once again, it turns out that people are more alike than different:

- Compensation was rated as one of the top three attracting factors for all groups.
- Benefits were rated in the top three for all groups (with the exception of workers under the age of 30).
- Having the opportunity to develop skills was rated in the top five for all groups.

A Word About Generation X

There's a great deal of buzz out there about how different "Generation X" is. People talk about their strange ideas and odd values and peculiar motivations. But the truth is that what we're seeing are the generational differences that occur in every era.

Generation X isn't really so different from other younger generations, but it has perhaps stirred up more commentary based on its unusual participation in this economy. A recent article in the *Economist* summed it up nicely: "Children have always been more expert than their parents at something, but it's usually a game or a fad, not the era's most important business tool (the Internet)."[2] These techie youngsters are much more in demand than young workers have ever been before.

So companies today have analyzed Generation Xers' needs and desires in a manner they have traditionally reserved for more senior top performers, obviously attaining somewhat different analysis results. Even so, GenXers share some top priorities even with those workers whose needs/desires one would expect to find at the other end of the spectrum—those over age 50.

The Bottom Line

Attract and Retain by Focusing on Fundamentals

The challenge of getting and keeping talent in place becomes simpler when companies stay focused on fundamentals. Companies that succeed in addressing the following four areas will find that

Figure 5-4. *Factors Affecting the Decision-Making Process of Top Performers Considering a New Job*

All	Managers/Directors/Sr. Managers
1. Compensation	1. Compensation
2. Benefits	2. Benefits
3. Opportunity to develop skills	3. Type of people/culture
4. Opportunity for promotion	4. Opportunity to develop skills
5. Vacation/PTO	5. Opportunity for promotion

Secretarial/Clerical/Production	Professional/Technical
1. Benefits	1. Opportunity to develop skills
2. Job security	2. Compensation
3. Compensation	3. Benefits
4. Vacation/PTO	4. Freedom to work independently
5. Opportunity to develop skills	5. Vacation/PTO

Men	Women
1. Compensation	1. Benefits
2. Benefits	2. Opportunity to develop skills
3. Opportunity to develop skills	3. Compensation
4. Opportunity for promotion	4. Vacation/PTO
5. Freedom to work independently	5. Freedom to work independently

Earn >$100K	Earn >$30K
1. Compensation	1. Job security
2. Type of people/culture	2. Benefits
3. Benefits	3. Compensation
4. Opportunity to develop skills	4. Opportunity to develop skills
5. Opportunity for promotion	5. Vacation/PTO

Over 50	Under 30
1. Benefits	1. Opportunity to develop skills
2. Compensation	2. Opportunity for promotion
3. Freedom to work independently	3. Compensation
4. Job security	4. Vacation/PTO
5. Opportunity to develop skills	5. Type of people/culture

Strategic Rewards® 2001

Figure 5-5. *What Do Top-Performing Employees Really Want?*

Under 30	Over 50
Skill development	Benefits
Promotions	Compensation
Compensation	Freedom to work independently
PTO/vacation	Job security
Culture/coworkers	Skill development

Strategic Rewards® 2001

they are meeting the most important needs of the great majority of their employees:

- *Company Effectiveness.* People want to work for a winner. They want to be a part of a success story, and they want to see leadership, strategy, and goals that will keep the company on the right track.
- *Personal Utilization/Effectiveness.* People want to be able to do a good job. That means they want work that will make the most of their skills, they want the resources necessary to be effective, and they want to know how their work contributes to the company's overall objectives.
- *Economic and Interpersonal Treatment.* People want to feel respected and valued. They want their opinions to count, and they want their contributions recognized.
- *Enjoyment of Work.* People want to like the job. That means they want to be interested in the work itself and to enjoy the environment and their coworkers.

The company that makes considerable strides in these basic areas will find they are winning battle after battle in the war for talent.

PART

Create a Total Reward and Accountability Orientation

6

CHAPTER

Link Rewards to Performance

Reward n. 1. Something given or received in recompense for worthy behavior.[1]

Salaries, bonuses, stock—they are loosely termed "rewards." But too often they fail to function as such because in dispensing them companies do not significantly distinguish between their true stars and their chronic nonperformers. Those firms are wasting valuable resources on a reward system that does not actually reward a thing. And they are disabling one of the most powerful tools in their arsenal when it comes to attracting, retaining, and motivating the best players.

The answer is as simple to say as it is difficult to do: Organizations should promise employees terrific rewards for terrific performance. They must warn them that poor performance will not be tolerated. Then they must follow through.

What the Numbers Say

Pay for Performance; Refuse to Tolerate Nonperformance

The Human Capital Index research suggests that companies that use the right reward systems will enjoy 9 percent higher shareholder value. What constitutes the "right" approach? Of the 10 specific reward practices the study identified (other than benefits, which are covered in Chapter 10), 9 fall under the category of "pay for performance." (See Figure 6-1.) The most successful companies create reward systems that reward good performance and refuse to tolerate poor performance.

The "Look" of Pay for Performance

Companies that embrace a "pay for performance" philosophy look and feel remarkably different than those who do not. For example:

Figure 6-1. *Links Between Clear Rewards and Accountability and Value Creation*

Practice	Impact on Market Value
High percentage of company stock owned by employees	1.3%
High percentage of company stock owned by senior managers	1.2%
Pay is linked to company's business strategy	1.1%
High percentage of employees eligible for stock options	1.0%
Company promotes most competent employees	0.9%
High percentage of employees participate in incentive/ profit-sharing plans	0.9%
Top performers receive better pay than average performers	0.8%
Company helps poor performers improve	0.7%
Company positions pay above the market	0.7%
Company terminates employees who continue to perform poorly	0.6%

Expected change associated with a significant (1SD) improvement in practice

Watson Wyatt's Human Capital Index®

A midcap global health care company experienced mediocre financial and stock market performance over several years. While there were other possible explanations for that performance, the company's reward system was certainly a prime suspect:

- Stock options and other stock incentives were reserved for top management.
- Restricted stock—stock awards contingent upon continued employment—was used as a retention device. While potentially appropriate in and of itself, the fact that the company did not adequately eliminate subpar performers meant the restricted stock had become an entitlement.
- While the company did have an employee stock purchase plan, it was poorly communicated and therefore participation was quite low.
- The annual incentive plan had also become an entitlement, with little variation over time and by person in actual payouts.

The executives were perplexed. The CEO wondered why his key executives would not make the tough calls to create growth and cut costs. The company was eventually bought out.

On the other hand...

A major regional retailer has experienced excellent performance over the past five years. During that period, a system of clear rewards and accountability has been in place:

- The company offered stock options and other stock incentives deep into the organization, to the level of assistant store managers. A recently implemented all-employee stock purchase plan offered a 15 percent discount and had been effectively communicated and highly subscribed to by a huge number of associates.
- A very aggressive annual incentive plan had actual payouts of 0 percent, 100 percent, 200 percent, and 150 percent of target bonus opportunities.

- The company continually weeded out subpar performers at both the corporate level and in the stores.
- High-performing employees, especially store managers, were targeted for salary increases and special stock option grants.
- Stock ownership was strongly encouraged, and as a result management and the board owned a large proportion of the company.
- The company's compensation philosophy offered modest base salaries combined with cash and stock incentive opportunities that allowed actual pay to be well above the 75th percentile. Top management had the exact same compensation programs as the rest of the company.

The result—better corporate financial performance.

Choosing the Best Reward Alternatives

It is not surprising that many companies "look" a bit more like our first example than our second. The number of alternatives available to management when it comes to setting up a reward system is almost overwhelming, leading to confusion, inconsistency, and a kind of paralysis in the face of poor results.

The Human Capital Index makes the task easier. While there may be several viable human capital program alternatives to consider, this study points the way to the financially advisable choice. What follows is a brief discussion of the practices suggested by the HCI and the alternatives chosen most often by successful companies.

Stock Plan Programs

Companies that have a high percentage of stock owned by employees, a high percentage of stock owned by senior managers, and a high percentage of employees eligible for stock plan programs are worth 3.5 percent more on the market. Stock is one of the clearest, most measurable ways to link pay to performance.

Methods for broad stock ownership include:

- ESOP (Employee Stock Ownership Plan)—A U.S. tax-qualified plan where shares of stock are offered—for free in nearly every case—to employees as part of their retirement package.
- Employee stock purchase plans (I.R.C. Section 423 plans in the United States or nonqualified plans)—A plan where employees buy stock, usually at a 15 percent discount, using payroll withholding.
- 401(k) (stock matches or investment choice)—A plan where the employer provides a match in company stock (typically 50 percent of the first 6 percent of pay) for amounts put in the plan by employees. The employer could also offer company stock as one of the investment alternatives.
- Broad-based stock option grants—An approach that extends stock option eligibility below the management level.

The research shows that these stock programs are very effective. Yet many companies choose limited eligibility instead. Why? One does not have to be a skeptic to argue that broad stock option grants represent future issues of large numbers of shares, thereby diluting their value. In contrast, stock options also create an incentive effect, motivating employees toward behavior that creates better performance. There is considerable academic literature addressing the trade-off between the incentive and dilutionary effects. However, the statistical findings from the HCI (and most academic articles) are clear: As employees who lead and manage the company become wealthier, so do outside shareholders. This is further discussed in Chapter 8.

Linking Pay to Strategy

Companies that link pay to overall business strategy are worth 1.1 percent more. It is one of the basic tenets of business strategy that all aspects of a company's tactics—operations, marketing, research, distribution, and all staff functions (e.g., finance, human resources) must align with that strategy in order to maximize economic value creation. We have always believed that this is true for a compensation strategy as well. Fundamentally, the theory goes that the pay system will both communicate the chosen strategy to all employees and reward successful strategy implementation.

The HCI provides support for that notion. If a company's strategy were to grow revenue, an annual incentive plan that only pays off for earnings per share (EPS—the most common measure of profits), would *not* be aligned or linked to the growth strategy. Most likely the company would be reasonably profitable but would not grow. There were many examples of such misalignment at consumer products companies in the late 1990s and early 2000s. A company in that situation should either give up on a growth strategy or take the risk and change the incentive plan to reward for that growth goal. (The risk being that the growth will come at the expense of profits!)

A lack of alignment is more likely due to lack of planning than to a specific mistake. The business strategy and the pay strategy may have been created by two different groups of people at two different points in time. Or the pay system is simply an ad hoc system for paying people, rather than a means of supporting or communicating strategy. Whatever the reason, companies that lack this linkage should get to work on it immediately, as its payoff is substantial relative to the efforts required to achieve it.

Promoting the Most Qualified

Companies that promote the best candidates are worth 0.9 percent more. Not only does this practice put the right talent in the most responsible positions, it has significant impact on overall employee satisfaction. "Promoting the most qualified employees" ranks as one of the leading factors in establishing trust in senior leadership, according to Watson Wyatt's *WorkUSA® 2000* research.

Offering Corporate Profit Sharing

Shareholder value is 0.9 percent higher at companies where employees participate in the company's success through profit sharing. This program capitalizes on employees' desires to be "part of the bigger picture." Corporate profit sharing—particularly when combined with stock incentives and employee participation programs (e.g., suggestion box, focus groups)—encourages employees to think like owners.

This area, like many others, has its controversies. Specifically, there is good reason to believe that employees perform better when their incentives are linked to "line-of-sight" objectives, namely those that are closer to home, rather than at the corporate level. This would include individual objectives and/or divisional/unit objectives. While this may be true, there is strong empirical support for corporate profit sharing's positive impact on TRS.

One of our energy industry clients has an excellent corporatewide profit-sharing program. It is quite simple. The plan uses only one financial measure—Earnings Per Share—for all employees, from hourly paid production employees to the CEO. The incentive opportunity, of course, varies from 5 percent of salary for the production employees to 75 percent of salary for the CEO. And most importantly, the top managers cannot receive a payment under the plan unless the hourly employees do as well. It is a perfectly aligned plan.

Are there successful companies that do not have corporatewide profit sharing? Of course there are. However, they are likely to have some other type of corporatewide plan, such as a stock option plan, an employee stock purchase plan or an ESOP.

And further, when we visit an unsuccessful company, we usually find an absence of any mechanisms for sharing overall corporate financial success. For example, we once visited a publishing company with no corporatewide incentive plan—no profit-sharing or broad-based stock-based incentive plan. Most of the "goodies" were reserved for top management. We were asked to develop an enhanced incentive plan for top management, but when we shared our ideas for that new plan, we advised the company to develop some type of broad-based incentive plan. We did not get the assignment. The company recently filed for bankruptcy. Cause and effect? Perhaps not, but certainly not an example of a best practices model.

Paying Top Performers More

When top performers are paid significantly more than average performers, shareholder value is 0.8 percent higher. This is accomplished by giving top performers larger salary increases, larger bonuses (higher payouts as a percentage of target bonuses), and larger stock option grants.

The alternative here, again, is the paternalistic one, such as the Japanese pay system (which is eroding over time) or the U.S. Civil Service system. Pay is targeted toward the middle, with a relatively small spread from highest to lowest pay level or pay increase. This model is highly dependent upon specialized cultural support and has had its uses. Obviously, the current data show that for most companies, those days are over.

Helping Poor Performers to Improve

Successful companies are strong at helping poor performers improve, and they are worth 0.7 percent more on the stock market as a result. How do companies help poor performers improve? A full discussion of performance management is discussed later, but suffice it to say that successful companies use clear goal setting, management coaching, frequent performance discussions, poor bonuses and salary increases, and shifting to new roles.

Paying Above the Market

Companies that position their pay above the market are worth 0.7 percent more. The data suggest that these companies are indeed attracting the best and the brightest—and that those people are more than making up for their higher salaries (or stock options, or incentives) with higher contributions to the firm's financial success.

The data show that hiring the more average candidate at a lower cost is a bad value. Those average employees are creating average productivity at best and are not creating any excess returns to shareholders. The stock price suffers.

Terminating Poor Performers

Companies that terminate employees who perform unacceptably are worth 0.6 percent more. The low productivity of poor performers is just the beginning of their negative impact on an organization—arguably more damaging is their effect on coworkers' productivity and morale, and the message their continued presence sends about management.

There is another important dimension to failing to terminate poor performers. If these poor performers are in management positions, their negative impact on management development, morale, and productivity is leveraged due to their position in the hierarchy. They also gain management development opportunities that could otherwise go to better candidates. According to the *McKinsey Quarterly,* "The War for Talent" (E. Chambers et al.), "It's hard to give all your high performers a great boss if too few of your bosses are high performers themselves...Our research suggests that taking action to deal with poor performers is the most difficult, least exploited talent-building lever for any company."[2]

That difficulty is the very reason so many companies opt for the alternative of simply allowing chronic nonperformers to stay on the job. The result is a paternalistic culture that tolerates mediocrity but is a "nice place to work." Turnover is probably low, but these companies lose their best performers and keep the rest. The results show that the paternalistic model punishes shareholders.

Paying for Performance Helps Attraction, Retention, and Motivation

The reward practices that increase shareholder value are those that make clear use of performance-based rewards (and punishments). That is particularly striking in light of the fact that most reward systems do not wield enough leverage on the upside to motivate superior performance. And on the downside, managers are frequently reluctant to confront employees about poor performance, much less terminate them for it. Those companies are missing one of their best shots at significantly improving shareholder value. Research confirms that the best reward plans put opportunities in front of workers to motivate them. If the worker pulls off a successful strategy, she wins high pay. If she fails, her pay suffers. According to our *WorkUSA® 2000* study, shareholder value is significantly higher at companies where employees believe that true pay for performance is practiced. (See Figure 6-2.)

One reason paying for performance improves the bottom line is that it helps companies attract and retain talent. When asked why they resign, 50 percent of top-performing employees say "dissatisfaction with pay" played a significant role, according to the *Strategic Rewards®* study. But companies are learning. The same study also shows that firms are slowly shifting to performance-based compensation and moving away from nonperformance-based rewards as part of a formal retention strategy. We are seeing small increases in group incentives, project incentives, exempt overtime (both cash and compensatory time), and stock options/grants.

Figure 6-2. *Employee Believes He/She Will Receive Better Pay for Performance*

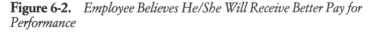

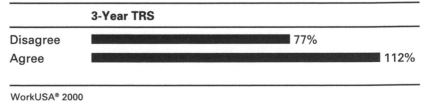

	3-Year TRS
Disagree	77%
Agree	112%

WorkUSA® 2000

Paying for performance may be particularly important—and underrated by companies—in the quest to attract talent. Top performers rated various reward plans on their effectiveness in attracting them to a company, and their response made it clear that these "stars" want compensation to be tied to performance.

Why It Works

Paying for Performance Harnesses Human Nature

Pay for performance works because it is based on human nature. People do things that are in their own interest. They do not do things that are not in their own interest. When companies structure their reward systems correctly, it becomes human nature for employees to work hard to achieve the company's—and thus their own—goals.

So why do so many companies fall into the trap of giving salary increases that range from 4 percent for almost unacceptable performance to 5 percent for phenomenal performance?

Figure 6-3. *Effectiveness of Compensation-Based Reward Plans in Attraction—Top-Performing Employees*

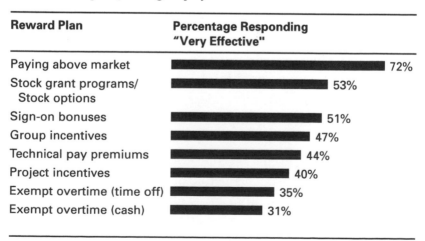

Reward Plan	Percentage Responding "Very Effective"
Paying above market	72%
Stock grant programs/ Stock options	53%
Sign-on bonuses	51%
Group incentives	47%
Technical pay premiums	44%
Project incentives	40%
Exempt overtime (time off)	35%
Exempt overtime (cash)	31%

Strategic Rewards® 2000

Why do some companies give annual Christmas bonuses regardless of performance? Why are so many organizations filled with dead wood? The answer to this, too, is "human nature." First, resources—rewards—are limited. Giving more to the stars leaves less for the others. That means a confrontation with nonperformers is looming. Second, evaluating performance means managers have to know, and communicate, what kind of performance they wanted in the first place. That is a great deal harder than it sounds, and managers know it. Unclear aims, conflicting goals, and unrealistic expectations from the top can all make it terribly difficult to create a fair performance evaluation system. And the more that is riding on that performance evaluation, the more important fairness becomes. So in the end, many companies opt for the easier road, where all levels of performance are met with roughly the same "reward."

We also think there is another more strategic—essentially historical—reason why companies fail to reward their top performers. It turns out that for any given short period of time—say a year or certainly a quarter—some companies may need large numbers of employees in the middle of the performance ladder. And in a drum-tight labor market like that of the past 10 years, even this middle can get better-paying jobs elsewhere. Basically, squeezing the pay of the middle 1000 workers to pay the top 100 best performers creates short-term risks to the revenue stream. That short-term risk needs to be balanced against losing any of the top 100, which creates even greater risks to the company's long-term revenue stream. This is because so many product innovations and other creative ideas—basically the company's future—come from this group.

This is how it works: Over the short term, costs tend to rise along with revenue, even if revenue levels have increased dramatically in the recent past. This pernicious trend is experienced by virtually every industry, from oil exploration to software, from pharmaceuticals to telecommunications and financial services. So companies feel the need to keep revenue growing or at least stable.

If a company loses too many middle-performing workers, revenue may fall faster than the cost savings, sending the company into the netherworld of revenue-cost gridlock or downward spiral.

The lesson is that companies need to assume a long-term strategic view of these issues by continuously upgrading their human capital. Further, they need to put incentive plans in place to motivate middle performers to rotate to the top. If they fail to do so, their middle performers can hold them hostage with inferior returns to shareholders.

This is a knowledge-based economy. Talent is all-important. The best and the brightest will work only where they receive appropriate reward for their efforts. Finding it "too hard" to implement a true strategic rewards program may end up putting a company in a position where it is "too hard" to stay in business.

Critic's Corner

It seems obvious to us that pay for performance works. But there are critics, the most well-known of whom is Alfie Kohn, who articulated his case in *Punished by Rewards* (1993). The author's fundamental conclusion is that any approach that offers a reward for better performers is destined to be ineffective. His reasons:

- Rewards manipulate people's behavior.
- Failure to receive a bonus is bound to have an adverse effect on subsequent performance.
- Horizontal relationships are damaged because rewards don't pay for cooperation.
- Vertical relationships are hurt because performers manipulate information and do not admit the need for help.
- The system fails to address underlying issues that lead to poor performance.
- The system discourages risk-taking and reduces creativity.
- The system undermines genuine interest in the work on the part of the employee.

"People who are trying to earn a reward end up doing a poorer job...than people who are not," says Kohn. "Extrinsic motivators are a poor substitute for genuine interest in what one is doing."[3]

His points are interesting and some contain a grain of truth. But we disagree with his conclusions. Our experience, our research, and the research of others indicate that companies are high performing specifically because they successfully deploy a portfolio of reward plans—including pay for performance—that are aligned with their business strategies. Rewards have provided a major source of competitive advantage for U.S. companies.

Annual Incentive Matrix

A tool that can be very useful in effectively managing rewards and accountabilities is a structured annual incentive matrix. This would be used instead of a subjective or discretionary bonus plan. A disciplined annual incentive process is not for every company; it requires a strong planning process and mostly quantifiable goals. Nevertheless, companies should strongly consider this type of plan, even if they ultimately and correctly reject it in favor of their discretionary plan. Or employers could incorporate aspects of the matrix into their discretionary plan.

What does a structured plan look like? Figure 6-4 is a sample matrix for a business unit executive. There are three different organizational levels on which performance will be measured, with each assigned a particular weight (percentage) for use in calculating the final award. For each area, measurable goals are established with both a threshold figure and a target figure. For example, revenue or EPS would be used to establish performance measures on the "company" level; revenue, margin, and departmental budget objectives would be used to

Figure 6-4. *Illustration of Award Matrix for Business Unit Executive*

Salary = $400,000
Target Incentive = 100% of Salary ($400,000)

Organizational Level/ Performance Measures	Weight	Percent of Target Incentive Achieved					
		Below Threshold	Threshold	Below Target	Target	Above Target	Maximum
		0.0%	25%	62.5%	100%	150%	200%
Company	40%	0	$40,000	$100,000	$160,000	$240,000	$320,000
Business Unit	30%	0	$30,000	$75,000	$120,000	$180,000	$240,000
Individual	30%	0	$30,000	$75,000	$120,000	$180,000	$240,000
Total Final Award	100%	0	$100,000	$250,000	$400,000	$600,000	$800,000

establish performance measures on the "business unit performance" level; and productivity, professional staff turnover, collections, cross selling, and succession planning might be used to establish performance measures on the "individual" level. The executive's monetary reward will fall into one of six categories for each of the three organizational levels, depending on how close results are to the target figure. The final award will be the sum of those three component incentives.

For example, if this particular executive came in above threshold but below target in the company level, on target in the business unit level, and above target in the individual level, the executive would be awarded $400,000.

How It Plays Out

The Game of Reward Hardball

One of the best turnarounds we have seen in the corporate world was by one of our retail clients who learned the pay-for-performance lesson well. Their long-standing annual incentive plan guaranteed employees very good bonuses for excellent performance. They also paid bonuses—not such great ones, but bonuses nonetheless—when the company did not do well. The rationale was that denying the bonuses would make employees too unhappy to be productive. When a new CEO came in, he decided a change in culture was needed. He set aggressive goals and let employees know that if they hit their goals, they would be paid extremely well, and if they didn't, they would be paid poorly. Lo and behold, one year they missed their goals. Many advised the CEO to continue the tradition of paying a modest bonus anyway, but he stood his ground. There was a lot of grumbling, but the next year they again set very aggressive goals and very aggressive bonus opportunities. This time, they made their numbers, attaining 200 percent of target. They have had outstanding results ever since. The CEO attributes a lot of that performance to that one year with no bonus payout.

Whether the subject is bonuses, salaries, stock options, or even keeping the job, the key is being very clear that only those employees who perform will be rewarded. That philosophy should underscore a company's approach to reward design. It will keep employees focused on business goals, keep top people happy, work to reform subpar performers, and keep morale high by getting rid of low contributors.

How to Implement a Performance Management System

Having a formal performance management system in place is an essential part of making a carrot-and-stick approach work. People often confuse performance management with performance appraisal, but they are very different. An appraisal is a distinct event—a meeting between a manager and an employee to review a performance evaluation. Performance management is a process with many interrelated activities. A comprehensive performance management system will help a company meet the following challenges:

- How can we get employees to focus on doing the "right" things?
- How can we improve those employee capabilities that are most important to the company?
- What can we do to reduce turnover rates?
- How do we better link performance to compensation?
- What is the best way to get better results out of a specific department/division?
- How can we help our managers to more effectively develop their people?

There are many different kinds of performance management systems, but the ones that work best include the following steps:

1. Clarify performance expectations, responsibilities, and standards.
2. Set goals and link them to business objectives.

3. Coach and give feedback on progress and performance.
4. Adjust goals as appropriate to shifting business priorities.
5. Solve problems of resources, time, and training.
6. Directly support the employee's development of competencies that are critical to the organization.
7. Evaluate performance contributions in terms of quantitative results as well as alignment with company values and operating principles.
8. Deliver pay or other rewards based upon the employee's performance.
9. Plan a future that meets the needs of both the employee and the organization.
10. Deal with issues of nonperformance either through a specific action plan or through termination/replacement.

So, whether it's the 360-degree performance review, Management by Objective, career development, individual performance appraisals or something else, it will have the basics in common. One of the most unusual—and difficult to implement—is a "forced ranking" system. Under this system, managers must rank all their employees, with those at the top being the best performers who receive rewards accordingly—larger salary increases, bonuses, and stock options. Those at the bottom receive the smallest—and possible termination. Forced ranking requires a special culture and lots of management discipline. Ford recently cancelled its forced ranking system under legal pressure. Others may follow suit.

Linking rewards to performance is an excellent way for managers to add to the economic value of their company—and continue to populate their organizations with productive high performers who are engaged in doing just that. Our research and our experience support specific best ways to make that happen.

7 CHAPTER

Demand That CEOs Hold a Significant Stake in the Company

> *"While there are many reasons American companies have flourished over the last two decades, it's no coincidence that the boom has come in the wake of the shift in executive pay from cash to equity."*
> —Brian Hall (2000, Harvard Business Review)

For maximum impact on shareholder value, paying for performance and ultimate accountability has to start at the top: Companies should combine stock ownership with stock option grants to give CEOs a significant stake in the company. Their fortunes must rise and fall with the value they create for shareholders.

Why is this the case? When the CEO is seen to be in the same boat as everyone else—whether battleship or lifeboat—morale and therefore productivity should soar. This includes both variations in pay as well as job security. On the other hand, if

CEOs are held harmless or insulated from the economic and job risks faced by their colleagues, morale, productivity and economic results generally plummet.

But is this the case? Does the compensation of CEOs vary as dramatically as the performance of their companies? And importantly, is there any support for the powerful concept that the structure and levels of CEO pay programs—especially their stock ownership and stock options—are actually driving CEOs to improve the performance of their companies? And equally importantly, are CEOs whose companies fail being held accountable? Are they being terminated for poor performance? The answers to these questions are among the most accurate predictors of future corporate success available.

We have been doing CEO pay studies for 10 years with consistent findings: **There is compelling statistical evidence that executive compensation programs and other methods of accountability management strongly motivate CEOs to improve corporate performance.** Our studies have uncovered a strong correlation between CEO stock ownership, levels of CEO pay, and changes in pay on one hand, and varying corporate performance on the other.* The upshot is clear: As investors have demanded greater accountability and returns for their money, boards of directors have forged better links between executive pay and performance, largely by shifting more pay into stock options and ownership, and by holding CEOs accountable.

Before we look at the statistics, however, what do these two distinct types of companies—CEO held accountable or not—feel like?

What the Numbers Show

High Stock Ownership = Higher Corporate Performance

See Figure 7-1. Watson Wyatt recently researched 1300 large public companies to determine the relationship between execu-

A midcap retailer had fallen on hard times. The board took aggressive action and terminated the CEO and most of his team. They then recruited a new CEO to create a new merchandising, branding, real estate, and cost-cutting strategy. The new CEO came in with impeccable credentials, but his intensely negotiated contract contained the seeds of future problems. For starters, the contract awarded him large amounts of restricted stock (stock awards contingent on continued employment) completely "for free." While restricted stock has its proper uses, it should have been an immediate "bearish" signal that he was unwilling to put any of his own money on the line. Even highly favorable terms, like a 50 percent discount on the stock price, would have been far superior. Second, he was given a special medical account that insulated him from the cost cutting—in health insurance and other areas—that was sure to follow. Needless to say, the company's financial performance and stock price continued to suffer.

A major financial services company was also in trouble, with weakness in both its income statement and balance sheet. Its stock price was collapsing, reaching a 20-year low. Its newly appointed CEO, promoted from within, invested several million dollars of his own money in the stock in open-market purchases. This was, of course, in addition to a fully competitive compensation package including a jumbo stock option grant. His open-market purchase turned out to be at the low. Flawless strategy development and execution yielded outstanding results. The stock price increased 20 fold and the CEO retired 10 years later as a centimillionaire.

tive stock ownership (excluding stock options) and company performance. We split these companies into high and low CEO ownership based on stock owned at the end of 1999. CEOs in the high ownership group had a median ownership stake of over $30 million. By contrast, the median holding of CEOs in the low ownership group was just 6 percent of that amount ($1.7 million).[2] We then looked at a host of financial variables for these two groups of companies, especially total returns to shareholders. The results: There is a strong, positive relationship between senior-level stock ownership and simultaneous corporate performance.

- Annualized total returns to shareholders over a five-year period (1994–1999) are three times higher in companies where CEOs own a significant amount of stock. In fact, higher-performing companies had CEOs owning 40 percent more stock than low-performing companies. (See Figure 7-3.)
- High CEO stock ownership was associated with superior corporate financial performance in 1999 as measured by Return on Equity (ROE), Return on Investments (ROI), One-Year Earnings-per-Share growth, and Tobin's Q*. Stock ownership by the other four highest paid executives at these companies is equally important. Higher levels of ownership are also correlated to better financial performance. High ownership CEOs are creating an ownership culture that spreads throughout the companies.

- We also looked at 1995 CEO stock ownership and subsequent financial performance. (See Figure 7-2.) The results are equally compelling in support of CEO stock ownership.
- In addition to stock ownership, TRS is correlated to high levels of CEO total pay and changes in CEO cash compensation. (See Figure 7-3.)

Finally, we compared the cumulative Total Direct Compensation (total cash compensation plus present value of long-term incentives such as stock options, restricted stock, and performance shares) of CEOs from 1995 through 2000 with their company's five-year annualized TRS. (See Figure 7-4.) This was designed to

---

*Defined in the Appendix.

Figure 7-1. *Executive Stock Ownership and Company Performance*

	1999 Ownership	Ownership-to-Salary Multiple	1-Year TRS
High	$30.5 million	46:1	5.8%
Low	$1.7 million	3:1	-9.2%
All	$7.7 million	13:1	-2.8%

Executive Pay 2001

Figure 7-2. *CEO Stock Ownership Correlates with Subsequent Corporate Performance*

	1995 Stock Ownership	5-Year Annualized TRS
High	$8.6 million	24.9%
Low	$5.2 million	3.5%
All	$6.7 million	12.9%

Executive Pay 2001

Figure 7-3. *High CEO Pay Correlates with High Corporate Performance*

	Median Value Total CEO Pay*	5-Year Annualized TRS
High	$3.3 million	18.3%
Low	$1.2 million	10.2%
All	$1.9 million	14.0%

*1999 salary plus bonus plus profit from stock options exercised

Executive Pay 2001

answer, as best we could, the question of whether pay opportunity in early years creates a higher level of performance. The resulting TDC is the best measure of future compensation opportunity. Therefore, we expect that TDC over the prior five years should be correlated with subsequent stock market performance. We found that CEOs with above-median TDC had a TRS almost nine percentage points higher than CEOs paid below the median.

Stock Ownership Guidelines

Over the past five years, more than one-third of U.S. companies have established policies that require their top executives to own and hold stock in their companies.' The theory is that as true shareholders—not just "option-holders"—executive interest will be even more highly aligned with shareholders. We heartily endorse this strategy and recommend it to most of our clients.

The percentage of companies establishing executive stock ownership guidelines appears to have leveled off recently at around 30 percent (See Figure 7-5.), although it still reflects a significant increase from 13.8 percent in 1998.'

Nearly 68 percent of companies use stock owned as a multiple of the base salary to establish the executive stock ownership guideline.× For example, an executive with a salary of $500,000 and a multiple of "4" would need to own $2 million worth of stock.

A study out of Wharton titled "Performance Consequences of Requiring Target Stock Ownership Levels," echoed our finding that companies that require CEO stock ownership have significantly better shareholder returns.*

The Greed Debate

Critics of U.S. executive pay have been particularly vocal in the past decade. At first, the argument was that CEO pay bore no

Figure 7-4. *Cumulative CEO Pay Opportunity and Total Return to Shareholders*

	5-Year Total TDC	5-Year Annualized TRS
High	$20.7 million	17.9%
Low	$5.6 million	9.2%
Median	$10.2 million	12.8%

Executive Pay 2001

Figure 7-5. *Stock Ownership Guidelines by Industry*

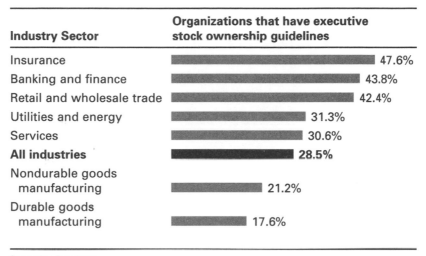

Industry Sector	Organizations that have executive stock ownership guidelines
Insurance	47.6%
Banking and finance	43.8%
Retail and wholesale trade	42.4%
Utilities and energy	31.3%
Services	30.6%
All industries	**28.5%**
Nondurable goods manufacturing	21.2%
Durable goods manufacturing	17.6%

Executive Pay 2001

relation to the company's financial performance. Everyone got into the debate: the media, the government, and institutional shareholders. While there were certainly some overpaid CEOs, this was not typically the case. Nevertheless, the public scrutiny led to a dramatic increase in the linkage between top executives' pay and corporate performance, largely through stock option grants and increased executive stock ownership. A massive increase in the value of the U.S. stock market followed.

That very success created a second round of criticism regarding executive pay: CEO pay is too high. CEO pay went up because the stock market went up—so they didn't deserve all that pay. CEOs get rich by downsizing; the gap between CEO pay and worker pay is too wide and widening. The stock market would have increased anyway; and CEO pay is still not related to true performance.

This time, however, one voice is largely missing from the chorus of naysayers: the shareholders'. That is because they have been benefiting from the dramatic increase in shareholder value. Better executive compensation programs have made the average

Figure 7-6. *Basis for Determining Executive Stock Ownership Guidelines—All Industries*

	Percentage of Responses
Multiple of base salary	████████████████████ 67.7%
Multiple of total cash	█ 5.1%
Other	███████ 27.3%

Executive Pay 2001

CEO more of a partner of shareowners, taking prudent risks and staying competitive to maximize value.

Despite its recent correction, the U.S. stock market has created trillions of dollars in value, much of which went directly into pension funds. In comparison, the CEOs of all the Fortune 500 companies in any given bull market year take home far less than 1 percent of the stock market increase[x]—certainly a small price to pay.

Those who support high pay opportunities argue that the way CEOs are paid—heavily through stock options—motivated them to improve their companies, thereby driving up the stock price, yielding high pay. One need only look at Japan, with limited stock incentives and low performance, for a very different and unattractive picture. Their critics counter that if that were true, a falling stock market would result in low CEO pay—which they do not believe will happen. We do. In fact, we have already seen declining CEO pay as a result of the stock market drop. But we also believe that maintaining strong incentives for top executives will help to minimize any market decline.

Premium-Priced and Indexed Stock Options

We strongly believe in the creative use of stock options balanced with executive stock ownership. Our data show that such an approach helps to maximize shareholder value.[x]

Some companies offer premium-priced or indexed stock options in lieu of or in addition to regular ("at-the-money") stock options. These have an exercise price above the market stock price on the date of the grant. For example, if the stock price is currently $20, a traditional stock option would have an exercise price of $20. A premium-priced option might have an exercise price of $30. The point? To deliver the message, both to executives and all employees, that some minimum level of return is expected by shareholders before the employees should get paid.

An indexed stock option has the exercise price of the option move up and down with a market index. So in our previous example, the exercise price would only go to $30 if the index (e.g., the Dow Jones Industrial Average) went up 50 percent. If the index went down 10 percent, the exercise price would be $18.

This is often touted as the obvious solution to the executive pay dilemma. If the CEO and the executive team, working with all employees, beat the premium or indexed stock price, they really deserve their pay. The problem is that to meet those goals, the management team would have to undertake a riskier business strategy than the market anticipates for the company. If that strategy succeeds, everyone wins. If it fails, the stock price will go down further than anticipated, and the real shareholders will lose more than the option holders. Our view: When used in conjunction with other programs, specifically real stock programs, premium and indexed options have their place.

Why It Works

Stock Ties CEO's Personal Fortune to Company Performance

Our 2001 study on U.S. CEO pay confirms our long-held belief that combining CEO stock ownership with stock options is likely to be the best method of linking executives' and shareholders' interests.[9] The core of the theory is simple: As shareholders become wealthier through an increasing share price, so do the CEOs and executives who lead and manage the companies.

CEOs Become the Agents of Shareholders

Under the U.S. system of corporate law and corporate governance, shareholders own a company and elect a board of directors to manage its regular business affairs. The board of directors, in turn, elects and hires management, including a CEO, to operate the day-to-day business. The scope of authority of the CEO and other members of management is defined—one can also say delegated, limited, or controlled—by the board. As a result, the CEO and management become agents of the owners of the company.

The relationship between owners and agents is grounded on the basic principle that agents act on behalf of—and in the best interests of—owners. But basic notions of human behavior challenge this principle: Agents may primarily act on behalf of owners and secondarily maintain self-interest, however consciously or subconsciously. Unmet expectations and unacceptable results occur when these primary and secondary interests conflict. For example, a CEO interested in managing a large and profitable company might make decisions that trade off profit for revenue growth. An owner is only interested in profits. CEO stock works to bridge that gap.

(One recent exception to this profit/growth trade-off was the superior—albeit temporary—stock market valuations that some high-tech companies achieved during the late 1990s. There was little or no gap between founders (owners) of these companies and executives (agents) with lots of stock, mostly options. For awhile, the stock market suspended its usual rules and rewarded growth for its own sake. But when the high-tech bubble finally burst, it became clear that even in high tech, growth without profits did not create lasting economic value.)

Stock Bridges the Gap Between Owners' and Agents' Interests

Stock options are a relatively low-risk form of compensation, since they pay off handsomely for success and not at all for failure. But direct stock ownership is essential for two reasons:

- First, executives holding solely stock options have only upside opportunities, compared to the shareholders they represent, who also face downside risks. This can result in more aggressive risk taking by executives because they have nothing to lose.
- Second, options generally do not result in ownership, since most employees, including executives, sell the stock shortly after they exercise options.

Grants of restricted stock, as opposed to purchases, also have drawbacks, the primary one being the negative perception that boards of directors are "giving stock away." In addition, the CEO faces even less risk with restricted stock than with options. Unless the share price drops to zero, the executive will always have a gain. Nevertheless, both stock options and restricted stock have their appropriate uses, such as in specialized recruiting and retention situations.

How It Plays Out

Real-Life Examples of CEO Pay for Performance

There is a fairly strong statistical relationship between pay and performance. But how does this happen? The reality is that this occurs one CEO, one company, one board, one compensation committee at a time. An incentive plan is developed, a stock option grant is sized and made, and a conversation takes place between the compensation committee or its chair and the individual CEO. The following two anecdotes describe the process more fully.

Large Stock Option Package Is No Guarantee of Performance

A health care company was anticipating dramatic growth in size, profitability, and TRS. The CEO had basically built the company from the ground up, doing a terrific job of expansion through organic growth and acquisitions. The stock price at the time was around $15 a share, and the market capitalization was around $500 million. This CEO anticipated dramatic growth in the demand for the health care services his company provided, and that the stock price would double or triple in the next two or three years. What was the best way to ensure he shared extremely well in this growth? The 50,000 to 100,000 stock options he had been getting every year did not begin to capture the upside opportunity he wanted.

We recommended a premium-priced stock option, which has an exercise price higher than today's stock market price. If the exercise price was 50 percent higher than the current $15 per share, or $22.50, and if the CEO did not take any additional stock options for five years, the board could be justified in awarding 1 million stock options in a lump sum grant today. That way, if the stock price tripled to $45, the CEO would make a $22.50 profit per share on 1 million options, or $22.5 million. That was exactly what he had in mind, and the board and shareholders approved the plan.

However, changes in the health care market were extremely damaging to this company. Instead of rising, the stock price fell by half, to around $7 or $8. Those stock options were now about $15 out of the money, or "underwater." Strategy and execution notwithstanding, the health care market moved out from under the company, which caused the stock market to do the same. Subsequently, the CEO became chairman, and the company brought in another CEO, who is in the process of turning the company around. The stock price moved to $15 or $16, and the company uses more traditional stock options. The former CEO's options will likely expire before they are valuable.

Clearly, a large stock option grant is no guarantee of success.

Stock Ownership Is a Win-Win

Another client is a multibillion-dollar chemical company. Its new CEO felt that the company's costs were bloated and that it had diversified inappropriately. He believed that there was a real opportunity to increase shareholder value substantially by streamlining the organization and selling business units. Anticipating that outcome, he wanted a plan for himself and his top management team where they could continue to get stock options, but more importantly, they would buy a great deal of stock at a small discount. After receiving approval, they bought millions of shares of stock at a 15 percent discount using pretax dollars. The CEO also converted his Supplemental Executive Retirement Plan (SERP) to stock. He then proceeded to implement his strategy to good effect. The company's stock went from $25 to $125 per share, a five-fold increase. The CEO's net worth went from a few million dollars to around $50 million. Today, the company is considered one of the great success stories in the chemical industry.

Obviously, an incentive plan, no matter how perfectly structured, cannot overcome a change in the marketplace outside the company's control, a poor strategy, or even a great strategy poorly executed. Compensation is only one of the management tools necessary for creating value in the company.

And it is important to measure the risk. In the health care company, the CEO received one million options. Yes, that created some potential dilution. But that is a relatively low-cost way to fund a program like this. Because of bad luck, those options turned out to be worthless, so there was no payment made and no significant risk. (Had things turned out differently, shareholders would certainly have been happy to give the CEO his $22.5 million in return for a stock price that tripled to $45, and ownership of a company worth $1.5 billion.) With the chemical company, the executives purchased huge amounts of stock at a small discount. It was an additional cost to the company, but obviously well worth it.

From a policy perspective, a board or shareholder needs to ask, "Is it worth the risk? Are we comfortable offering these programs to our executives with the hope of motivating them to execute the right strategies? Is it worth giving the top managers 1, 2, or even 3 percent of the increase in market value to see if those strategies will be implemented?"

The answer, in almost every case, is clearly yes.

Academic Research Review[10]

There is considerable existing academic research on the topic of CEO pay. The studies generally try to answer one of six questions. Below is a summary of some of the best work:

Question #1: Is there pay for performance?

Is a CEO's pay sensitive to company performance? Is there a correlation?

Typical findings:

- CEO pay (including stock) is highly sensitive to performance.
- Sensitivity of compensation in one year is positively related to corporation performance in the next year.

Authors: Leonard; Abowd; Abowd et al.; Kahn et al.; Hall et al.; Murphy (1999); Himmelberg et al.; Joskos; Weibach; Hubbard

Question #2: Does stock ownership matter?

In other words, can companies ignore CEO stock ownership and solely grant stock options? If stock ownership is important, do stock ownership guidelines work? Do stock ownership guidelines create CEO ownership, which improves company performance?

Typical findings:

- Stock ownership has increased dramatically.

■ Firm performance is positively related to the percentage of equity held by managers.
■ Stock ownership guidelines increase ownership, which improves performance.

Authors: Mehran; Murphy; Core/Larker; Holderness et al.; McConnell; Morck

Question #3: Are there motivational differences between stock ownership and stock options?

Are executives afraid to buy stock if the price is volatile? Do large stock option grants motivate expensive company stock repurchase programs?
Typical findings:

■ Stock options cause increased volatility.
■ Increased volatility causes less ownership.
■ Stock options motivate lower dividends and increased repurchases.
Authors: Fenn et al.; Himmelberg et al.; Aggrawel; Demsetz

Question #4: Do stock options create ownership?

Typical findings:

■ No. Stock options do not create stock ownership but tend to serve as an imperfect proxy for stock ownership.

Authors: Ofek/Yermack
Stock options must be combined with executive stock ownership guidelines and vehicles to help executives achieve the required ownership levels. One way to promote stock ownership is a management stock purchase plan, which allows executives to purchase discounted company stock with a portion of their cash bonus and/or salary. This plan has significant tax, accounting, and financial planning advantages.

Question #5: Are poorly performing CEOs terminated?

Typical findings:

■ Yes

Authors: Denis/Denis

Another CEO myth is that poorly performing CEOs are never terminated. Some companies do keep their CEOs too long after poor financial performance begins. But many well-known and powerful CEOs lost their jobs in the 1990s at General Motors, American Express, IBM, and dozens of other companies. This study found statistical support that CEOs at poorly performing companies do indeed lose their jobs.

Question #6: Is the U.S. model being exported?

Typical findings:

■ Yes, but the "performance sensitivity" is much lower. (In other words, a y percent increase in stock price yields a 3-times-y percent increase in the CEO's pay. If the stock price went up by 5 percent, the CEO's net worth would go up by 15 percent. This sensitivity is much higher in the United States than elsewhere.)

Author: Kato

Comparisons of U.S. and overseas CEO pay packages are difficult given the vastly different size of the countries and companies. Because CEO pay tracks with company size, given the complexity and risk involved, the U.S. CEO pay packages are likely to be larger than those found overseas. In addition, international studies often do not account for differences in culture, local welfare benefits, and tax rates.

Does Pay Really Cause Better Performance?

Many critics of executive compensation argue that there is only a modest link between a company's performance and the compensation of its chief executive officer. The most well known of these critics is Graef S. "Bud" Crystal, a widely quoted former executive compensation consultant who is now a journalist. As publisher of *The Crystal Report,* he documents examples of companies and industries that show very little pay for performance. For example, *The Crystal Report* evaluated 424 large-market capitalization firms, comparing the CEO's base salary, total cash compensation (salary plus bonus) and total direct compensation or TDC (total cash compensation plus the value of stock plans, particularly stock options at grant) to the size and performance of the company.

In evaluating TDC, *The Crystal Report* found that only one-third of the variation in TDC could be explained by company size, performance (shareholder returns), and CEO tenure, leaving fully two-thirds unexplained. The study concluded that there is limited pay for performance.[11]

A few points should be made:

- *The Crystal Report* has been studying this issue for years, while pay for performance has increased substantially over time. In fact, Bud Crystal should be congratulated for his part in promoting pay for performance, since he has been such an articulate critic of overpaid CEOs over the past decade, even influencing legislative efforts restricting executive pay.[12]

- The primary dispute relates to the TDC definition, including the *hypothetical grant value of options,* or "grant valuation" approach, which uses the Black-Scholes option valuation method.[13] While all compensation experts agree that option grants have economic value (even at grant, when most have no intrinsic profit built in), we disagree that it is appropriate to correlate this hypothetical *future* value with *past* financial performance. This is explored further below.

Our own studies of top management compensation, as well as many academic studies, show a very different finding. As detailed in the beginning of this chapter, Watson Wyatt's survey of top management compensation shows first that total cash compensation for CEOs, which is their base salary plus bonus, is indeed sensitive to the stock market performance of their companies in terms of TRS. (See Figure 7-3.) When we looked at TDC, our definition did not use the *hypothetical future* value of the options but the *historical actual* value. Our data show that those companies with the highest paid CEOs outperformed the lowest paid ones in many industries. Companies that paid CEOs at a higher-than-median level registered nearly five percentage points higher in terms of TRS. For large capitalization companies, this difference can mean hundreds of millions of dollars of increased shareholder value. Since much of the pay was delivered via exercised stock options, companies appear to be directly linking executive and shareholder interests. While it is impossible to say with certainty that the higher pay opportunity *caused* the better stock performance, there is a strong statistical relationship. Most importantly, such an outcome is so favorable to shareholders that it is certainly worth the risk. We believe that this difference in methodologies—theoretical grant value of options versus actual historical value, each of which is then compared to historical TRS—explains some of the differences in findings among the various studies.

To show what we mean, take two companies, Company A and Company B, each with different histories, strategies, products, and management styles, but with an identical goal to increase TRS. The CEOs of each company are granted 500,000 stock options (with proportional grants for all other employees at Company A and only top management grants at Company B), each at the fair market value of, say, $20 for both companies, and each with a Black-Scholes value on their options of $10, for a hypothetical grant value of $5 million. Over the next year, Company A performs brilliantly, partly due to an excellent strategy and execution and partly due to its team culture from broad-based stock options. Its stock price rises fivefold, to $100, and the CEO realizes $40 million in pretax option profits. During that same year, Company B poorly executes a flawed strategy and experiences some unfortunate circumstances (turnover of key sales personnel to option-granting companies, price wars, bad weather, and a loss in a lawsuit). Its stock price plunges to $11, and it becomes a takeover target. Naturally, Company B's CEO's stock options are worthless.

As we look back on these two companies and perform our statistical analysis, what can we conclude?

1. The highly paid Company A CEO worked for a company that performed substantially better than the lower-paid CEO.
2. Stock options or any incentive plan are no guarantee of success for shareholders. Overall strategy execution is essential.
3. Stock options are a relatively low-risk form of compensation, since they pay off handsomely for success and not at all for failure.
4. The Company B CEO did not walk off with nothing. It is very likely he received a competitive salary and benefits, which we favor, despite his company's poor performance. It is important, however, to structure salary and benefits so that they do not diminish the motivational impact of a stock option program, because stock options have the highest probability of driving a successful strategy. In this case, total pay for performance eventually wins the day, because the Company B CEO probably lost his job because of poor strategy and execution.

5. Executive pay experts who value options at grant would have completely missed the boat on this one. Their analysis would have valued the two option grants at about $5 million for each CEO (500,000 × $10 estimated per option value). The one-year look-back using the "grant valuation" approach would have shown two identically paid CEOs, with one company performing in a stellar manner, the other performing terribly. They would have concluded that there is no pay for performance. They would, of course, have been wrong. To be fair, Bud Crystal occasionally studied stock option grants and subsequent stock price increases *over time* for the same individuals. He typically found no pay for performance using this method as well. His explanation usually related to the timing of option grants and stock price fluctuations. This timing of option grants can clearly have a major impact on their ultimate value. Nevertheless, the primary studies that critics use are indeed the intercompany comparisons as described above.

6. However, we still cannot conclude that the high pay opportunity caused the high performance. Might Company A's stock have gone to $100 if the CEO had been granted only 100,000 stock options, or even none? Of course, this question is impossible to answer, but we have come full circle: Is it worth the risk that the board would take on behalf of shareholders? In this simplistic example, the answer is obviously "yes." Real life, of course, is much more complex. But what is the policy alternative for the board? Follow the Japanese or German model of limited stock option grants for executives? That model has not worked for the Japanese, and we believe it certainly would not work in the United States either, in today's globally competitive economy.

This methodological dispute is more than just an arcane argument among experts: It defines the nature of the argument.

Specifically, if the entire stock market goes down, and if companies continue granting stock options, the grant methodology will show even lower linkages of pay for performance. Our methodology, as seen in the example, would show ever-rising links, even as pay declines with the market. This more meaningful methodology is the one used in the above analysis, Figures 7-1 to 7-4.

CHAPTER

Offer Significant Stock-Based Incentives Across the Board

"...it is inconsistent to require much higher commitment and involvement without offering a dollar payoff if the performance is positive."
—Tom Peters in *Thriving on Chaos*

Make it worth their while, and employees will focus on shareholder value. The obvious answer is to link compensation to stock price through stock options. But the concern is obvious as well: the resulting dilution of the stock could well hurt total return to stockholders more than it helps.

A growing body of research provides the answer: a clear, but careful, "yes" to broad-based stock options. They are a tremendously important tool, but should be used judiciously.

What the Numbers Say

Broad-Based Stock Programs Increase Productivity

Watson Wyatt's most recent studies show broad-based stock plan programs play a key role in increasing shareholder value. The Human Capital Index found that companies emphasizing stock programs for employees were worth 3.5 percent more. (See Figure 8-1.)

Our *Strategic Rewards®* research also gave stock high marks:

- Fifty-three percent of top-performing employees say stock options are a "very effective" recruiting tool.
- Fifty-one percent of top-performing employees say stock options are a "very effective" retention tool.
- Of all the monetary rewards at companies' disposal, the one that grew the most in usage from 1999 to 2000 was stock grants: from 40 to 48 percent.

Echoing our results are those from the first comprehensive study to evaluate whether and how broad-based employee stock option programs affect corporate performance. Among the research findings, which are available from The National Center for Employee Ownership (NCEO), are the following:

- Seven to 10 million employees actually received stock options as of May 2000. This represents a substantial increase since 1991, when the NCEO estimated that about 1000 companies with 1 million employees offered such plans. This number of employees probably surpasses the 8 million plus employees in ESOPs and stock bonus plans.[1]

Figure 6-1. *Links Between Stock Programs and Value Creation*

Practice	Impact on Market Value
High percentage of stock owned by employees	1.3%
High percentage of stock owned by senior managers	1.2%
High percentage of employees eligible for stock options	1.0%

Expected change associated with a significant (1SD) improvement in practice

Watson Wyatt's Human Capital Index®

- Broad-based stock option companies demonstrated statistically significant higher productivity levels and annual growth rates than public companies overall and than their industry peers. This is particularly important because individual employees and groups of employees influence productivity, via active components such as work practices and employee effort and/or passive components such as their acceptance of and participation in downsizings, reorganizations, and new technologies.[2]
  - For a specific two-year period, broad-based stock option companies had significantly higher productivity **levels**—9.3 percent greater—compared to all companies.[3]
  - In the same time period, they also had 2.2 percent higher annual productivity **growth.**[4]
  - At the end of 1997, broad-based stock option companies had 31 percent higher productivity than all public companies.[5]
  - Surveyed stock option companies with more than 50 percent nonmanagement employees receiving grants had 20 percent higher productivity than all public companies and 21 percent more than their peers.[6]
- The total shareholder return findings are that over the 1992-1997 period, broad-based stock option companies performed at least as well as public companies overall and their industry peers, and sometimes outperformed these two comparison groups.[7]

The authors of the NCEO report conclude: "When companies implement broad-based stock option programs, they are taking an action that should, all other things being equal, dilute total shareholder returns. We see clearly that the drop that might have been expected in TRS did not take place over the long run. It would appear that the positive performance of the broad-based stock options companies—especially in the productivity area—may have counterbalanced the dilution that these plans would have been expected to cause."[8]

Why It Works

Stock Options Engage and Empower the Troops

We have seen stock options expand positively in the United States over the past three decades. In fact, as of mid 2000, 7 to 10 million employees actually received stock options, according to the NCEO.[9] That is up from just 1 million in 1991, and may make it the leading form of employee ownership in America today.

Employees at all levels—including unionized employees—have embraced the idea that stock options and stock ownership will provide them a larger slice of the corporate pie than paychecks, making wealth an achievable goal for more American workers than ever before. Executives embrace risk with excitement and commitment, knowing the payoff is within their reach. This opportunity creates empowerment, demands open communication, and minimizes bureaucracy.

A Caution: Too Much of a Good Thing

Led by the proliferation of technology firms, the U.S. stock market has experienced phenomenal growth in the past decade. Despite the recent market correction, much of this growth can be attributed to the increased use of stock-based incentive compensation, especially stock options, to link the interests of employees and shareholders. One measure of stock option usage is called "overhang," which is defined as stock options granted, plus those remaining to be granted, as a percentage of the total shares outstanding at a given company. Overhang has grown dramatically over the past decade because of much larger executive option grants and increased option eligibility.

In general, option expansion has been a healthy development, getting employees to think more like owners, thereby improving company performance. Nevertheless, stock options are not without their controversy and challenges. As is the case for all scarce resources—such as financial capital and human capital—optimum usage and allocation of stock options by boards of directors are absolutely required by the equity markets.

To understand the impact of stock options, it is important to note their two countervailing effects:

1. Incentive effect. Stock options motivate employees to create superior financial performance, placing upward pressure on stock prices.
2. Dilution/volatility effect. Stock options represent a potential future issuance of shares, thus creating dilution and exerting downward pressure on stock prices.

The overall effect of a stock option grant on a firm's value depends on many factors, including grant size, the condition of the stock market, the company's performance, corporate culture, and levels of employee stock ownership. Boards of directors must be sensitive to these issues as they determine how many shares of stock and stock options to issue.

- Stock option overhang has grown dramatically over the past 10 years to an average of more than 14 percent at a typical firm.[10]
- The rate of increase in overhang has slowed recently. Almost 40 percent of the firms in our sample decreased their overhang between 1997 and 1999. These overhang-decreasing firms tended to have had above-average overhang in 1997.[11]
- There appears to be a limit to the economic benefits from very high overhang, which varies significantly by industry and the extent of its human capital intensity (a firm is said to be human-capital intense if its primary value is in its employees' intelligence or skills). The reason growth in overhang has slowed is because more firms have reached this limit.[12]
- Stock options appear to have motivated top managers to undertake riskier business strategies, including more debt, lower dividends and higher stock repurchases.

These riskier strategies have yielded higher levels of
stock price volatility, which are not in the best interests
of general shareholders.[13]

■ Companies with higher direct ownership of stock tend to
have higher financial performance, lower volatility, higher
dividends, and more balanced stock repurchases.[14]

Watson Wyatt's study, "Stock Option Overhang—Shareholder
Boon or Shareholder Burden?" illustrated that—up to a certain
point—there is a positive relationship between Total Return to
Shareholders (TRS) and stock option overhang.[15] Beyond that
"sweet spot," increases in overhang actually lead to a decrease in
firm value.

To illustrate how the optimal overhang level works, let's
focus on 70 large companies in the technology industry, specifically a comparison of 1997 overhang to 1999 TRS (a bull market
year) and 2000 TRS (a bear market year). (See Figure 8-2.) Our
data indicate that the optimal level of overhang for 1997 was
approximately 25 percent in this industry. If we divide the firms
into three groups based on their proximity to this level, we see
that firms at the approximate optimal level, say between 21 and
29 percent, have the highest TRS for both years. Firms that are
substantially below the optimal level have an overhang of less
than 21 percent and a lower TRS, while firms that are substantially above the optimal level have even lower levels of TRS.[16]

While successful firms will continue using stock options to
motivate employees to think like owners, they need to control the

Figure 8-2. *Overhang and Total Return to Shareholders—
Technology Industry*

Actual overhang level vs. optimal	1997 overhang	1999 TRS (median)	2000 TRS
Significantly below optimal	16%	+27%	-8%
At or near optimal	26%	+50%	+6%
Significantly above optimal	38%	-6%	-30%

Stock Option Overhang 2001

size of their grants to avoid excessive dilution and motivating risky behavior. Value-maximizing firms need to effectively manage both the levels of their stock-based incentive compensation and the mix between stock options and stock ownership. As the willingness of shareholders to suffer dilution reaches a limit, as reflected in the slowdown in the growth rate of overhang, there will be even more pressure to increase stock ownership at all levels, perhaps by using formal ownership guidelines, and to slow down the increase or even reduce the size of stock option grants.

How It Plays Out

Doing It Right; Doing It Wrong

A premiere professional services firm had been a partnership for the three decades since it was founded. The traditional partnership model had served them well—the firm had a superior reputation and financial performance, the partners were extremely well paid, and the likelihood of—and payoff for—becoming one of those highly paid partners served to attract, motivate, and retain employees at all levels of the career ladder. The "Golden Rule" of partnership was working—"do unto the next generation as was done unto you." In this case, that meant leaving the partnership in the same or better condition for the next generation.

However, retirements, competition, and the need for capital forced the firm to initiate an Initial Public Offering (IPO). While extremely attractive to current partners—their $2 book value stock was now worth $20—it broke the Golden Rule. How to salvage or at least replace that partnership model?

As a matter of generosity (or firm survival, depending on your perspective), the partners created several stock-based programs. First, they granted massive amounts of "founders" stock options to all employees at the firm, yielding more than 20 percent overhang. They also put in place a special senior level (but below partner) stock purchase plan that had favorable terms including a matching stock option. Finally, they established an all-employee global stock purchase plan, also with highly favorable terms. All of these stock programs were highly dilutionary to the former partners. But did it work?

The stock price has quadrupled since the IPO, with vast numbers of employees sharing in the gain. Turnover is at an all-time low. All in all, it was a great success.

On the other hand, a well-known consumer products company had a successful history of stock option grants and financial performance. Performance turned sour in the late 1990s for a host of reasons. The stock price plunged. In addition, many e-commerce companies viewed them as a recruiting playground, luring their key employees away with visions of riches. The company panicked, making large grants of stock options to numerous employees as its stock price dropped. They were continually assuming that the most recent grant was at the bottom price. They were wrong. Eventually, as the e-commerce world faced its own problems, things went back to normal. But not before a great deal of stock option overhang was created. Again—stock options are a great tool, but they must be viewed as a scarce resource to be used judiciously.

CHAPTER

"Synchronize" Pay

The CEO of one of our admired clients has a salary, the opportunity for a bonus, and stock options. It is a competitive and motivating package. And in its structure, it is identical to those of his division managers, his sales people, and his secretary.

We call it "synchronized pay," and when it is done well, it unites a workforce. Allowing most or even all employees to participate in reward plans puts the entire workforce squarely in the same boat. The employees share risk, and they share reward. They are similarly motivated toward what is in the company's (and the shareholders') interests.

Furthermore, synchronizing pay creates the opportunity to reward—and therefore attract, retain, and motivate—outstanding employees at all levels. If variable pay and stock options are only available at the top of the company, then the only reward for the rest is their salary program (and perhaps the opportunity to move up). That is not enough to create the kind of high-performance culture that produces top shareholder returns.

On the flip side, failing to synchronize pay can result in a demoralized and less productive workforce. In his book *Strategic*

Pay, Edward Lawler notes that the typical organization offers incentive pay to only a part of the workforce: "This often leads to a 'we-they' split in the workforce that can be counterproductive and can lead to non-cooperative work relationships. In one plant I studied, the conflict degenerated into open warfare. Occasionally the support people would purposely delay their work, thereby holding up incentive workers, so that the workers on incentive would not make more than they themselves did. The incentive workers, on the other hand, would constantly complain to management about the support workers and at times even threaten them."[1]

Wherever there are wide discrepancies in the manner in which employees are compensated, there are rumors, squabbling, and general "noise" about who has what kind of deal (and how unfair it is). That saps productivity and poisons the atmosphere.

Synchronizing pay, on the other hand, demonstrates a spirit of fairness—a crucial component of the "trust in senior leadership" so important to shareholder value, employee commitment and effective change management. (See Chapter 14.) In early 2001, two major banks (BankOne Corp. and First Union Corp.) cancelled their supplemental executive retirement plans. In the March 2001 issue of *American Banker*, a spokesman for BankOne explained why: "It is a fairness issue. The executives should not have a pension plan the average employee does not have."[2]

Leading companies are clearly beginning to recognize that synchronized pay is a key component in achieving a true pay-for-performance culture.

The Effects of Synchronized Pay

Synchronizing pay does not mean, of course, that all employees are paid the same amounts. It means designing compensation plans that allow broad—perhaps even total—participation in most reward plans. It also means that special perquisites for top executives probably have negative returns on investment in terms of the morale problems they create.

Positive Impact on Morale

In our experience, employees do not resent their CEOs becoming wealthy from stock options as long as they have an opportunity to reap proportionate rewards. As then-President Clinton remarked to *USA Today*, "I don't think working people…resent people who run companies making a lot of money. What they resent is any feeling that they are being treated unfairly."[3] The worst morale problems we've seen are in companies where top management received all of the stock options granted and then tried to reduce costs through downsizing. Layoffs are never welcome, of course, but most employees understand that companies must respond to global and other competitive pressures. Having stock and other incentives in place throughout all levels of the company makes for a very different reaction from both "survivors" and those losing their jobs.

The morale boost from synchronized pay is not limited to certain employee groups. Those on the way up as well as those in relatively permanent career positions—whether production/clerical jobs, supervisory, or even middle management—want to share in the overall success of their company. The impact on morale and productivity has been obvious.

Flat Versus Steep Pay Structure

Optimal synchronicity does not require pay equality or even a very flat pay structure. Some organizations do maintain a low ratio of CEO pay to entry-level pay, such as government agencies, a few idiosyncratic (but successful) companies such as Ben & Jerry's Ice Cream and, of course, Japanese and many European companies (although pay structures in European countries tend to be less flat than the Japanese model). At a typical, large, successful American company, the CEO-to-average-worker pay ratio has grown dramatically over the past 20 years and is now around $200:$1.[4] The question is whether this relatively high (and still growing) ratio is a problem.

Pay inequality has been debated extensively in books and in the media (for example, *Created Unequal* by James K. Galbraith[5] and *CEO Pay and Shareholder Value* by Ira Kay[6]). Some CEO pay critics argue that a steep pay structure (high CEO pay ratio) damages morale and therefore productivity. This viewpoint appears to have been proven false by the outstanding financial and stock market success of the U.S. economy and companies.

Japanese companies were very successful financially at the same time they emphasized pay equality from highly synchronized pay programs, from 1970 to 1990. Given their economic tumble of the past 12 years, either the equality model failed or it was never helpful in the first place, and other factors accounted for Japan's historical success. We do not know. We do know that the United States succeeded with "optimally" synchronized pay systems, but unlike the Japanese, they had uncapped pay opportunities at all levels including the CEO. Cisco, Microsoft, Enron, Lowe's, Home Depot, and hundreds of other companies have created tens of thousands of millionaires at all employee levels, not just executives, through their stock options, ESOPs, employee stock purchase plans, and so on. Even Ben & Jerry's had to abandon their low CEO/employee ratio model a few years back to recruit an external CEO who could respond to their own unique competitive pressures.

Pay synchronicity works wonderfully; excessive synchronicity leading to pay equality will most likely fail.

Top Performers Attracted and Retained

As mentioned, synchronized pay has another crucial attribute: It allows the company to reward—and therefore attract, motivate, and retain—top performers at all organizational levels.

Those division managers and sales personnel mentioned in the first paragraph are not all paid the same. They are all **eligible** for stock options, but only 80 percent of the division managers and 50 percent of the sales personnel actually **received** them. They also received very different bonuses and salary increases.

The net result is that the top performers at all position levels make two or three times as much as the bottom performers. And 1 of those division managers and 10 of the sales people just might have taken their skills to an e-commerce competitor if they had not been given these pay opportunities.

Convergence of Old and New Economies

So, we are seeing a trend toward similarly designed compensation packages up and down the corporate ladder within a given company. In addition to motivating employees, there is another important benefit of this trend: It is creating a convergence of what used to be widely varied compensation systems across companies in both the old and new economies. What is causing the convergence? The fight over the top-performing employee.

With a shrinking talent pool as a backdrop, the digital world has been trying to lure the best people from traditional firms, which try just as hard to retain them. Program after program aimed at keeping and motivating top performers has been instituted at both ends of the spectrum. The result? There has been a convergence of the two labor markets around the mechanism of rewarding the top-performing employee. As a part of that convergence, the compensation systems at these companies are beginning to look alike. And the stock market correction that started in early 2000 has accelerated and basically completed this convergence.

And what do these compensation systems look like at their point of convergence? A well-designed synchronized pay system.

What the Numbers Say

Synchronizing Pay Can Help with Attraction and Retention

Companies have always been after high-performing employees, but never before has that pursuit had the power to dramatically alter the compensation landscape. Why now? Because the war for talent has escalated, given both shrinking supply (demographics) and the rising demand in the knowledge enonomy. According to *Watson Wyatt's Strategic Rewards®* research, companies of every kind are reporting difficulty in both attracting and retaining critical-skill employees. (See Figure 9-1.) Those that win the battle for these key employees will substantially outperform those that do not.

Complicating matters is the fact that employers and employees have very different ideas about what works most powerfully in attracting and retaining the best. We asked two groups—employers and top-performing employees—which types of compensation programs were most effective when it came to attraction and retention. The gaps between the two sets of answers were telling. The data reveals a startling disconnect in viewpoint between bosses and the very workers they most wish to keep.

As a general rule, employers try a little bit of everything to attract and retain employees. High performers want a specific group of programs—especially career advancement opportunities, high pay, and stock options—and lots of them.

For example, a full 72 percent of high-performing employees say that paying above the market will be a very effective tool in attracting them to a certain company. In contrast, only 33 percent of the employers feel above-market pay has that strong of an impact. Another enormous gap is in the area of group incentives. While only 15 percent of employers view them as very effective, almost half of the top-performing employees rate them that highly. (See Figure 9-2.)

Figure 9-1.   *Attracting and Retaining Critical-Skill Employees*

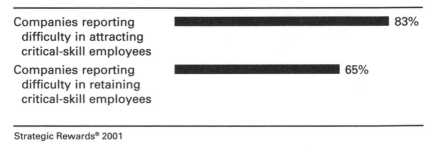

Companies reporting difficulty in attracting critical-skill employees	83%
Companies reporting difficulty in retaining critical-skill employees	65%

Strategic Rewards® 2001

Figure 9-2. *The Perception Gap: Comparison of Rewards Programs in Attraction*

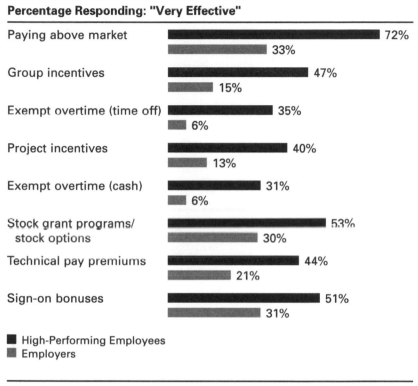

Percentage Responding: "Very Effective"

Paying above market — 72% / 33%

Group incentives — 47% / 15%

Exempt overtime (time off) — 35% / 6%

Project incentives — 40% / 13%

Exempt overtime (cash) — 31% / 6%

Stock grant programs/ stock options — 53% / 30%

Technical pay premiums — 44% / 21%

Sign-on bonuses — 51% / 31%

■ High-Performing Employees
■ Employers

Strategic Rewards® 2000

The results are similar in the area of retention. Again, top-performing employees say paying above the market is tremendously effective (69 percent), while employers give it a lukewarm rating (29 percent). (See Figure 9-3.)

The disconnect is not only in the area of compensation-based rewards. Most employers do not recognize the importance of enabling employees to advance and learn new skills. (See Figure 9-4.)

We took a look at the programs top performers said were most important in attracting and retaining them, and then we looked at the gaps associated with those practices. The most important programs also happen to be some of the ones with the

Figure 9-3. *The Perception Gap: Comparison of Rewards Programs in Retention*

Percentage Responding: "Very Effective"

Paying above market — 69% / 29%

Group incentives — 38% / 5%

Exempt overtime (time off) — 46% / 20%

Project incentives — 44% / 24%

Exempt overtime (cash) — 51% / 32%

Stock grant programs/ stock options — 41% / 26%

Technical pay premiums — 26% / 9%

■ High-Performing Employees
■ Employers

Strategic Rewards® 2000

widest gaps we had found between top performers and their employers. (See Figures 9-5, 9-6, and 9-7.)

Study the gaps, and a powerful competitive advantage in the attraction/retention fight begins to emerge. Top performers in this new economy want, in fact, what top performers have always wanted: terrific opportunity to earn based on their contribution, plus the chance to learn and advance. The gaps show that most employers do not recognize how important these basics are to their key talent. That means a synchronized pay system with strong pay for performance elements should provide a significant competitive advantage. Since corporate resources are always scarce, we believe that focusing on these key five or six areas would yield a high return on both attraction and retention.

Figure 9-4. *The Perception Gap: Comparison of Noncompensation-Based Reward Plans in Retention*

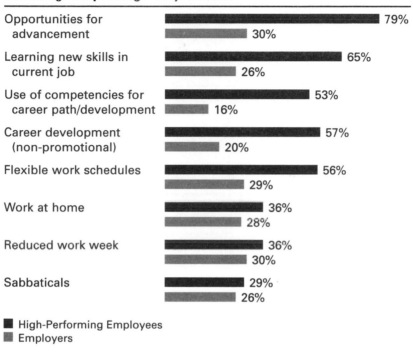

Percentage Responding: "Very Effective"

Opportunities for advancement	79% / 30%
Learning new skills in current job	65% / 26%
Use of competencies for career path/development	53% / 16%
Career development (non-promotional)	57% / 20%
Flexible work schedules	56% / 29%
Work at home	36% / 28%
Reduced work week	36% / 30%
Sabbaticals	29% / 26%

■ High-Performing Employees
■ Employers

Strategic Rewards® 2000

It's important to note that the number-one program that high performers want—career advancement opportunities—is very closely related to high pay opportunities. It is impossible to imagine that any employee—especially a high performer—would take a promotion and not expect to be paid for it. Creating career opportunities and paying for advancement are essential to all levels of the organization, and are therefore another part of a synchronized culture.

But does this synchronized pay-for-performance culture really work? We looked to the high-tech companies to find out. The stock market correction of the past two years has taken some of the bloom off of this sector, but high-tech companies have

Figure 9-5. *High-Performers' Top Three Issues in Attraction*

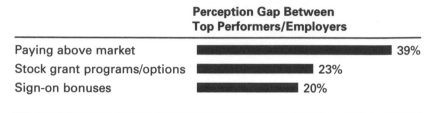

Strategic Rewards® 2000

Figure 9-6. *High-Performers' Top Three Compensation-Based Issues in Retention*

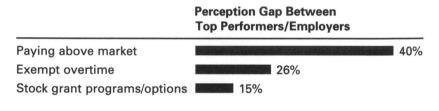

Strategic Rewards® 2000

Figure 9-7. *High-Performers' Top Three Noncompensation-Based Issues in Retention*

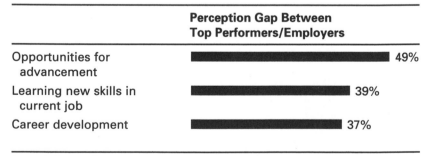

Strategic Rewards® 2000

done an excellent job of managing their human capital via their pay programs. There are valuable insights to learn from them. These firms were the first to move whole-heartedly into a philosophy of synchronized pay, and since then it has become a distinguishing characteristic of employment in that sector. It turns out that these companies are in fact experiencing less turnover (moreover, it is even declining) and less difficulty in retaining employees than most. (See Figures 9-8 and 9-9.)

What, exactly, are the technology companies doing differently when it comes to compensation? They're offering more of everything, but especially more sign-on bonuses, more stock options, and more spot bonuses. (See Figure 9-10.)

Look down the list: Almost every type of compensation program is offered more consistently by technology companies than by others. Ten percent more tech companies offer sign-on bonuses than other companies. Twenty-two percent more tech companies offer broad-based stock options. Fourteen percent more tech companies offer spot bonuses. High-performing technology companies are obviously focusing on pay for performance—exactly what high-performing employees say they want.

The good news: It is working.

Synchronized Pay Emphasizes Pay for Performance

In the early 1990s, when those high-tech companies began offering stock options to most of their workers, it was a stunning turn of events. That kind of incentive used to be a reward for getting to the

Figure 9-8. *Average Turnover Rates*

Technology companies — 12%
All other companies — 14%

Strategic Rewards® 2001

Figure 9-9. *Difficulty in Retaining Noncritical Skill Employees*

Technology companies — 38%
All other companies — 45%

Strategic Rewards® 2001

Figure 9-10. *How the Technology Companies Are Different*

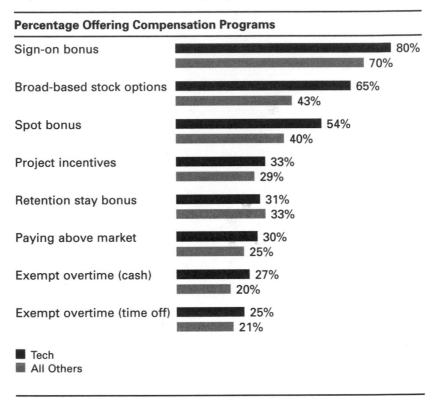

Percentage Offering Compensation Programs

Sign-on bonus — 80% / 70%

Broad-based stock options — 65% / 43%

Spot bonus — 54% / 40%

Project incentives — 33% / 29%

Retention stay bonus — 31% / 33%

Paying above market — 30% / 25%

Exempt overtime (cash) — 27% / 20%

Exempt overtime (time off) — 25% / 21%

■ Tech
■ All Others

Strategic Rewards® 2001

top. Stock options, special stock purchases, annual bonuses and special benefits were the perquisites of those at the very highest level of the company. Everyone else just moved along, receiving small raises regardless of company or individual performance.

The high-tech leaders were the first to recognize that a new business model emphasizing a team-based environment demanded a different approach. If human capital is indeed the key asset in this knowledge-based economy, it must be treated as such throughout the company—not just at the top. The legions of workers below top management are not interchangeable pawns that can be easily or cheaply replaced. They need to be motivated and rewarded fairly or they will pack up and take their talent elsewhere. Making use of all of the attraction, motivation, and retention tools previously used only with high-level executives gives an organization much more power in directing its workforce toward important objectives.

Many of today's compensation programs reflect that shift in philosophy, and even at the executive level, there have been dramatic changes. An executive program may still target salaries at the market average, but it may have career bands that allow for significant differentiation between average and star performers. These broadbands reduce the number of salary grades but increase the amount of money available in each grade. Under this system, individuals can be rewarded on their own competence level instead of according to a narrower job classification. The highest-performing executives today also receive larger annual incentive payments, and very large stock option grants.

Similarly, companies have moved toward the "band" concept for all-employee programs as well. Establishing annual incentives for a majority of workers—certainly nonhourly employees—has become common. Stock purchase plans are commonplace, particularly the opportunity to buy stock at a 15 percent discount. And stock options, formerly the sole province of very senior managers, are now becoming routinely available to all employees, and not just in start-up and high-technology companies.

The common thread that runs through the changes outlined above is the growing emphasis on pay for performance—the most critical attribute of a synchronized culture.

Rules for Synchronizing Pay

Many organizations, then, are beginning to adopt elements of a synchronized system. To formally establish this type of consistent pay structure, the following guidelines should be used:

1. *Maintain three basic types of compensation programs for all employees: salary, annual incentives, and long-term*

incentives (typically stock options or some type of stock purchase vehicle). This structure gives everyone the same opportunity, but can easily enable top performers to earn much more than average performers. Under this system, where everyone has the same "deal," the star can receive a 10 percent salary increase when the average performer gets 4 percent. The star gets a 20 percent bonus when the average performer gets 10 percent. And the star gets 1000 stock options when the average performer gets none. Not only does this system reward (and therefore retain) key talent, it strongly encourages poor performers to improve.

2. *Performance measures should be identical, if possible, and the same for all employees from the top down.* Establishing objective performance measures is key to the crucial concept of fairness behind synchronized pay. There are two types of measures we recommend: organization-wide results such as total return to shareholders, earnings per share, net income, return on equity and economic value added; and "line-of-sight" measures that reflect a smaller business unit. They should always be used in combination.

   (The line-of-sight measures are an important motivator because that's where the employee has a larger impact.) If an employee in the New York office has a terrific year, paying him using line-of-sight measures will ensure he gets rewarded for his performance. But using line-of-sight measures alone creates two problems: (1) One employee's terrific year may coincide with a devastating year for the corporation as a whole, but the company still has to pay him. (2) Business that would be handled best in, say, the Philadelphia office may end up in the New York office because the New York decision-maker wanted to get paid for the work. That's why line-of-sight measures should always be used in conjunction with traditional organization-wide measures.)

Profit sharing is an ideal way to reward every employee based on the same measurement. And the Human Capital Index research found that corporate-wide profit sharing is associated with a 0.9 percent increase in market value.

3. *Executive perquisites and benefits should be eliminated or reduced, if possible.* For example, executive medical benefits should be eliminated and replaced with salary. We once worked with a company whose CEO had a special $50,000 fund for medical benefits. Imagine how it looked when he tried to raise his employees' deductibles. This is consistent with the status issue discussed in Chapter 12.

4. *Performance management programs should cover all employees, including CEOs.* You can't have a pay-for-performance culture without performance appraisals. And you don't have a synchronized system if some employees get reviewed and others do not. Boards of directors should establish special committees to review the CEO's performance every year. Probably fewer than 25 percent of companies do this now, and that is not enough.

The hallmark of the synchronized system is consistency. But beware "foolish consistency," as Ralph Waldo Emerson called it. The goal is to have programs with similar structures, not identical payouts, across the board.

Introducing the New System

Like any change, moving to a synchronized culture is threatening for those comfortable with the current system. Top executives may feel their status is being stripped away when entry-level workers are suddenly offered bonuses and options. Long-term employees who've been happy to coast along on a guaranteed salary may feel panicky at the idea of pay for performance.

Make It Simple

To ease the transition, management needs to take care in introducing the system. Good communication is crucial at the start. The task of articulating the plan and gathering support will be much easier if it is designed simply. In the quiet of the planning stages, the temptation to add more and more to the program can be strong. The following test should be used: Imagine detailing this plan to 200 employees in an auditorium. How does it feel? If you begin to wish you didn't have to go into the next paragraph, you have your answer.

Present the Upside

When making that initial presentation to employees, make the upside clear. As with any major culture change, start by identifying the burning platform. After establishing the pressing nature of the situation, management can outline the tremendous opportunity this offers to each employee. Management shouldn't shy away from detailing how different the paychecks may look in a few years, as money begins shifting from nonperformers to star performers.

Focus on Performance Measurement

Another key architectural element is educating employees about the measures on which their compensation will be based. In *Strategic Pay,* Lawler emphasizes the importance of this issue: "Fundamental to an effective merit pay system are credible, comprehensive measures of performance. Without these, it is impossible to relate pay to performance. There is a great deal of evidence that in most organizations performance appraisal is not done well and that, as a result, no good measures of individual performance exist...The entire usefulness of merit pay rests on the performance appraisal system. Yet all too often, rather than providing a firm foundation, it is the weak link."[7] It takes time and effort to establish appropriate performance measurements. It takes even more time and effort to communicate them thoroughly, and to use them correctly. But the payoff—a true pay for performance culture—is enormous.

When it comes to organization-wide measurements, the work is easier. No matter which numbers a company is using, the results are the results. The key is to make sure employees have an easy way to access the information, and they have the help they need to understand it.

Don't Rest on Your Laurels

Finally, the program's impact and outcome should be reviewed regularly, with a view toward modifying the plan in years to come, as different needs emerge.

How It Plays Out

Various Companies Succeed with Synchronicity

Companies have approached synchronized pay in slightly different ways, reflecting their own cultures and needs. Below are a few more examples we've witnessed.

- A U.S.-based insurance company was bought by a European parent. Before the purchase, the American company provided stock options only to top management. It was a successful company, but the European parent wanted to see stock incentive plans at all levels on a global basis, including stock ownership and not just stock options. The American subsidiary implemented a broad-based stock purchase plan with a 15 percent discount for all employees. Morale, productivity, and financial performance have all improved.
- A professional services firm was switching from a partnership model to a publicly traded stock. Pre-IPO, only the

partners were owners. The post-IPO culture was intended to be a broad-ownership culture. The firm implemented a number of stock option and stock ownership plans that have been very well received. Their financial performance should continue to be excellent.

■ A utility company developed an annual cash incentive program for all employees—including union workers—using the exact same performance measure: Return on Equity (ROE). If the company earned 15 percent ROE, everyone made their predetermined "target incentive." If the company fell short, employees earned less. If the company beat the ROE goal, then each employee earned an above-target incentive. The program was very well received and helped produce excellent financial and stock market results.

CHAPTER

Don't Treat Benefits as "Fringe"

What does a stealth weapon in the war for talent look like? It looks like this: Life insurance. Pension plan. Health insurance. Savings plan. Compared to a media darling like stock options, benefits are routine. But the smartest firms understand that great benefits, when emphasized properly, play a crucial role in attracting and retaining the best performers.

So what constitutes "great benefits?" Fifty years ago, all plans looked alike—some were more generous than others, but their architecture was the same. Not any longer. Benefits today are anything but standard. While companies are getting more creative—and often more generous—those improvements are not enough.

Like all other aspects of an organization's foundation, benefits need to reinforce and support the human capital strategy—and, in turn, the primary business goals. Benefits also need to differentiate an organization from the competition in order to attract new talent and keep current employees from walking away. And perhaps most importantly, over the long term, benefits can have an effect on the configuration of your workforce—as well as help to communicate the culture to current and potential employees.

But here's the rub: too often even beautifully conceived benefits packages fail to pay off in better recruiting and retention, because candidates (and employees) usually do not recognize their true value. Maybe they assume all plans are alike. Perhaps they don't understand the details. Whatever the reason, the result is that some companies—especially those that put expensive programs into place without any strategic alignment—are throwing money down the drain.

To optimize their benefits, companies must devise a strong communications program that educates employees and candidates about what makes their package different and better. How does the program align with the direction of the organization? What type of service or behaviors does it recognize and reward? Why? When employees see that benefits are in sync with the organization's vision and approach to the marketplace, shareholder value jumps substantially.

What the Numbers Say

Where There Are Good Benefits, There Is High Shareholder Value

Great benefits are great for business. Our HCI research indicates that the better the benefits, **and the sharper the company's focus on using them for attraction and retention,** the higher the firm's market value. In fact, companies that emphasize benefits are worth 7.3 percent more. (See Figure 10-1.)

But having a great benefits program in place is only part of it. The companies that get the biggest return on their investment in these programs are those that also commit resources to making

Figure 10-1. *Links Between Benefits and Value Creation*

Practice	Impact on Market Value
Health benefits are important for recruiting and retention	2.8%
Defined contribution and defined benefits plans, combined, important for recruiting and retention	1.3%
Defined benefit plan important for recruiting and retention	0.9%
Employees have choice regarding benefits	0.8%
Defined contribution plan important for recruiting and retention	0.8%
Company positions benefits above the market	0.7%

Expected change associated with a significant (1SD) improvement in practice

Watson Wyatt's Human Capital Index®

Figure 10-2. *Employees' Satisfaction with Benefits and ECI*

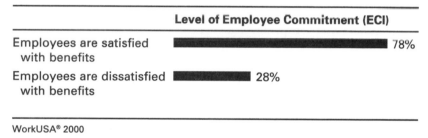

WorkUSA® 2000

Figure 10-3. *Employees' Satisfaction with Benefits and TRS*

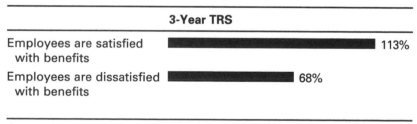

WorkUSA® 2000

sure employees understand those benefits and their linkage to a company's desired culture. Shareholder value and employee commitment are markedly higher at companies whose workers know how much their package is worth and what their benefits mean to them personally. (See Figures 10-4 and 10-5.)

Figure 10-4. *Knowledge of Reward Package Value and ECI*

Level of Employee Commitment (ECI)	
Employees know the value of reward package	███████████████████████████ 76%
Employees do not know the value of reward package	████ 12%

WorkUSA® 2000

Figure 10-5. *Knowledge of Reward Package Value and TRS*

3-Year TRS	
Employees know the value of reward package	███████████████████████ 102%
Employees do not know the value of reward package	███████████████ 67%

WorkUSA® 2000

When employees better understand the value and features of their benefits, they become better benefits consumers. For example, providing employees with targeted communications and specific advice about the company's 401(k) plan is just as likely to convince them to save as a high employer match, according to Watson Wyatt research. A recent study examined 401(k) plans at 15 U.S. firms, ranging in size from 700 to 10,000 employees. Employees who received targeted 401(k) communications saved two percentage points more of their pay than those who did not. Raising match rates from 25 to 100 percent achieved exactly the same effect—but at considerably higher cost to the employer. (See Figure 10-6.)

Benefit Package Design

Must-Haves versus Success Differentiators

There are two important trends affecting how organizations design and deliver their benefits programs.

Figure 10-6. *Communications Programs Versus Higher Match in Motivating Contributions*

Employees who received targeted 401(k) communications
contribute 2% more pay

Employees who were offered 100% match instead of 25%
contribute 2% more pay

401(k) Value Index™

1. Company leaders are looking for the substance in benefits programs. They will not implement new initiatives merely because they sound good—corporate leaders are looking harder for the link to the bottom line.
2. The aging of the baby boom, together with the baby bust that follows, creates an interesting dynamic. Many organizations are waging a ferocious battle to attract new, young, technically proficient talent, while simultaneously trying to retain, engage, and deploy experienced, seasoned employees for as long as possible.

We often hear senior executives express goals that appear contradictory:

- "Our benefits programs must be bottom-line oriented."
- "We want to be an employer of choice."

To resolve these different goals, we advocate using emerging research to identify the most effective benefits, in terms of recruitment, retention, and shareholder value, together with a focused approach to program design.

We often see "me-tooism" drive decisions. Employers copy programs adopted by other employers, without solid business justification. Employers should examine a new plan design trend, such as cash balance retirement plans, increased portability, or 401(k) broker windows, with an eye toward their contribution to organizational success. A well-designed benefits program should motivate the workforce to pursue the company's business strategy. And a poorly designed program actually may interfere with business objectives. For example, a company that wants to encourage long career commitments rather than instill a culture of employability will send the wrong message—and end up with the wrong people with the wrong values—if benefits are disproportionately "portable" and do not reward long-term service.

This leads us to an effective framework for making decisions on any benefit initiatives. Employers should categorize their programs into two groups:

1. Must-haves. These are programs that employers simply must have to attract and retain good talent. Examples include competitive base pay, a medical plan, and a 401(k) plan. Different industries have different must-haves. For example, a defined benefit plan is a must-have at large, Fortune 100 companies, but not necessarily everywhere. An effective strategy fixes any problems with the must-haves, but acknowledges their limitations. Spending too much money on must-haves doesn't lead to competitive advantage—usually it is simply spending too much money.

2. Success differentiators. These are the programs that provide competitive advantage by attracting, retaining, and engaging the right employees. This is where employers should focus their creative energy.

The choice of success differentiators should be driven by their contribution to organizational success. Often they uniquely fit a certain workforce—one company's success differentiator might be meaningless to another.

One more word on success differentiators: once companies get them in place, they should not get too complacent. Over time, these programs often turn into must-haves. For example, in the early 1980s, a 401(k) plan was a success differentiator. Today it is a must-have.

Communicating Benefits

Making the Most of Them to Help Recruiting and Retention

Finessing the design of the benefits package is just the beginning. To make effective use of the investment for recruiting and retention, it is critical to communicate the rationale and the value associated with the offerings.

Employees and candidates essentially have one question when it comes to a company's benefits package: "What does this mean for me?" That one question should guide the creation of the communications strategy. To cut through the haze of confusion hovering over most employee handbook benefits descriptions, companies should do everything they can to personalize information. Using case studies, showing examples, and playing out scenarios will illustrate more memorably just what the company is offering team members.

A focus on simplicity and the answers to fundamental design and operational questions provides the most compelling story and the quickest return on the communication dollar. Companies should help employees understand why the company offers these particular benefits, and how they are in sync with the company's overall strategy and culture. They should tell employees what type of support is set up to help them, and where to go for which kind of information.

Organizations should also take this opportunity to build employees' literacy in terms of benefits. To truly value what the company is offering, employees need to know the landscape: What economic/demographic factors have changed benefits? How does this package compare to what the competition offers?

Putting all of that information into a tidy little booklet delivered to new employees is not enough. To make benefits work hard for retention requires ongoing, active, frequent communication and education. Individuals need to be encouraged to ask questions about the different costs the organization encounters, its strategies, and how they relate to benefits. Passive or spotty communication runs the risk of substantially neutralizing the power of benefits in the war for talent.

How It Plays Out

McGraw-Hill Boosts 401(k) Participation Through Great Communications

Here are two ways to communicate the company's retirement plan to employees:

1. Tell them, "You can start saving now for retirement."
2. Send them a note that says, "Here's $42,762 for your retirement."

A hint: one is more effective than the other.

The McGraw-Hill Companies found that out a few years ago, when they explored the lower-than-expected level of participation in their 401k plan. The problem was not the plan itself—which was generous. The stumbling block was that employees truly did not understand how the plan could affect their finances and ultimately their lives. Which meant that the plan wasn't serving as a retention tool, either.

McGraw-Hill wanted to do something dramatic. Understanding that traditional "retirement talk" was not getting employees' attention, the corporation adopted a different approach. David Letterman was the inspiration behind a bulletin titled "Top 10 Excuses for Not Saving." Highlights included:

- Who needs savings when there are credit cards?
- I can't afford to save any money!
- Investing is too complicated.

The humor got the employees focused, and the bulletin got the key point across. But it was personalized savings plan statements—using the employees' own information—that rocketed

401(k) participation and savings rates to new levels during a campaign that began in early 1999.

The statements were quite detailed. For example, an employee currently saving 3 percent of pay got a statement showing employee and employer contributions based on 4, 5, and 6 percent. Someone already saving 5 percent got to see what would happen if she bumped her percentage up to 6, 8, or 10 percent. Bar charts showed the compounding effect of individual and corporate contributions over the course of 5, 10, and 20 years based on the employee's salary and existing savings plan balances. It was a remarkable departure from the hard-to-comprehend verbiage in the employee handbook.

Adding a final, convincing touch to the effort was a letter to employees from Harold McGraw III, the chairman, president and CEO. Regarding the company's matching program, he wrote: "If you're not saving six percent of your pay, you're turning down money the company wants to give you."

The response was immediate—and so were the long-term results. The company expected 10 percent enrollment from nonsavers; instead, 23.5 percent started saving within three months. Equally remarkable, the average savings rate for those former nonsavers went from zero to 6.6 percent of pay.

Take note: McGraw-Hill didn't change one single element of the benefits program. But benefits have just become one more reason for talent to stick with McGraw-Hill.

PART

Establish a Collegial, Flexible Workplace

CHAPTER

Understand That Employee Satisfaction Is Critical to Any Business Goal

"Pleasure in the job puts perfection in the work."
—Aristotle (384–322 BC)

"How many CEOs do you know who come into the cleaners' break room at 3:00 am on a Sunday, passing out donuts or putting on a pair of overalls to clean a plane? If employees feel like they are respected and dignified, cared for and loved, then they will take good care of outside customers."
—Teamsters Local 19 President Tom Burnette on Southwest Airlines' Herb Kelleher[1]

Companies cannot please their shareholders unless they satisfy their employees.

It is a deceptively simple concept: Satisfied employees deliver superior service, which creates satisfied clients. Satisfied clients create growth in revenue and earnings, leading to increased shareholder value. First articulated in the *Harvard Business Review* in 1994, the "Service-Profit Chain" intuitively makes sense.[2] And now the numbers from Watson Wyatt and others can back it up.

That means "employee satisfaction" has come of age. No longer a secondary corporate goal, it has become one of the key factors examined by leading companies when shareholder returns are not what they should be. The link has never been clearer: satisfied employees result in a better bottom line.

What the Numbers Say

High Employee Commitment = High Shareholder Value

The numbers in Watson Wyatt's *WorkUSA® 2000* survey of 7500 workers show that companies whose employees are highly committed to their employers deliver dramatically higher returns to shareholders. Firms with a high Employee Commitment Index (ECI) rated 36 percentage points higher Total Return to Shareholders (1996-1998) than those with a low ECI. And firms with a high ECI actually outperformed the S&P 500 by 24 percent-

Figure 11-1. *Relationship Between Employee Commitment and Shareholder Value*

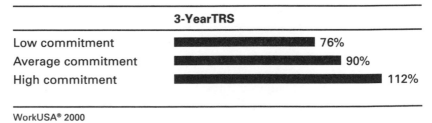

	3-YearTRS	
Low commitment		76%
Average commitment		90%
High commitment		112%

WorkUSA® 2000

age points (the S&P 500 had an average three-year TRS of 88 percent).

The HCI results corroborate these findings. Firms with high employee satisfaction and low voluntary turnover have decidedly higher market value:

Figure 11-2. *Links Between Employee Retention and Satisfaction and Shareholder Value*

Practice	Impact on Market Value
Company has high employee satisfaction	1.3%
Company has low voluntary turnover of managers/professionals	1.7%
Company has low voluntary turnover of employees in general	1.5%

Expected change associated with a significant (1SD) improvement in practice

Watson Wyatt's Human Capital Index®

Fortune magazine confirms that the companies where people like to work markedly outperform their less popular competition on the stock market. In their 2001 study on the "100 Best Companies to Work For," the magazine found a direct link between higher levels of employee satisfaction and higher shareholder returns:

Figure 11-3. *Links Between Employee Satisfaction and Shareholder Value*

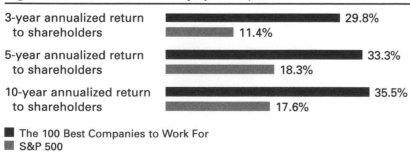

3-year annualized return to shareholders: 29.8% / 11.4%

5-year annualized return to shareholders: 33.3% / 18.3%

10-year annualized return to shareholders: 35.5% / 17.6%

■ The 100 Best Companies to Work For
▨ S&P 500

Source: "100 Best Companies to Work For," *Fortune*, January 2001

In a 1998 study, the Gallop Organization also found a link between employee satisfaction and financial performance. The research showed that the most satisfied employees also worked in business units with higher levels of productivity, profit, retention, and customer satisfaction.[3]

While researchers were not surprised to find a link between employee satisfaction and productivity, they were impressed with the link between satisfaction and profitability: "After all, many believe that profit is a function of factors that lie far beyond the control of individual employees: factors like pricing, competitive positioning, or variable-cost management. But the more you think about it, the more understandable this link becomes. There are so many things one employee can do to affect profit—everything from turning off more lights, to negotiating harder on price, to avoiding the temptations of the till. Simply put, these will happen more often when each employee feels truly engaged."[4]

Clearly, the body of research linking employee satisfaction to business results is growing. But here is the rub: Only about one-half of the workers polled say they are committed to their employers. The good news is that only half of the competitors' people are committed to their companies. A company that makes it a priority to increase employee satisfaction will have a true competitive edge.

The not-so-good news is that a third of the workforce feels neutral—neither committed nor uncommitted. Perhaps the best

Figure 11-4. *U.S. Employees' Commitment to Company*

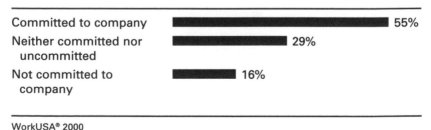

Committed to company	55%
Neither committed nor uncommitted	29%
Not committed to company	16%

WorkUSA® 2000

way to understand this neutral level of commitment is through the kinds of statements we hear when interviewing these groups:

- "It's a job like any other."
- "This company is okay, I suppose. I've worked for worse and I've worked for better."
- "It's not like I hate the place, but it's hard to get worked up about it."
- "If something better came along I'd take it, but it's alright for now."

Ranging from compliant to apathetic, these workers are decidedly an underperforming asset, representing a target to win over during a culture turnaround.

The truly alarming news is that one-sixth of the workforce is not happy to come to work and may, in fact, be angry—worse than apathetic. They may be withholding effort, and deliberately sabotaging management's efforts.

- We spoke with a company's engineering group, where people complained that they couldn't get anything done because the hourly workers hated the exempt workers so much. The engineers couldn't get their tests done on time because the hourly workers would say, "Oh, you know what? We forgot to turn the computer on last night. I think we lost the test results."
- We witnessed what can only be described as a "war" between employees and management when we worked with a large suburban rail transport company. So committed were workers to not helping the company, that they had devised schemes so that employees could have side businesses on company time. Workers would literally clock in and then leave to run their private business. Not surprisingly, their performance was a fraction of that of the competition.

Figure 11-5. *Key Drivers of Employee Commitment*

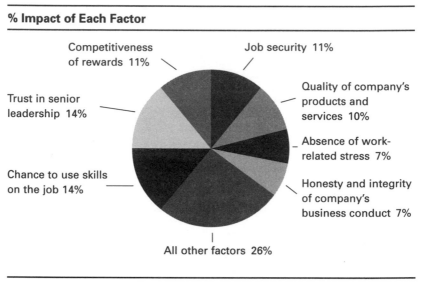

% Impact of Each Factor

Competitiveness of rewards 11%

Job security 11%

Trust in senior leadership 14%

Quality of company's products and services 10%

Absence of work-related stress 7%

Chance to use skills on the job 14%

Honesty and integrity of company's business conduct 7%

All other factors 26%

WorkUSA® 2000

The question for every executive is: What share of your own workforce is in this danger zone? One-sixth of the workforce is a lot of employees. What if your faction is even higher? How much business are you losing because of them?

So how do companies get satisfied workers? There are seven key factors affecting commitment. (See Figure 11-5.)

Organizations that work hard (and smart) to cultivate employee satisfaction will have an engaged, committed workforce willing to go the extra mile for the good of the organization. Organizations that do not will pay the price...literally.

Why It Works

Service-Profit Chain Connects Employee Satisfaction with Business Results

How does a committed employee have such a strong impact on the bottom line? Employee satisfaction drives whether someone is going to stay or leave, perform to the fullest or withhold effort, serve customers well or poorly, and commit or disengage from company objectives. As a result, there is a direct feedback loop that cycles between high levels of employee satisfaction, high levels of customer satisfaction, and positive business results. This, of course, is the well-known "Service-Profit Chain."

Here is how the authors of the theory put it: "Profit and growth are stimulated primarily by customer loyalty. Loyalty is a direct result of customer satisfaction. Satisfaction is largely influenced by the value of services provided to customers. Value is created by satisfied, loyal, and productive employees. Employee satisfaction, in turn, results primarily from high-quality support services and policies that enable employees to deliver results to customers."[5]

The authors point out that the impact of customer loyalty can be astronomical over time. "For example, the lifetime revenue stream from a loyal pizza eater can be $8000, a Cadillac owner $332,000, and a corporate purchaser of commercial aircraft literally billions of dollars."[6]

Furthermore, a 5 percent increase in customer loyalty can increase profits from 25 percent to 85 percent, according to research by Frederick F. Feichheld and W. Earl Sasser, Jr., also cited in the *Harvard Business Review.*[7]

Studies have also shown that highly satisfied customers are six times more likely to repurchase a company's product than customers that are merely satisfied.[8]

Committed, motivated employees will produce better, more efficient service for customers, and higher service levels will in turn yield tangible financial improvement. The best firms go one step further, reinvesting the added returns in reward programs and other measures that will continue to ensure employee satisfaction, continuously refueling the service-profit connection. They know that if they can keep this cycle operating smoothly while other organizations struggle to catch up, they will retain their competitive advantage.

Figure 11-6. *Links in the Service-Profit Chain*

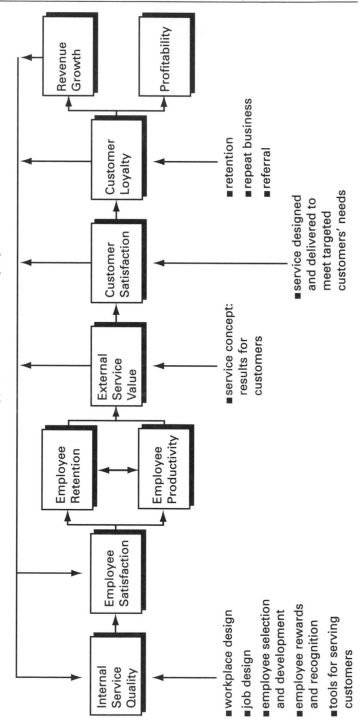

Operation Strategy and Service Delivery System

The Chain on Display

Employee Satisfaction Measurement Proves Crucial in Improving Commitment

If employee satisfaction is critical, it must be managed. And if it is to be managed, it must be measured. And in order to make the measurements count, people must be held accountable for them.

The powerful payback from that simple approach was highlighted in a recent *Harvard Business Review* article, "The Employee-Customer-Profit Chain at Sears." The study showed how a 3.5 percent improvement in employee satisfaction led directly to a 1.3 percent improvement in customer satisfaction, which in turn yielded a 0.5 percent increase in revenue growth. In the case of Sears, a focus on "Total Performance Indicators"—a set of measures gauging the satisfaction of employees, customers, and investors—improved employee satisfaction, which paid off at the store level by significantly increasing per-store revenue. Multiplied by Sears' network of several thousand stores, this case history demonstrated the enormous financial power that grassroots efforts to improve employee satisfaction can wield in large organizations.

"The basic elements of an employee-customer-profit model are not difficult to grasp," say the article's authors. "Any person with even a little experience in retailing understands intuitively that there is a chain of cause and effect running from employee behavior to customer behavior to profits, and it's not hard to see that behavior depends primarily on attitude. Which is not to say that implementing an employee-customer-profit chain, or model, is easy. One big problem is measurement. Unlike revenues and profits, soft data are hard to define and collect, and few measures are softer than customer and employee attitudes, or 'satisfaction.' In many businesses, it is difficult to measure even relatively hard behaviors like customer retention, and the inevitable result is that many companies are unwilling to expend the time, energy, and resources to do it effectively. Not surprisingly, many companies do not have a realistic grasp of what their customers and employees actually think and do."[9]

The solution: a well-designed and executed employee survey. It is the best way to determine an organization's strengths and weaknesses on the four major factors that influence employee satisfaction:

1. **Working for a Winner.** Employees want to know that they are working for a successful, well-managed organization. Clarity of strategy, customer service quality, business ethics, and social responsibility all play a part.

2. **Being Enabled to Do a Good Job.** Employees are more satisfied when they have the resources required to get their own job done effectively. This includes the required information, training, equipment, authority, teamwork, and staff.

3. **Feeling Respected and Valued.** Satisfied employees feel that their pay and benefits are competitive, that their rewards are commensurate with their contribution, and that they have a reasonable level of future financial security. They also want to be treated respectfully and fairly by managers and coworkers. They want to be recognized for good performance and coached on how to develop and improve. Policies and practices that enhance treatment, such as work/life programs, tend to increase satisfaction.

4. **Liking the Job Itself.** To be satisfied at work, it is important that employees enjoy their work. When employees dislike or are bored by the nature of the work, they are likely to become dissatisfied. In most cases, employees "self-select" work they enjoy or, at least, work they do not actively dislike. However, given the current competition for talent, some firms will glamorize and misrepresent a job in an attempt to lure more recruits (e.g., telling recruits they are going to be "customer consultants" when they are actually going to be telephone sales

reps). This practice ultimately creates dissatisfaction and turnover.

A good survey program will show how an organization is doing in all four of these categories. We identified six key ingredients that contribute to a successful survey:

1. **Link it to key business objectives.** For example, customer service improvement, turnover reduction, productivity improvement, cycle time reduction, and strategy alignment. Line managers need to know how this process will help them, so the survey should focus on things they believe are important.
2. **Keep senior management involved and accountable.** HR should facilitate but not *own* the program. Senior management needs to be involved in the creation and analysis of the survey. They have to buy into it if they are to commit to accountability later.
3. **Provide personalized data cuts for all key managers.** This increases accountability at all levels of the organization.
4. **Streamline the process.** To be repeatable, the survey process cannot be so elaborate that it dies of its own weight.
5. **Survey regularly.** The survey process must be integrated regularly into business planning to show where the company has been, and how things have progressed over time.
6. **Effectively communicate results and actions taken.** This is often overlooked but tremendously important. Employees need to have closure. It is harmful if they think their survey answers are just dangling out there somewhere, irrelevant. Companies need to help employees link their survey responses with direct corporate actions.

Once a company has these results, it has overcome the first hurdle: It knows where the problems are. Then, of course, the real challenge begins.

Branching Surveys Offer More Insight

The trouble with surveys is that time and space keep people from asking everything they would like to ask. But technology is changing that.

"Branching" technology creates, in essence, individualized questionnaires for each respondent. It allows for the follow-up questions you would ask if you were conducting a personal interview—but it does not sentence other respondents to wading through lots of irrelevant questions.

Here is an example of a branching survey:
Question #1: From the list below, please select the five factors that contribute most to your dissatisfaction at Company A:

> Compensation
> Benefits
> Career development opportunities
> Immediate supervisor
> Confidence in management of the company overall
> Confidence in management of my business/division
> Job security
> Personal empowerment/ability to act
> Job challenge
> Stress
> Lack of teamwork/cooperation
> Personal impact on the company's success
> Work/personal life balance
> Bureaucracy
> Physical working conditions
> Work location
> Lack of resources to get the job done
> Other

Follow-up #1: You identified compensation as contributing to your dissatisfaction at Company A. Which aspects of your compensation package are in need of significant improvement?

(Please check all that apply.)

> Base salary
> Incentive bonus/compensation
> Stock programs
> Link between compensation and performance

Follow-up #2: Where is the weakness in the link between compensation and performance? (Check all that apply.)

> Between individual performance and compensation
> Between team performance and compensation
> Between company performance and compensation

Detailed follow-ups like these allow companies to maximize their investment in a survey by cutting down on assumptions and guesswork.

How It Plays Out

Satisfaction Measurement and Accountability Produce Results

Company:	*ACNielsen*
Revenues:	*$1.5 billion*
Number of Employees:	*21,000*
Industry:	*Market research/Marketing information*
Location of Headquarters:	*Stamford, CT*

It was November 1996, and ACNielsen had just returned to its roots as an independent company trading on the NYSE. "Those were dark days for ACNielsen," according to Bob Chrenc, executive vice president and chief administrative officer. "We were delivering our products late and wrong." Clients were dissatisfied, profits were depressed, and employee morale was at a low. For a proud company with a 75-year heritage, the state of affairs was worse than sad. "It was time to go back to the basics," Chrenc recalls. In charting the turnaround, then-chairman and CEO Nicholas L. Trivisonno (since retired) turned to the service-profit chain. To restore its reputation as a global market research powerhouse, executives at the Stamford, Connecticut-based company committed to providing client service that is second to none—and embraced employee satisfaction as the key driver of that service.

They fueled a remarkable turnaround in the process: Operating income, return on equity, and return on assets have tripled. Net income has nearly quintupled.

First Step: The Satisfaction Survey

The foundation of their program is the Business Effectiveness Survey (BES). Administered annually since 1995, the BES is a critical measurement of employee satisfaction—so critical, in fact, that survey results are linked directly to executive compensation. A full 25 percent of incentive compensation for the company's top 1500 leaders depends on achieving an ever-improving Employee Satisfaction Index (ESI).

"Our senior leadership has created a culture that not only supports the Business Effectiveness Survey but also embraces it—weaving it into the fabric of the organization," says R. James Cravens, senior vice president and chief human resources officer. "They know that we can only create shareholder value by first creating a satisfying environment for our employees. Line management is committed to acting on survey results because they recognize the validity of the service-profit chain."

ACNielsen's 50-question Business Effectiveness Survey covers 12 work-related dimensions:

- Pride and commitment
- Career development
- Leadership

- Reward and recognition
- Support for innovation
- Communication
- Change management
- Business conduct
- Teamwork
- Performance enablement
- Client satisfaction and quality
- Performance management

Each dimension, made up of about five questions, is equally important. The scores for each dimension are averaged together to produce the final Employee Satisfaction Index. ESI scores can be generated for groups as small as 10 people all the way up to countries, geographic regions, major business units, and the company as a whole.

Typical Questions

The following questions for the Leadership dimension illustrate the degree of scrutiny the company expects from its employees:

1. To what extent do you have trust and confidence in the overall job being done by the senior leadership team of ACNielsen? (to a very great extent, to a great extent, to a small extent, to a very small extent, or don't know/not applicable)
2. Has senior leadership clearly communicated ACNielsen's business vision, strategy, and objectives?
3. Do you have confidence that ACNielsen's strategy and objectives will position it for business success?
4. Is senior leadership flexible and open to change?
5. Is senior leadership making the changes necessary to ensure that ACNielsen will achieve its short-term business objectives?

6. Is senior leadership making the changes necessary to ensure that ACNielsen will be a winner in the marketplace over the long term?
7. Does senior leadership demonstrate personal visibility in your part of ACNielsen?
8. Do you understand how your work fits into ACNielsen's strategy and objectives?

The survey process itself is streamlined and user-friendly. It begins with a month-long internal communications campaign in August. Posters, letters, e-mail messages, one-on-one conversations, and even games are used to generate awareness and interest. The survey is administered in September to all 20,700 employees, in more than 100 locations around the world, and translated into more than 20 languages.

Survey Results Lead to Action Plans

By mid-October—only two weeks after the surveys have been distributed—Watson Wyatt produces top-line global and regional results that are e-mailed to 2000 managers worldwide and presented to the board of directors. More specific results for countries and corporate headquarters departments are generated through November. Electronic survey reports allow managers to quickly navigate to their own strengths and weaknesses.

"The most significant aspect of the survey is what is done with the results," says Cravens. "Each manager must develop an action plan aimed at achieving measurable improvement in time for the next survey."

Employee satisfaction scores worldwide have soared since 1995, when the survey was first instituted. The Employee Satisfaction Index has increased from 42 percent to 65 percent. Participation continues to be record-breaking too, with a 91 percent participation rate last year, up from 80 percent in 1995.

CHAPTER

Minimize Status Distinctions

"We insult employees with executive parking spots, heated, no less; with executive dining rooms; with bonuses and 'strategy meetings' in lavish settings for the top 100 officers and their spouses even after lousy years...How do you humiliate and demean someone and then expect him or her to care about product quality and constant improvement?"
—Tom Peters, in *Thriving on Chaos*[1]

Is there a CEO in existence who would not trade a reserved parking spot for a 3 percent increase in shareholder value? We think not. Yet most companies are still clinging to systems and behaviors that emphasize status distinctions between employees—and their shareholders are paying for it.

To be sure, in response to the rapidly increasing pace of business, many companies have begun to move away from a strongly hierarchical management system. But change is slow, and vestiges of the old ways typically remain in place for quite some time: perks, titles, dress, office space, and countless unwritten behavior patterns.

Individually, these things seem fairly harmless: a habit of wearing a suit, a "VP" on the office door, or the fact that he's "Mr. Smith" and she's "Mary." But collectively, they draw attention to the existence of a hierarchy. They build and reinforce walls that block innovation and inhibit the sharing of knowledge. Status distinctions communicate loudly and clearly that all employees are not valued the same way, demoralizing the troops and effectively shutting off the organization's access to their ideas and energy.

Leading companies are making a concerted effort to remove all of those unnecessary status distinctions. They are making both a substantive and symbolic movement toward a culture that welcomes and encourages the contributions of every employee. If people are to work together, the walls between them must be torn down.

Empowering the entire workforce in this manner is typically threatening for executive leadership initially, but ultimately rewarding. As Jack D. Orsburn and Linda Moran write in *The New Self-Directed Work Teams,* "...managers have to get used to the idea that instead of managing people, they'll be managing ideas, standards, systems, and technology...Once managers begin taking on new, vitally important duties, and once they see that status doesn't necessarily depend on how many people they manage, the need for perks begins to fade."[2]

What the Numbers Say

Market Value Higher When Organization Is Flatter

What we are describing is the shift from a control system to what has become known as a commitment system. Control systems are hierarchical and emphasize status distinctions. In a control system, managers direct employee actions in order to make the numbers. Commitment systems aim to increase productivity through increased employee satisfaction and engagement. They stress decentralization and the creation of employee commitment to the firm. Commitment systems emphasize teamwork and reciprocal loyalty. Managers are used as coaches or mentors for employees.

Watson Wyatt research shows that companies using commitment management systems have higher market value than those using control systems. The Human Capital Index reveals that companies can increase market value by almost two percent if they reduce status distinctions through just four practices. (See Figure 12-1.)

A culture that emphasizes teamwork and cooperation returns half a percentage point more to shareholders. A key step in encouraging that culture is stripping away the status distinctions that work against the "team" concept.

At companies where titles are not used to designate authority, market value is half a percentage point higher. Some companies remove all titles (all employees become, for example, "associates"), and others just attempt to remove some of the layers. Whatever the approach, it de-emphasizes hierarchy. It also

Figure 12-1. *Links Between Minimized Status Distinctions and Value Creation*

Practice	Impact on Market Value
Company culture encourages teamwork/cooperation	0.5%
Company avoids using titles to designate authority	0.5%
Company avoids varying perquisites by position	0.5%
Office space does not vary according to position	0.4%

Expected change associated with a significant (1SD) improvement in practice

Watson Wyatt's Human Capital Index®

empowers employees by expanding their roles beyond those defined by traditional job titles and descriptions, allowing companies to leverage their talent.

(A related practice has employees on a first-name basis with top management. When we mention this in presentations as an example of the reduction in status distinctions that is linked to higher value, we inevitably have some CEO ask, "So, if I tell my employees to call me "Bob," my shareholder value will jump?" The answer, of course, is no. But in a culture where employees actually feel comfortable calling the CEO by his first name, it is likely that employees will feel comfortable communicating their thoughts and ideas.)

Companies where the perquisites do not vary with position are worth half a percentage point more in market value. That means the parking spots, executive dining rooms, penthouse offices, and vacation condos that make executives feel they have made it to the top are keeping the company from doing the same.

In addition to these findings from the *Human Capital Index,* Watson Wyatt's *WorkUSA® 2000* study also supports the financial benefits of replacing the control system with a commitment system. We studied the impact of self-directed work teams—an example of a commitment system—on shareholder return. The results support our HCI findings: TRS is higher when there are self-directed work teams. Employee commitment is higher as well, which partially explains the better financial performance—a link we cover in Chapter 11. (See Figures 12-2 and 12-3.)

Figure 12-2. *Self-Directed Work Teams and Shareholder Value*

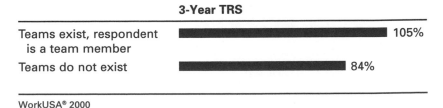

WorkUSA® 2000

Figure 12-3. *Self-Directed Work Teams and Employee Commitment*

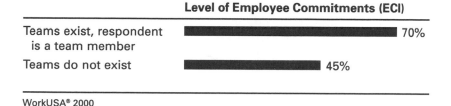

	Level of Employee Commitments (ECI)
Teams exist, respondent is a team member	70%
Teams do not exist	45%

WorkUSA® 2000

Why It Works

At Flat Organizations, Workers Are Empowered

The truth is that the movement away from hierarchy is coming whether companies seek it out or not. The reason? Technology. The new connectedness is both the cause and the effect of a reduction in status distinctions. Access to information is no longer limited, and the mechanism through which employees can be empowered is here. Even companies that would like to keep strict levels in place will find they cannot do it successfully anymore.

But smart organizations will meet the trend halfway. And not just because it is coming anyway, or because it seems more "fair." They will do it because it is the wise business choice. Companies that want to capture the ideas, the minds, and the energy of their entire workforce will knock down the explicit and implicit prohibitions that keep workers from contributing.

Hierarchy Blocks Information Sharing

Certain perks and practices have the effect—whether intentional or not—of preventing any interaction between senior management and the rest of the workers. The resulting atmosphere is a problem on both substantive and symbolic levels.

Let's say the company's management is cloistered on the 50th floor, and the workers are at the plant. There is a security guard in the executive parking lot and a secretary in the anteroom. There is a well-appointed executive dining room. And visiting senior managers who come to corporate headquarters are shuttled in limos to off-site meetings at luxury hotels.

The substantive problem: information flow. All informal means of information sharing are effectively blocked. Senior management cannot possibly have an accurate view of what is going on at the company.

In fact, our research demonstrates that the view of the world from that 50th floor is remarkably different, showing an alarming gap in perceptions between executives and all other workers on a wide range of issues. Not surprisingly, the higher-ups are dramatically more positive about the workplace than the rest of the workforce. (See Figure 12-4.)

This gap should sound an alarm bell. If people have such different perceptions of the organization as it is now, how could management hope to align the organization around any future goals? And if executives are this far from workers in their views about the workplace, how far apart are they on their views of the work itself? Business decisions are being made by managers, who may view the situation very differently than the people on the ground. How much is that costing the company in mistakes and lost opportunities?

Speed Unattainable Under Hierarchy

Hierarchy has a purpose: to slow things down. When those in control do not want anything to change, a hierarchical system is the choice. It works well for a company with dominant market share, little competition, and proprietary products. It has built-in status distinctions and layers of approvals that reward implementation rather than innovation. If there is a premium on controlled discipline and few errors, a hierarchy works.

But predictability and an absence of error are two things that are currently very far down on any company's list of must-haves. Instead, organizations are living and dying based on their success in achieving speed, innovation, creativity, and responsive-

Figure 12-4. *Perception Gap Between Executives and Others*

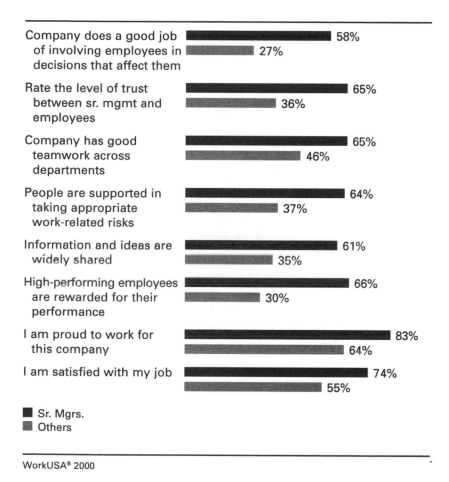

Company does a good job
of involving employees in
decisions that affect them
— 58% / 27%

Rate the level of trust
between sr. mgmt and
employees
— 65% / 36%

Company has good
teamwork across
departments
— 65% / 46%

People are supported in
taking appropriate
work-related risks
— 64% / 37%

Information and ideas are
widely shared
— 61% / 35%

High-performing employees
are rewarded for their
performance
— 66% / 30%

I am proud to work for
this company
— 83% / 64%

I am satisfied with my job
— 74% / 55%

■ Sr. Mgrs.
▨ Others

WorkUSA® 2000

ness. And none of these things is possible in an old-style control
system.

One of our associates left last year for a job with a very traditional type of organization. She finds, for example, that she can
no longer simply pick up the phone and call a colleague. If she
calls someone who is one layer above her in the company, the call
will be returned to her boss. Her days remind her of one long version of the kids' game "Telephone." Information is scrambled,
things are lost in the translation, time is wasted, and frustration

runs high. If she could simply and directly share information with her coworkers, they could all work more effectively to build the company's bottom line.

Another example of the speed-killing, money-wasting effect of a strict hierarchy: We did some work for a company where the chief executive was enamored with dramatic status distinctions. He did everything he could to distinguish himself from the troops: isolated office, limo, corporate jet, etc. He successfully created the impression that he was unapproachable. The result? When it came time for us to prepare our major presentation, his junior executives refused to make a quick phone call to sound him out regarding his expectations. Instead, they chose to spend triple the amount of money necessary, instructing us to prepare three different versions of our work so that we could switch gears at the last minute depending on his response at the meeting. By his emphasis on status distinctions, the CEO had eliminated the casual call from his employees' behavioral repertoire—and sent the bill to his shareholders.

Hierarchy Undermines "Team" Message

Aside from the very substantive problems with information sharing and speed that arise from status distinctions, there is an enormous symbolic issue. Overt status distinctions communicate quite clearly—regardless of any official company rhetoric—that "we" are not, in fact, all one team. "We" are not all reaping the rewards and shouldering the burdens of the work. The impact of that message is devastating to employee commitment.

At one company we saw workers toiling in plants without air conditioning as the executives watched from behind their air-conditioned windows. There were signs on the executives' building instructing hourly workers to wash their hands before entering. Plant workers needed to bring a note from the doctor if they were sick, and they had to ask their supervisor's permission to go to the bathroom. That kind of caste system, where adults are treated like children, makes people angry. The result? At best, people will not offer discretionary effort. At worst, they will actively sabotage the business.

The Pretense of Empowerment

In some companies, the official line is egalitarian. But unofficially, everyone knows what the rules are. There may be a pretense of empowerment, but information is still hoarded, and the real decisions are still made by an elite group of higher-ups. In this situation, employees view their work as unnecessary and superfluous. Why submit an idea that will not be considered? Why try to make the decision yourself when it will be decided by others anyway?

How to Do It

Flattening the Organization

When an organization attempts to minimize status distinctions, the first steps are the easiest: open up the reserved lot to all employees, convert the executive dining room to a coffee-break kitchen, move to a casual dress code, stop paying for limos, and hold meetings on-site.

Those are all examples of the important first symbolic steps away from a control system. It gets more complex when organizations truly begin to delayer the way they do business. As Hamel and Prahalad write in *Competing for the Future,* "…managers often forget that reducing the layers of management (reducing levels in the hierarchy) is not the same thing as reducing the dysfunctional consequences of hierarchical behavior. Hierarchical behavior avoids an active multilevel dialogue on critical issues and uses power to settle issues rather than broad debate and high-quality analysis. The conservative, idea-strangling, time-wasting phenomenon of 'managing upward' can be observed in many organizations, whether they have three organizational levels or a dozen."[3]

Intel has become famous for delayering on both substantive and symbolic levels. Visitors to the company's Web site see the absence of status distinctions celebrated in a list titled, "Intel Is...Intel Isn't..."[4]:

Intel isn't...

- Hierarchical management—our environment is informal and egalitarian. The best idea wins, whether it's from an intern or a senior manager.
- Suits—neckties get in the way of thinking. Success at Intel is based on your performance, not appearances.
- Closed offices—nobody gets an office with a door. Don't believe us? Here's Chairman Andy Grove's cubicle. (The site offers a link to Grove's office, which is indeed a standard cubicle.)
- Priority parking—Yes, that's yours, the first slot. And President Craig Barret's is way out there in the corn (unless he got to work first).

Intel is...

- Teams—many different people working together toward common goals.
- Open communication—people are always wiling to help or answer questions, every idea counts, and being straightforward is valued.

CHAPTER

Make Work Arrangements Flexible

"The focus is on results, not face time."
—Ernst & Young's Denny Marcel, of the company's
Office of Retention, on E&Y's flexible work
arrangements

When *Fortune* first published its "100 Best Companies to Work for in America" in the 1980s, exactly two of those companies (Federal Express and Northwestern Mutual Life) offered flextime to employees.[1] The concept was new, and it was vaguely threatening.

In *Fortune's 2000* version of the list, 89 out of 100 companies offered a compressed workweek, 87 offered telecommuting, 72 offered job sharing, and 70 offered flexible schedules.[2] Clearly, flextime has come of age. Far from being threatening to management, it has proven to be a lifeline for companies struggling to keep talent on board.

With experience showing that flexible arrangements increase productivity and commitment, the question is not whether companies should experiment with it. The question is how exactly to design programs that will ensure companies make the most of this powerful opportunity to attract and retain top performers.

What the Numbers Say

Top Performers Want Flexibility

Our Human Capital Index research suggests that a significant improvement in "flexible work arrangements" is associated with a 3.5 percent increase in market value. That is the highest-ranked item in our group of practices designed to create a "collegial, flexible" workplace. (See Figure 13.1.)

The fact that flexible work arrangements are an increasingly important element in the new world of work is evidenced by the differences seen between the 2001 HCI and the initial study conducted in 1999. Two years ago, a significant difference in work arrangement flexibility was associated with 1.7 percent greater market value. Today it is associated with a 3.5 percent impact.

Figure 13-1. *Links Between Collegial, Flexible Workplace and Value Creation*

Practice	Impact on Market Value
Company shows flexibility in work arrangements	3.5%
Company has high employee satisfaction	1.6%
Trust in senior leadership in actively engendered	1.2%
Managers demonstrate company's values	1.1%
Company culture encourages teamwork and cooperation	0.5%
Company avoids using titles to designate status and authority	0.5%
Company avoids varying perquisites by position	0.5%
Company avoids varying office space according to position	0.4%

Expected change associated with a significant (1SD) improvement in practice

Watson Wyatt's Human Capital Index®

How do flexible arrangements improve financial performance? Part of the reason is a surge in productivity. When their time is their own, people tend to use it more wisely. A second key reason flexible arrangements are linked to better business results is that they keep top performers from leaving. These key employees report that lack of flexibility is one of the top reasons they would consider resigning from their present firm, and that the availability of flexible arrangements would be a top reason they would consider another offer. (See Figures 13-2 and 13-3.)

Our research further indicates that companies are unaware of how prominently flexible work arrangements figure into the attraction/retention picture for top performers. We asked top performers and their employers to rate various non-compensation-based

Figure 13-2. *Top Four Reasons Top Performers Resign*

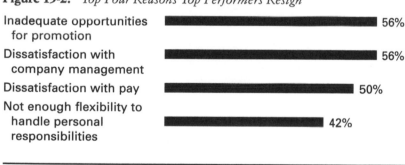

Inadequate opportunities for promotion — 56%
Dissatisfaction with company management — 56%
Dissatisfaction with pay — 50%
Not enough flexibility to handle personal responsibilities — 42%

Strategic Rewards® 2000

Figure 13-3. *Top Four Reasons Top Performers Would be Tempted to Join Another Firm*

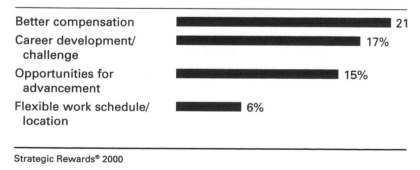

Better compensation — 21
Career development/ challenge — 17%
Opportunities for advancement — 15%
Flexible work schedule/ location — 6%

Strategic Rewards® 2000

reward plans on their effectiveness. While 56 percent of these key employees rated flexible work arrangements as "very effective" in motivating them to stay, only 29 percent of the employers believed they were that important. (See Figure 13-4.)

According to the Society for Human Resource Management (SHRM) 2001 Benefits Survey, organizations offering flextime are now in the majority, with the use of flexible work arrangements on the rise.[3] (See Figure 13-5.)

Figure 13-4. *Gap Between Employers and Top Performers*

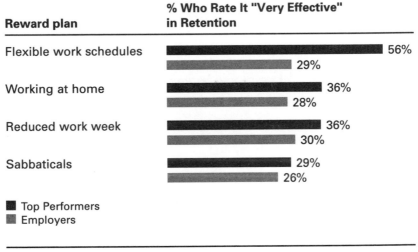

Strategic Rewards® 2001

Figure 13-5. *Flexible Work Arrangements Increasing*

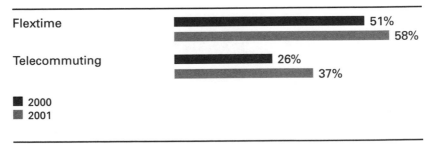

Source: SHRM Benefits Survey

And technology companies continue to be at the forefront of flexible work arrangements. Our own *Strategic Rewards®* study shows that alternative/flexible work arrangements are widely used and on the rise there as well. (See Figure 13-6.)

Companies are flocking to flextime, and not for altruistic reasons, either. The business case for flexible arrangements is solidly based on higher productivity, stronger employee commitment, and better retention. Many studies are confirming the anecdotal evidence that flex is a win-win:

- The British Industrial Society and The Resource Connection studied senior executives with flexible work arrangements. Their managers rated those who shared jobs and/or worked from home higher in productivity, resilience, leadership, and commitment.[4]
- Boston College conducted a two-year study, "Measuring the Impact of Workplace Flexibility." Six companies

Figure 13-6. *Flexible Work Arrangements Increasing at Technology Companies*

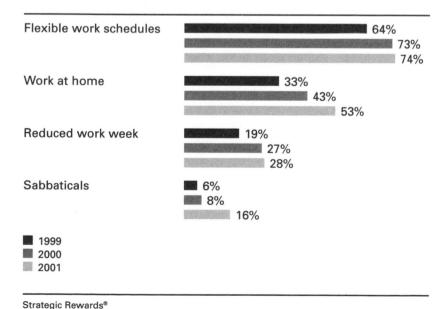

Flexible work schedules — 64% / 73% / 74%

Work at home — 33% / 43% / 53%

Reduced work week — 19% / 27% / 28%

Sabbaticals — 6% / 8% / 16%

■ 1999
■ 2000
□ 2001

Strategic Rewards®

(Amway, Bristol-Myers Squibb Company, Honeywell, Kraft, Lucent Technologies, and Motorola) took part. Results showed the use of flexible arrangements had a positive impact on productivity, work quality, and retention.[5]

■ The Society for Human Resource Management found flexibility to be the most effective recruiting tool in a 1999 survey.[6]

Companies That Resist Flexibility

Managerial anxiety regarding flexible work arrangements almost always rests on the presumption that most employees dislike work and therefore will avoid it if not monitored and controlled. Flexible work arrangements are seen by these managers as enabling delinquent employees to fulfill their true desire: to loaf while still collecting a paycheck.

But employees see resistance to flexible work arrangements as a clear sign of disrespect. A plant worker at a steel company told us: "My manager thinks nothing of the fact that he might come in at 11 a.m. because he had a doctor's appointment. I need to get approval from him and personnel a week in advance and then bring in proof of the visit."

This approach is not only disrespectful, it is simply wrong. Research shows that most people actually enjoy the work they do and want to do a good job—assuming the organization does not get in their way.

What's Out There

Various Options Taking Shape

In its early manifestations, flextime usually meant allowing an employee to quietly duck out early on occasion to pick up the kids. As the arrangement has proven itself, the official options have grown to reflect the needs of an increasingly diverse workforce.

Flexible Scheduling

The idea of flexible scheduling is essentially to alter the core hour requirements of the job. Instead of nine to five, Monday through Friday, companies allow floating hours at either end of the business day. Another practice that is becoming common: compressing the workweek into fewer days with longer hours.

Job Shares

With a job-sharing arrangement, two employees share the workload of one position. They might split the workday, with one working mornings and one afternoons, or they might split the workweek.

Virtual Office/Telecommuting

The option of a "virtual office" or telecommuting consists of employees working outside the office almost exclusively, usually only coming into the office for meetings.

Sabbaticals

In some cases, it is not a daily or weekly break from the office that employees want—it's one large block of time. Perhaps they want to travel, earn a degree, become involved in charitable work, or remodel a house. They do not want to quit, but they don't want to miss this opportunity either. The answer is a sabbatical.

Sabbaticals can be paid or unpaid, and are usually earned after working for some number of years or attaining a certain position. Employees are typically guaranteed either the same position or an equivalent one upon their return.

Phased Retirement

Employees nearing retirement age can be the most skilled and knowledgeable a company has. Rather than losing the people who know the business best, some companies are finding ways to redeploy them. These workers are stepping back from a full-time position to provide mentoring, participate in special projects, or take on global assignments. Companies that facilitate this kind of transition find it increases overall worker satisfaction by illustrating a company's commitment to ongoing employee development and retention of intellectual capital.

Seasonal Employment

Some companies are offering seasonal employment. Workers may want to have the summer off to take care of the kids, or teachers may want summer jobs.

Unofficial Flexibility

A final practice is more along the lines of on-the-spot flexibility. Managers do not have to have company-approved flexible work arrangements to be flexible, but can rearrange work hours for a day or give free time off at their discretion.

How to Make It Work

Support It with Policy, Technology, Systems

When flextime first came on the scene, managers were dubious. How could they retain control when they could not physically oversee their workers? How could they make sure workers in fact worked? How could their team work together when they rarely saw each other? By and large, these have turned out to be nonissues. Far from being more difficult to oversee, managers are reporting that flextimers often require less oversight and therefore free up managers' time for more strategic work.

Why? Because flextimers are motivated. Flexible work arrangements are enormously valuable for people seeking a better work/life balance, and their commitment to making it work is very strong.

The second factor smoothing the transition to flexible arrangements is technology. It is now easy and relatively inexpensive to tap into the office from anywhere using a laptop, a cell phone, and a pager. Web technology has made it simple for teams to relate via their own constantly updated site.

Nevertheless, flexible work arrangements can fail. Some positions simply are not suited to them. In other cases, the infrastructure isn't there. At times the team has not developed the necessary communications systems. Thinking through the arrangement thoroughly in advance can dramatically increase the odds of success.

Formalize the Process

Rather than letting each manager handle individual requests on a case-by-case basis, companies should formalize the process. Some companies have gone so far as to have a "flextime" section on their company Intranet, complete with a questionnaire that helps employees analyze their own likelihood of succeeding with various flexible options (which allows employees who are hesitant to approach their own managers to investigate the idea on their own).

A typical form should cover the following areas:

- How will the desired arrangement affect workflow?
- What potential problems could arise, and what is the plan for addressing them?
- Will there be an impact on clients/customers?
- What is the backup plan when the employee is unavailable for something that requires immediate action?
- Will the employee be available for meetings and travel? If not, what is the plan for coverage?
- How will communication be maintained with the office?
- What kind of investment in equipment (laptop, mobile phone, pager, phone lines, etc.) will be required?

Make Use of Experienced Flextimers

No one understands the benefits and challenges of flexible work arrangements better than those who have used them. Companies should maximize that resource by formalizing the use of mentors—both those who have used flextime, and the managers who have supervised them. Some companies have identified an official mentor who is available to answer anyone's questions, and others have sought to pair any employee considering a flexible work arrangement with a personal mentor. Flexible work arrangements work differently depending on each company's corporate culture, which is why mentoring is particularly helpful.

Let Employees Design Their Own Plan

A critical success factor in flexible work arrangements is letting employees design their own plans. Employees who are completely invested in the arrangement are more likely to make it work. Employees need to create a plan where they describe current and proposed work schedules. They must summarize their current workload and client/customer responsibilities and any proposed changes.

Make the Business Case

A key component of the plan is articulating the business case for the flexible arrangement. How, precisely, will it benefit the organization? This keeps everyone involved focused on the right priorities. It will keep managers from griping that they are doing employees a favor, and it will keep employees from acting as if this is a much-deserved perk. What this is, instead, is a business arrangement that works as long as both parties get what they need out of it.

Use It to Recruit

One of the most powerful incentives luring companies into flexible arrangements is that they will help with attracting talent. That is true, but flextime will only help if the talent finds out about it. The company's recruiting efforts should mention flexible offerings as pointedly as possible. Even when space is limited—as in a newspaper listing—"flex" should appear so that the company does not miss out on the enormous pool of candidates interested only in flexible positions.

Use It to Retain

Keep in mind that external candidates are not the only audience the company needs to woo. Current employees need to hear the message that the company is open to and supportive of flexible arrangements. The increased productivity and employee commitment that go hand in hand with flexible arrangements only happens if employees actually use the program. Companies should seek out success stories and profile them in newsletters or the company Intranet.

Measure the Results

As with any initiative with a goal, flexible work arrangements should be monitored and their results measured—and publicized. Has retention improved? Has flextime enabled the company to reduce overtime costs? Are workers reporting higher satisfaction? If the benefits that are supposed to flow with the adoption of flexible arrangements are not surfacing, companies should take another look at the design of their programs to find out why.

What's Ahead

Taking Flexibility a Step Further

Companies that hope to compete for talent must offer flexible solutions. But those just adding on policies and programs are missing a golden opportunity. Flexible work arrangements can be a first step in completely redesigning work systems in a way that makes them much more rewarding for both companies and employees.

The Work in America Institute has conducted a two-year investigation of what it calls "work/life policies," and the findings paint a picture of what is ahead for flexible work arrangements. The organization studied U.S. employers that "have moved beyond simply adding a work/life program or policy" and have instead "adopted a strategic work/life approach designed to accomplish a dual agenda: to simultaneously improve business results and employees' work/life integration."[7]

While many companies theoretically offer flexible arrangements, the report says they often fail because they are not truly rooted in business strategies and, in fact, clash with the corporate culture. The research report profiles 10 leading companies that have redesigned work processes, altered corporate culture, or worked harder at integrating flexible arrangements with core business strategies and human capital systems. The results: greater retention, improved productivity, better customer service, and reduced absenteeism.

The structural, systematic approach to flexible work arrangements represents an enormous commitment. But there is no question about the direction in which we are headed: flexible arrangements are becoming the norm. In the not-too-distant future, they will represent an integral part of the way companies do business. The organizations that work hardest now at capitalizing on flexible work arrangements will be at a substantial competitive advantage in the future.

How It Plays Out

How Different Companies Make It Work

Companies approaching flexible solutions need to take a look at their own environment to see what will succeed. What follows is a glimpse of a few actual programs (and results):

Ernst & Young's Office of Retention has created two Lotus Notes databases to guide interested employees through flexible work arrangements (FWAs). The FWA database features profiles and quotes from existing flextimers about their experiences. The database addresses the myths surrounding flexible arrangements, hosts a discussion board, and offers links to the firm's administration policies regarding work/life issues. The FWA Road Map has a self-assessment tool that helps interested employees decide whether they have the skills and personality to succeed on a flexible schedule. It outlines options and addresses the challenges linked to each. The FWA Road Map includes a template employees can use to write the required business case, and offers access to 12 FWA specialists who can help craft the plan and negotiate the terms. Eighty-four percent of the flextimers say the program is the primary reason they stay with Ernst & Young.[8]

Lexis-Nexis cut its operating expenses by more than 45 per cent by implementing a telecommuting program and a flexible work environment. Telecommuters get equipment, two telephone lines, and an allowance for home furnishings. The cost cutting resulted from higher productivity, fewer facilities, greater geographical hiring pools, being able to hire workers with disabilities, and better use of technology.[9]

PriceWaterhouseCoopers has a 25-page document on planning and implementing flexible work arrangements. It includes approval guidelines, discussion tools, compensation adjustment information, types of plans, and tips from other flextimers at the company. The policy demands that employees take responsibility for their relationships with both team members and clients.[10]

CHAPTER

Don't Underestimate the Crucial Importance of Senior Leadership

Most U.S. corporations today are overmanaged and underled.
—John Kotter[1]

Conventional wisdom says that when it comes to employee commitment, what counts is the direct supervisor. Some say it matters less if senior leadership is uninspired, or if there is some dysfunction in the upper ranks. Give somebody a good manager, they say, and he will stay and be productive. It seems to make sense.

Except it is not true anymore.

The manager is, of course, important. But these days it is *senior* leadership that research reveals to be the key component in employee satisfaction. It is senior leadership—even more so than individual managers—that can make or break a transformation effort. And it is trust in senior leadership that has a statistical link to higher shareholder value.

What the Numbers Say

Trust In Senior Leadership = High Employee Commitment = Higher TRS

The results are impossible to ignore: The firms where employees see real leaders at work return 42 percent more to shareholders after a three-year period (1996-1998), according to Watson Wyatt's *WorkUSA® 2000* study. (See Figure 14-1.)

Certainly, part of the explanation is that good leaders make good business decisions, which pay off on the bottom line. But an enormous component is that having good leadership creates high employee commitment—and we have already shown what high employee commitment does to shareholder value in Chapter 11. (See Figure 14-2.)

The Human Capital Index underscores the tie between leadership integrity and better financial performance. The study found that companies that focus on building trust in senior leadership, and companies where managers actively demonstrate the company's core values in their everyday behaviors, are worth significantly more. (See Figure 14-3.)

Again according to the *WorkUSA®* study, there are seven key factors driving employee commitment, and trust in senior leadership tops the list. (See Figure 14-4.)

Figure 14-1. *Trust in Senior Leadership and Shareholder Value*

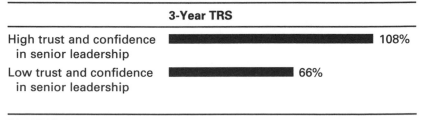

3-Year TRS		
High trust and confidence in senior leadership	████████████████████	108%
Low trust and confidence in senior leadership	██████████	66%

WorkUSA® 2000

Figure 14-2. *Trust in Senior Leadership and Employee Commitment*

	Level of Employee Commitment (ECI)
High trust and confidence in senior leadership	████████████████████████ 78%
Low trust and confidence in senior leadership	████ 17%

WorkUSA® 2000

Figure 14-3. *Links Between Leadership Integrity and Value Creation*

Practice	Impact on Market Value
Trust in senior leadership is actively engendered	1.2%
Managers demonstrate company's values	1.1%

Expected change associated with a significant (1SD) improvement in practice

Watson Wyatt's Human Capital Index®

Figure 14-4. *Key Drivers of Employee Commitment*

Factor	% Impact on Each Factor
Trust in senior leadership	14%
Chance to use skills on the job	14%
Competitiveness of rewards	11%
Job security	11%
Quality of company's products and services	10%
Absence of work-related stress	7%
Honesty and integrity of company's business conduct	7%

WorkUSA® 2000

So great leadership creates high employee commitment, leading to high shareholder value. Unfortunately, only half of the employees in the country trust those holding the reins at their corporation. (See Figure 14-5.)

Those numbers are not lost on today's senior executives. Respondents to Watson Wyatt's 1997 survey on "Leadership in the Global Economy" cited leadership development as the single

Figure 14-5. *U.S. Employees' Trust in Leadership*

WorkUSA® 2000

most important human resource issue facing their company in the second half of the 1990s.[2] (See Figure 14-6.)

It seems clear that senior leadership is fast becoming a top issue in the workplace. Why is it suddenly so important?

What's Behind the Trend

Big Decisions Now Have Greater Impact on Employees

The direct supervisor is still a critical component in employee commitment—it obviously detracts from an employee's satisfaction at work if she does not like her boss. But a shift has occurred: Our studies show that trust in *senior* leadership has become a better predictor of commitment than satisfaction with the immediate supervisor.

Why? Two main factors: a phenomenal increase in the incidence of capital restructuring—mergers, acquisitions, spin-offs and divestitures—and the extraordinary pace of business in general. Because of those factors, senior leadership now has more to do with giving employees a satisfying experience. Decisions made at the very top now have a direct—and almost immediate—effect on whether a business succeeds or fails. Key actions by senior executives determine whether an employee's job will remain or not; whether there will be career opportunities or not; whether there will be an opportunity for wealth creation or not. It used to be that senior management would make a decision, and over the next few years, the effects trickled down to employees. Now, a company can be bought, sold, made public, spun off, repur-

Figure 14-6. *Organizational Leadership Priorities: People*

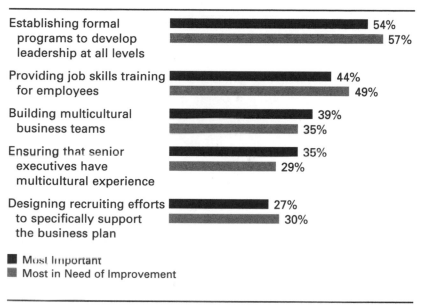

Establishing formal programs to develop leadership at all levels — 54% / 57%

Providing job skills training for employees — 44% / 49%

Building multicultural business teams — 39% / 35%

Ensuring that senior executives have multicultural experience — 35% / 29%

Designing recruiting efforts to specifically support the business plan — 27% / 30%

■ Most Important
■ Most in Need of Improvement

Leadership in the Global Economy

chased or all of the above at any time, and the impact on employees is instantaneous. These deals are in constant play, and the ball is moving at lightning speed.

So, employees are naturally interested in the strategy and tactics of the company at a broader level. We have seen employees in town meetings challenge executives on the direction of the company. They want to know what their organization is doing to meet the demands of the competitive marketplace, because they have the choice to join a winning team elsewhere. They want to know that the decisions made by their leaders will safeguard their job security, expand opportunities to use their skills and ultimately support their wealth creation. Executive leaders have a tremendous influence on those things in the way they chart the course of an IPO, handle a merger or acquisition, develop a new product line or decide where to invest. All of which explain employees' sudden interest in the skills of those many rungs above them on the corporate ladder.

How to Address the Problem

Understand Leadership, Then Focus on It

Leadership versus Management

People know leadership when they see it. And these days, employees know they are not seeing it enough.

Harvard's John Kotter agrees. The professor widely acknowledged as the world's foremost authority on leadership says the problem is dire: "After conducting 14 formal studies and more than a thousand interviews, directly observing dozens of executives in action, and compiling innumerable surveys, I am completely convinced that most organizations today lack the leadership they need. And the shortfall is often large. I'm not talking about a deficit of 10 percent, but of 200 percent, 400 percent or more in positions up and down the hierarchy."[3]

Kotter believes that the emphasis is on management rather than leadership. The purpose of management, he says, is to keep the current system running well. The purpose of leadership is taking charge of change. The two disciplines are distinct, and complimentary. "Leadership works through people and culture. It's soft and hot. Management works through hierarchy and systems. It's harder and cooler."[4]

What Employees Want in Leaders

The numbers tell us that all companies have "leaders," but many of them are not leading. And while the commentary on leadership cited above is illuminating—even inspiring—it is not easy to put into practice. Telling your senior executives to start "leading change by working through people and culture" may not produce exactly the results a company is after.

How does a company begin to hire great leaders, or teach its current executives to begin leading? Given the ambiguousness of the subject, we find the surest footing in the research. In our *WorkUSA® 2000* study, we asked employees what made them trust their senior executives, and here are their answers. (See Figure 14-7.)

Looking down this list, two key characteristics jump out: communication and fairness. Great leaders know how to talk to employees, to listen to them, and to persuade them. And they play fair: They promote employees for the right reasons, and they do not eliminate jobs casually.

What Senior Executives Want in Leaders

Watson Wyatt's "Leadership in the Global Economy" study offers additional insight. Here, we asked senior leaders themselves to offer their observations about leadership.

Respondents believe there is no substitute for the hard work of demonstrating through actions—rather than mere words—which personal leadership qualities are needed for organizational success. They said that effective leaders must themselves exhibit the work habits, attitudes, and priorities they expect from their subordinates. Exhibiting confidence in an increasingly uncertain

Figure 14-7. *Key Drivers of Trust in Senior Leadership*

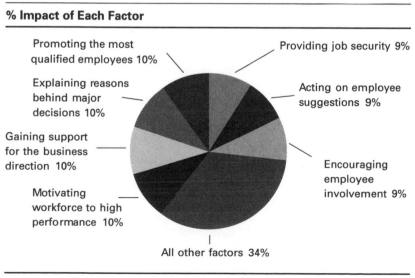

% Impact of Each Factor

Promoting the most qualified employees 10%

Providing job security 9%

Explaining reasons behind major decisions 10%

Acting on employee suggestions 9%

Gaining support for the business direction 10%

Motivating workforce to high performance 10%

Encouraging employee involvement 9%

All other factors 34%

WorkUSA® 2000

world is the second most frequently noted personal leadership quality.[5] (See Figure 14-8.)

Leaders need to act as teachers and coaches, conflict mediators, and consensus builders. According to top executives, the most important factor in influencing others is inspiring people, followed closely by managing effective two-way communication. (See Figure 14-9.) A few regional differences are worth noting: Top executives in North America assign more importance to two-way communication, while top Asian executives place more importance on engendering common goals and values in the workforce.

Top executives believe creating a "culture for learning and innovation" is the key leadership behavior involved in mobilizing people.

Focusing on Leadership

Getting employees on board, committed, and moving in the same direction is the most vital objective for top executives in today's knowledge-based economy. To keep executives focused on that one goal, the most successful companies have instituted leadership development programs.

Figure 14-8. *Personal Leadership Qualities*

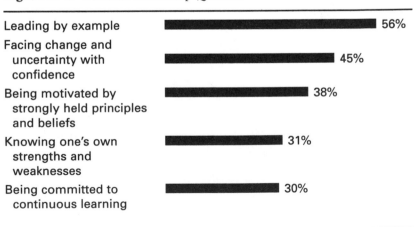

Leading by example	56%
Facing change and uncertainty with confidence	45%
Being motivated by strongly held principles and beliefs	38%
Knowing one's own strengths and weaknesses	31%
Being committed to continuous learning	30%

Leadership in the Global Economy

Figure 14-9. *Factors in Influencing Others*

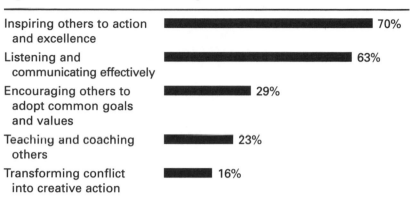

Inspiring others to action and excellence — 70%

Listening and communicating effectively — 63%

Encouraging others to adopt common goals and values — 29%

Teaching and coaching others — 23%

Transforming conflict into creative action — 16%

Leadership in the Global Economy

Figure 14-10. *Factors in Mobilizing People*

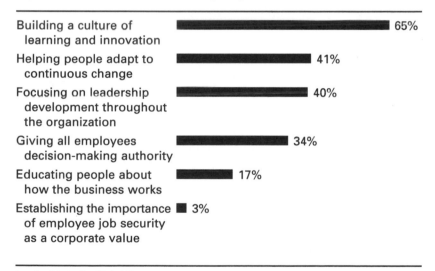

Building a culture of learning and innovation — 65%

Helping people adapt to continuous change — 41%

Focusing on leadership development throughout the organization — 40%

Giving all employees decision-making authority — 34%

Educating people about how the business works — 17%

Establishing the importance of employee job security as a corporate value — 3%

Leadership in the Global Economy

The effort starts with recruiting. The best companies profile their leaders. They probe to discover more about the motivations and styles of these stars, and why they are able to create such a productive work climate. They develop leadership competency models based on these top performers, and tie them back to the company's business strategy. These models are used rigorously to hire employees with the "right stuff" to succeed as leaders in the company.

The next element of the effort involves an ongoing program to develop the leadership skills that the job demands. A rotational system for job assignments enhances experience. External "executive" business school programs, development programs run by outside consultants, and in-house "universities" add knowledge and refine talents. These programs work to hone communication skills and "unlearn" behaviors that torpedo trust. But perhaps what they do most effectively is reinforce to the top players that leadership is indeed part of their job description, and the company's financial performance depends on it. Finally, the best companies keep their leaders focused on leading by setting up related performance measures tied to rewards.

How It Plays Out

The Familiar Ring of Poor Leadership

We recently conducted an organizational analysis including interviews and survey of the top 100 managers at a Fortune 500 company that was experiencing a dramatic slide in financial performance. Looking at the data, it quickly became clear that the CEO and his top lieutenants were the problem. Here are some comments (with names/places changed) taken directly from the focus group:

- "Our CEO is out looking at new businesses to acquire while our flagship operation goes down the toilet. I'm not sure he knows we have a problem."
- "I don't even know what business we're in anymore."
- "Our decision-making process is: 1) Form a committee with too many people on it; 2) Gain consensus, which takes months; 3) Come up with a compromise or hedged solution or go back to the drawing board and start over."

- "The direct reports to our CEO spend their time managing up, and don't have time to focus on the business."
- "There is no performance accountability at the top; they have geared it so they get rich whether we succeed or fail."
- "The CEO is very smart, but he doesn't want to hear bad news, so he surrounds himself with people who will tell him what he wants to hear."
- "The fact that leadership ties our hands with ineffective policies indicates that they don't have the slightest idea what it takes to get this done."
- "I am perplexed by their stance. I don't know what their plan is or what they expect."
- "These guys have squandered their credibility. They may even be telling us the truth, but at this point no one believes them."
- "xI do want more communication from our executive team—but I don't want to hear again that we must achieve double digit growths and huge margins. I want to hear specifically how we are going to do that."

This is the kind of list that makes executives cringe. Why? Because it has the ring of truth. This goes on everywhere, and we all know it. "Leaders" are out of touch, feathering their own nests, and are failing to communicate a strategic vision to their employees. The result: a lack of trust in senior leadership that dramatically impairs the company. Until a company repairs that crucial breach, no other new business effort stands a chance.

Leaders "Walk the Talk" of Mission and Values

One of the surest ways to torpedo faith in senior leadership is clear evidence that management does not practice what it preaches. In contrast, companies who get high marks for leadership make it a habit to develop and showcase ways in which the company stands behind everything it says.

Fortune's "World's Most Admired Companies" research provided dozens of examples of corporate leaders modeling the policies and behaviors they endorsed verbally.[6] A few examples:

- Citibank demonstrates its belief in the value of global thinking by ensuring that more than half of its senior executive team is comprised of non-Americans.
- Procter & Gamble backs up a key principle in its mission statement—to make the company's and employees' interests synonymous—by using stock ownership as a key building block of its retirement program.
- Sony's long-standing reputation for technical leadership and innovation stems from a Founding Prospectus, written in 1946, that established the framework for a "free, dynamic and pleasant" culture "where technical personnel…can exercise their technological skills to the highest level."
- General Electric's dynamic former CEO, Jack Welch, set an unmistakable cultural tone within his organization by declaring, "Making your numbers, but not demonstrating our values, is grounds for dismissal."

There are plenty of companies out there with inspiring mission statements posted on the wall. Most of the time, those statements do more harm than good. When they're not backed up by obvious, definitive action by a committed leadership, those posters inspire ridicule rather than commitment.

CHAPTER

Learn How to Manage Change

"Nothing endures but change."
—Heraclitus (540–480 BC)

"Whosoever desires constant success must change his conduct with the times."
—Machiavelli

"If you want to make enemies, try to change something."
—Woodrow Wilson

Reengineering. Restructuring. Restrategizing. Quality programs. Mergers. Acquisitions. It is all change, and it has become the one constant in business.

It stands to reason that all of this would make executives more comfortable with change. But having been through it, managers now understand just how damaging change efforts can be. Even the change programs that are eventually termed successful suffer through periods of general chaos, poor customer service, and high employee turnover. The concept of change may be full of promise, but its reality is threatening to employees, executives, and shareholders alike.

It doesn't have to be that way. The very frequency and prominence of these change efforts means that we have, in fact, learned something. At this point, corporate transformation does not have to be undertaken with crossed fingers and a hope for the best. The smartest companies are putting programs and practices in place that allow them to excel at change, and they are keeping their employees on board and productive throughout.

What the Numbers Say

Good Change Management = High TRS

Two-thirds of all organizations have experienced some type of "trauma" in the past year, whether it is a merger, acquisition, management restructuring, or downsizing initiative. Learning how to manage change effectively has never been more important, but less than half of employees say that change is implemented well. Doing it right has a highly positive effect on employee commitment and economic value. When change is handled well, commitment levels are almost four times higher, and three-year total returns to share-

Figure 15-1. *Effective Change Management and Employee Commitment*

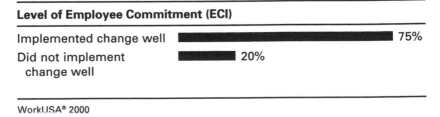

Level of Employee Commitment (ECI)

Implemented change well — 75%

Did not implement change well — 20%

WorkUSA® 2000

Figure 15-2. *Effective Change Management and TRS*

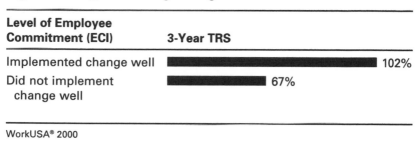

WorkUSA® 2000

Figure 15-3. *U.S. Employee Perspective on Change Implementation*

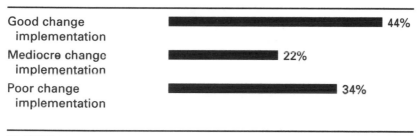

WorkUSA® 2000

holders are a dramatic 35 percentage points higher. (See Figures 15-1, 15-2.)

Despite its importance to commitment and value creation, only about two-fifths of employees say that change has been implemented well. (See Figure 15-3.)

How to Do It Right

Establish Trust, Respond to Emotional Needs, Communicate

Identifying the factors that contribute to effective change management is vital to an organization's success. Watson Wyatt isolated seven critical factors that largely account for whether change is viewed as well executed or not:

Figure 15-4. *Key Drivers of Effective Change Management*

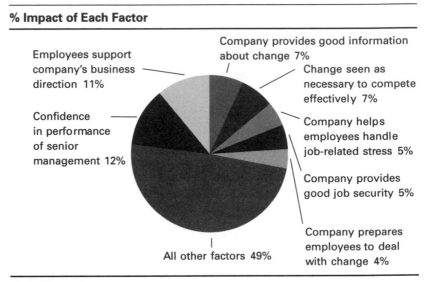

% Impact of Each Factor

Company provides good information about change 7%

Employees support company's business direction 11%

Change seen as necessary to compete effectively 7%

Confidence in performance of senior management 12%

Company helps employees handle job-related stress 5%

Company provides good job security 5%

All other factors 49%

Company prepares employees to deal with change 4%

WorkUSA® 2000

Looking at this list, it is clear that changing the organization without losing the employees along the way boils down to a focus on three factors: 1) establish trust in the leadership and where it is taking the company, 2) communicate effectively, and 3) respond to employees' emotional needs surrounding change.

Establish Trust in Leaders and Business Direction

Particularly when there are major changes in the works, people need to feel confidence in their leaders. Employees want to feel certain that those at the helm will do what is strategically best for the company. And they want to be able to trust that leadership will be true to its word.

We consulted with a railroad company that had not created an atmosphere of trust between workers and leadership. In fact, the workers hated management. When the company came up against a competitive situation—and truly needed concessions from the union—that lack of trust came back to haunt them. Rather than engaging employees in a face-to-face, open dialogue, management actually made a videotape—featuring an executive in a suit, no less—asking for concessions. Not only did the union not respond to the call for "help," it displayed a banner in a very public arena with pejorative messages about the railroad's CEO.

Trust in leadership is essential to a successful change effort—much like getting in shape is a precursor to running a marathon. You simply cannot embark on the effort without doing the preparation first. Companies struggling with these leadership issues need to begin a coordinated effort to rebuild trust. The first step is to disarm cynicism by addressing the issues head-on. ("We know we've made some mistakes. Here's how they happened. Going forward, we've got a new approach, and we need your help.") Management's behavior must be aligned behind the new message and must reinforce it daily at all levels. Eventually, with repeated, consistent messages backed up by a new style of leadership, companies can reestablish the trust they need to move forward.

Communicate Effectively

A key to maintaining that crucial trust in leadership throughout the challenging period of a change effort is to communicate openly and honestly. In order to have faith in management, employees need to understand the competitive and strategic issues the executives are facing, and to comprehend the rationale behind any painful decisions.

The communications segment must provide employees with the "burning platform"—the pressing reason for the change. Management should explain why the change is necessary for business success or survival and urgent for all concerned. (In order for a patient to willingly submit to the disruption, pain, and expense of an operation, he must first view the alternative as worse.) So through open, honest communication, executives need to focus employees on a) what happens if they do not undergo change, and b) the upside for them personally when the company achieves change.

As much as possible, leadership must explain exactly what will be involved and what employees can expect to happen. That reduces uncertainty and increases trust, conveying that there is, in fact, a plan. (When a doctor details exactly what is involved in an operation, the patient may well tune out the medical minutiae, but nevertheless find it soothing to hear that the doctor clearly knows what he is doing and has a plan.)

Rather than trying to sugarcoat or deny the potential impact, leadership must describe, honestly and openly, how the change may affect employees. If jobs will be lost, employees should be told. Stress is largely fear of the unknown. If leadership demonstrates right off the bat that employees will be told the unvarnished truth as soon as it is available, levels of stress will go down and levels of trust will go up.

In January of 1996, the Dun and Bradstreet Corporation announced that it was restructuring the company into three separate businesses. The change was well received by management, employees, and Wall Street as a smart move. Employees in the separate business units were largely unaffected by the changes, as they had always operated independently from corporate. On the other hand, the corporate office was about to undergo massive change as the "head" of something that no longer existed. We were in the audience as Mike Connors, then the senior vice president of HR (now chairman and CEO of VNU Media & Information Group) made the announcement to the almost 300 corporate employees. It could not have been a more potentially explosive moment, but Connors demonstrated the leadership that creates successful change. With an open, honest, forthcoming demeanor, he explained exactly what was going to happen. He let employees know that the organization was very concerned about their careers, and described at length the processes by which they could bid for jobs in the new operation units. He outlined the "safety nets"—including career guidance programs, support hot lines, and career centers—that had been set up for them. At the end of the speech, those 300 employees (some of whom were about to lose their jobs) amazed us by applauding him. We turned to one of them to ask why employees would applaud—rather than boo—an executive in these circumstances. "They trust him," was the simple response.

Help Employees Cope, Occupationally and Emotionally

The first question in every employee's mind will be: how will this affect me? Employees will fear losing their jobs (and their status). They will worry about having their pay cut. They will be concerned about how their managers or work teams will change, and about what new skills might be required.

If management fails to address these questions, employees will be distracted by their fears, and productivity will fall. Candid communication is crucial—even hearing "we don't know yet" from a leadership team that has established credibility will relieve stress. Once answers become clear, companies must help employees transition with change management training, hot lines, stress management workshops and, when necessary, generous outplacement and severance programs.

Something that can go a long way in helping employees cope with change is for a company to remain clearly committed to job security. That doesn't mean guaranteeing that everyone's job is safe. It means a recognition of the seriousness of eliminating a job. Some executives have become cavalier about this, but it is not something to be approached casually. A 45-year-old factory worker making $25 an hour may not have a big nest egg. His wife may not be contributing a second paycheck. He may have three kids and could be living paycheck to paycheck. If management closes his plant, he faces economic disaster. If the local economy doesn't offer comparable employment, the factory worker's next option may be fast-food service at $7 an hour. This scenario is why "trust in senior management" is so critical to successful change efforts.

About 20 years ago, during the 1980s recession, a company was "forced" to close a few plants. In a spectacular display of bad timing and even worse judgment, management actually allowed a major architectural design publication to do a story on the firm's new executive offices. As workers in the factory towns were being handed their pink slips, they were reading about the exotic wood that was being used in the new executive conference rooms. It takes a very, very long time for a company to recover from that kind of breach of trust.

The Big Picture

World's Most Admired Companies See Culture Change as a Constant

The most successful organizations not only master the art of change; they demonstrate an understanding and acceptance of change as a constant. Leading organizations understand that different stages of organizational development require different cultures. And rather than minimizing "culture" as neutral or irrelevant, these companies view culture as an asset that can play a crucial role in achieving business objectives.

Fortune's "World's Most Admired Companies" research specifically examined how 18 world-class corporations handled change.[1] Remarkable similarities were revealed. In approaching major cultural transformation, successful firms:

- Get consensus at the highest levels about where they are, and where they want to be.
- Seek to drive and reinforce behavior in as many ways as possible, through systems, staff, structure, and processes.
- Systematically measure what they are trying to change.

- Ensure that their basic human resources practices—
  reward systems, career development systems, selection
  procedures, performance management strategies, and
  leadership styles—support the new behavioral directions.

Consensus Is Critical

The common assumption is that the hard part is agreeing on
where the organization should be headed. Oddly enough, that
turns out to be the easy part. What is much more difficult is
reaching consensus on just where the company is today. In fact,
agreeing on a vision for the future can actually be counterproductive, possibly creating a false sense of alignment when in fact
there is major disagreement under the surface.

For example, an entire management group might agree that
employee trust in senior leadership is a crucial component of the
firm's plans for the future. One executive may leave that meeting
thinking that a top priority will be putting programs in place that
will build that trust. Another executive, who happens to think
employees already trust senior leadership, will consider the matter
settled and done with.

What differentiates successful firms from the rest? They
make sure everybody leaves a meeting like that with the same priorities in mind. Achieving consensus on where the company is,
and how far it is from the goal, is a hallmark of the leading firms
studied in the *Fortune* research.[2] Until this consensus is reached,
it is virtually impossible to assign the correct sense of urgency to
specific issues.

Research has shown how difficult it is for an organization to
gauge its distance from its cultural target. One study by the Hay
Group, in which executive teams ranked 56 internal cultural elements to form snapshots of both desired and current cultures,
found that 9 out of 10 executive teams were more divided on
defining their current cultures than in describing future cultural

priorities. In almost half of these organizations, the difference was quite pronounced, by a factor of 33 percent or more.[3]

Culture Is Tenacious

Multiple Interventions Must Affect Systems, Staff, and Structure

Insight into where the organization is in relation to its goals, then, is the first step. But when the object is changing behavior, insight is not enough. There has been so much written about the high return/low cost of communication that people sometimes feel that communication is enough. In other words, if we tell people why we need to change the culture—if we have the right posters, and the CEO makes the right speech—somehow change will magically occur. This model of learning is psychoanalytically based, relying on insight to change behavior. It doesn't work. Communication is critical to a transformation effort, but it is not enough.

Changing the behavior of even one individual is tricky. Changing the collective behavior of an entire workforce is even more complex. Culture is tenacious, and behavior patterns are reinforced by many nonverbal, nonintellectual factors that are tough to work against. In short, any new program targeted to changing deep-rooted cultural patterns will be sabotaged at every level, both consciously and subconsciously. The only way to succeed is to battle on as many levels as possible. The critical individual and organizational competencies that will form the core of the new culture must be established, communicated, and then—most importantly—reinforced in every conceivable way through new structures, systems and processes.

As James A. Belasco writes in *Teaching the Elephant to Dance*, "Organizational systems give people the tools to use the new vision. They give people permission to use those tools. Performance systems guide day-to-day activities. They must expect, measure, and reward using the new vision. Human resource/personnel policies give permission to use the new vision tools. Selection, orientation, training, promotion, and compensation policies encourage the use of the vision. Last, the cultural system—heroes and symbols—subconsciously reinforces the use of the new vision."[4]

In other words, in addition to telling people what to do, a company has to make sure they have the ability to do it, and the motivation for doing it. That means the organization has to hire the right people. It has to give them resources. And it has to reward and punish performance appropriately.

Let's say a company wants orders to be fulfilled faster. A manager can communicate that simple idea to workers many times over, but employees can't speed things up if the outdated computer program keeps freezing the screens while customers are on hold. Instead, those seeking speedier performance must also budget for problem-free equipment that will help workers move faster. They must develop training programs to teach employees shortcuts and to emphasize the goal of moving faster. And they must redesign compensation so that it rewards speed instead of freedom from error.

Expectations, Behavior, and Consequences

In setting up the systems and structures that will keep change on track, companies must pay close attention to the critical relationships between expectations, behavior, and consequences.

Expectations: Tell People What You Want

Leadership is critical in communicating expectations during change. That doesn't mean executives simply reminding employees what is expected of them in the new culture (although that is important, too). It means that executives must live, eat, and breathe the new behaviors. Every day, in each interaction, senior leadership must take the opportunity to reinforce the new way of doing business.

Behavior: Make Sure They Have the Ability to Do It

Research has shown us that the most successful firms keep culture change in mind when recruiting. Rather than acting as if the transformation effort has nothing to do with new hires, the best companies focus on finding and attracting workers whose attitudes, goals, and expectations are consistent with the desired culture. If the culture is risk-oriented, admired firms take care to select risk-takers, rather than risk-avoiders. If the culture is team-based, the selection process emphasizes the need to find team players, rather than individual contributors.

Hiring people with the right basic mix of skills, experience, and attitude is the first half of making sure employees are able to meet the new expectations. The second half is to support those individual competencies with organizational resources. Leading firms marshaled the staffing, structure, systems, information, and physical resources to support their employees.

Rewards and Consequences: Encourage Them to Do It

The final step in changing collective behavior is to make it in the employee's self-interest to "get with the program." Through the careful use of compensation systems and career development opportunities, the most successful firms reward the desired behavior—and discourage anything else.

Measure What You Seek to Manage

Culture change is vast. It can feel very ambiguous. That is why it is so important for a company to identify precisely what it is that it seeks to change. Then, sometime in midcourse, it needs to measure whether change is in fact taking place. Say the goal is to speed up decision-making. There are ways for a company to measure whether it is on the right track. Is the organization getting back to customers more quickly about decisions on refunds? Are employees saying they are freer to make decisions? Do managers find they are spending less time in meetings seeking approvals? Whatever indicators are chosen, the company needs to monitor and measure them in an active way. If change is not taking place, some adjustments in the change effort are clearly required.

As a side note, just the act of measuring something will help to make people feel accountable. It communicates that people are watching, and they are watching something concrete.

In his book, *Leading Change: Why Transformation Efforts Fail,* widely acclaimed leadership expert John Kotter reviews the most common mistakes corporations make when trying to change. To steer clear of those errors, Kotter suggests eight "Steps to Transforming Your Organization."[5] Here is a summary:

1. **Establish a sense of urgency.** Examine market and competitive realities. Identify and discuss crises, potential crises, or major opportunities. "When is the urgency rate high enough? From what I have seen, the answer is when about 75 percent of a company's management is honestly convinced the business-as-usual is totally unacceptable," writes Kotter.

2. **Form a powerful guiding coalition.** Assemble a group with enough power to lead the change effort. Encourage them to work together as a team. "Efforts that don't have a powerful enough guiding coalition can make apparent progress for a while. But, sooner or later, the opposition gathers itself together and stops the change," says Kotter.

3. **Create a vision.** Use a vision to help direct the change effort, and develop strategies for achieving that vision. "A useful rule of thumb: If you can't communicate the vision to someone in five minutes or less and get a reaction that signifies both understanding and interest, you are not yet done with this phase of the transformation process," writes Kotter.

4. **Communicate the vision.** Use every vehicle possible to communicate the new vision and strategies. Teach new behaviors by the example of the guiding coalition. "Communication comes in both words and deeds, and the latter are often the most powerful form," advises Kotter. "Nothing undermines change more than behavior by important individuals that is inconsistent with their words."

5. **Empower others to act on the vision.** Get rid of obstacles to change. Change systems or structures that seriously undermine the vision. Encourage risk taking and nontraditional ideas, activities, and actions.

6. **Plan for and create short-term wins.** Plan for visible performance improvements. Create those improvements. Recognize and reward employees involved in the improvements. "Most people won't go on the long march unless they see compelling evidence within 12 to 24 months that the journey is producing expected results," writes Kotter.

7. **Consolidate improvements and produce still more change.** Use increased credibility to change systems, structures, and policies that don't fit the vision. Hire, promote, and develop employees who can implement the vision. Reinvigorate the process with new projects, themes, and change agents. "Don't let up," Kotter says, "until the all the work is done."

8. **Institutionalize new approaches.** Articulate the connections between the new behaviors and corporate success. Develop the means to ensure leadership development and succession. Kotter says, "In the final analysis, change sticks when it becomes 'the way we do things around here,' when it seeps into the bloodstream of the corporate body."[6]

How It Plays Out

Dramatic Culture Change Results in Financial Turnaround

Company:	*Reader's Digest*
Revenues:	*$2.6 billion*
Number of Employees:	*5000*
Industry:	*Publishing*
Location of Headquarters:	*Pleasantville, NY*

Tom Ryder knows all about culture change. The corporate culture was very well established at Reader's Digest when he came in to head the company in 1998. The 78-year old, paternalistic company coddled its employees. The corporate offices were on a beautiful campus in Pleasantville, New York. Picasso paintings and Giacometti sculptures from founder DeWitt Wallace's prized art collection adorned the hallways. Employees who had never flown before were treated to jaunts on the corporate jet.

And then Ryder came in. He sold 38 of the company's most valuable paintings and sculptures for $100 million. He sold the jet. He sold off unprofitable operations, slashed the dividend by nearly 80 percent, cut marginal customers, and reduced the workforce by several hundred workers. To add insult to injury, he put a sign on his coffee table that said, "No whining."

Then something remarkable happened: morale improved.

The Burning Platform

When Ryder came to Reader's Digest, he had no need to manufacture a "burning platform" to convince the troops that change was imperative. The company's share price had plunged from a high of $56 in 1992 to $16, profits had dropped by about 75 percent to $100 million, revenues were down, and the flagship's circulation had fallen by 5 million. Employees knew the situation was untenable. Still, selling the Picassos?

"I did something that was very scary," says Ryder. "But I knew exactly what I was doing, and I told people far in advance that I was going to do it. What I said was we are going to make this a smaller, more profitable company."

His initial plans alarmed the board and some big investors: It was risky and counterintuitive. And the new no-fluff, no-whining culture was threatening to employees who were used to a very different way of life.

And yet, two years later the company reported eight straight quarters of operating profits, two quarters of revenue growth, and a share price at $40, close to its 52-week high. Marta Nichols, an analyst for Donaldson, Lufkin & Jenrette, explains: "What Ryder did differently was to get employees on his side and improve morale. He has brought discipline and focus."

Expectations, Behavior, and Consequences

How did he do it? How did he take away the employees' toys and end up as their hero? By approaching change the right way. He had a clear vision of how to fix a broken company. He communicated it in every way available to him. He kept employees informed about what was expected of them and what changes they could expect to see. Finally, he made sure that there would be consequences for behavior. Below are some of the elements of Reader's Digest's change program:

- A survey was conducted that focused specifically on culture. The goal was to gauge current culture as well as to shape the attributes of ideal future culture. Five main goals came out of the Culture Survey: communicate better, manage performance more effectively, focus on customers more, emphasize long-term goals, and be more innovative.
- A Worldwide Employee Survey followed with 83 percent participation (3600+ people) that supplied feedback on employee satisfaction and commitment. Responses illuminated current strengths and weaknesses.

- Managers were held accountable for creating and implementing business unit action plans based on survey results.
  Action plans laid out a clear itinerary for the coming
  months, identifying two or three key developmental areas.
  Progress was made measurable.
- Those who did well were rewarded through the Management Incentive Plan.
- In a letter to all employees, Ryder referred to the "Change
  starts with me" initiative. "Each one of us should be doing
  at least one thing differently than we were doing before,"
  he wrote. To help focus employees on that concept, he
  initiated the Great Performers Awards, including the
  Chairman's Award, which is given to a handful of
  employees who make the most significant contributions
  to the company's business success in ways that personify
  the new culture.

A key element of Ryder's approach: hiring the right person to head
Human Resources during a period of change. He brought in Gary
Rich, who quickly went to work aligning human resource practices
with the new culture. Among other things, Rich changed how
employees were compensated by making all U.S. employees eligible for bonuses, implemented career development programs, and
introduced new performance management techniques.

By the beginning of 2001, Reader's Digest had reduced its cost
base by $350 million, increased operating profit by $150 million,
delivered 10 consecutive quarters of operating profit growth, and
four straight quarters of revenue growth.

Clearly, change can be handled well.

CHAPTER

Don't Assume Workers No Longer Care about Job Security

"What employees hear is that they're the firm's most valuable assets; what they know is that they're the most expendable assets."
—Gary Hamel and C.K. Prahalad in *Competing for the Future*[1]

There used to be a deal: If workers performed well, they got to keep their jobs. But then the world changed—it got faster, bigger, and more competitive. Suddenly it became harder for executives to keep their end of the deal.

Amid a sea of media attention in the mid-1980s, managers everywhere began to suggest that job security was no longer something a worker could expect. There was a general switch away from the company-as-a-family metaphor to the company-as-a-team metaphor. The distinction? Players can be cut from a team.

This new generation of management seemed to suggest that they were merely adapting to a changing marketplace. But eliminating job security because it is a challenge to commit to it isn't particularly smart business.

World-class leaders recognize the following: The most productive relationship between employee and employer is one of reciprocal commitment. This is the era of the knowledge worker, where the discretionary efforts of countless individual employees will determine an organization's financial success—or failure. Management is continually asking for more creativity, more problem solving, and more initiative from workers. If there is not an equivalent commitment offered in turn, employees are more likely to seek a fair deal elsewhere.

Leading organizations, therefore, actively demonstrate a long-term commitment to job security. They show employees that they are doing everything they can to avoid layoffs. The result: higher employee commitment and increased shareholder value.

Providing job security does not, of course, mean letting an employee perform poorly. Nor does it mean guaranteeing that, no matter what the business conditions, jobs will never be lost. After all, things do change, and there are times when avoiding painful layoffs could result in an entire company going belly-up.

What the Numbers Say

Job Security Dropping, but Still Just as Important to Employees

We may have entered a new millennium, but job security is just as important to employees now as it was 100 (or for that matter 1000) years ago. Unfortunately, managers today often find themselves in the position of rationalizing rampant downsizing, sometimes suggesting that it's the employees who aren't interested in long-term commitments. The research suggests otherwise.

According to the Human Capital Index, companies who emphasize job security are worth 1.2 percent more on the market.

Our *WorkUSA®* study echoes that finding and builds on it: companies whose employees feel good about the security of their jobs have both higher TRS (see Figure 16-1) and a higher Employee Commitment Index (see Figure 16-2) than companies whose employees are worried about losing their jobs.[2]

Job security is so fundamental that it is a key driver of three of the most sought-after organizational characteristics: employee commitment, trust in senior leadership, and effective change management: (See Figures 16-3, 16-4, 16-5.)

What's more, worries about job security not only add stress to the lives of employees but also encourage them to pack up and take their talent elsewhere (most likely to the competition). A survey on retention practices by the Society for Human Resource

Figure 16-1. *Job Security and Total Return to Shareholders*

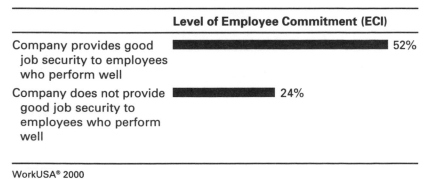

3-Year TRS

Company provides good job security to employees who perform well	106%
Company does not provide good job security to employees who perform well	69%

WorkUSA® 2000

Figure 16-2. *Job Security and Employee Commitment*

Level of Employee Commitment (ECI)

Company provides good job security to employees who perform well	52%
Company does not provide good job security to employees who perform well	24%

WorkUSA® 2000

Figure 16-3. *Key Drivers of Employee Commitment*

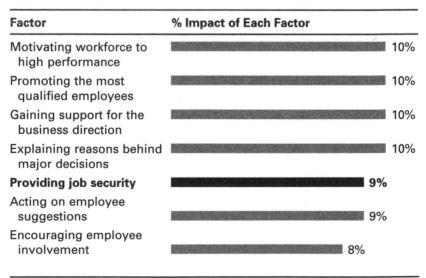

Factor	% Impact of Each Factor
Trust in senior leadership	14%
Chance to use skills on the job	14%
Job security	11%
Competitiveness of rewards	11%
Quality of company's products and services	10%
Absence of work-related stress	7%
Honesty and integrity of company's business conduct	7%

WorkUSA® 2000

Figure 16-4. *Key Drivers of Trust in Senior Leadership*

Factor	% Impact of Each Factor
Motivating workforce to high performance	10%
Promoting the most qualified employees	10%
Gaining support for the business direction	10%
Explaining reasons behind major decisions	10%
Providing job security	**9%**
Acting on employee suggestions	9%
Encouraging employee involvement	8%

WorkUSA® 2000

Figure 16-5. *Key Drivers of Effective Change Management*

	% Impact of Each Factor
Confidence in performance of senior management	12%
Employees support company's business direction	11%
Company provides good information about change	7%
Change seen as necessary to compete effectively	7%
Company helps employees handle job-related stress	5%
Company provides good job security	5%
Company prepares employees to deal with change	4%
All other factors	49%

WorkUSA® 2000

Management found that loss of job security is one reason employees give up on a job. "Job security fears" was cited by 10 percent of workers who left their jobs, making it one of the most common reasons for leaving.

That means job security plays a role in virtually every crucial category: market value, employee commitment, trust in senior leadership, change management, and retention. And yet, companies appear to be offering less of it. In the California Management Review, Sanford Jacoby writes, "The share of employees who say they are frequently concerned about layoffs has risen from 12 percent in 1981 to 37 percent in 1999."[3]

Watson Wyatt's research shows the same trend: (See Figure 16-6.)

It comes down to equilibrium. Workforces at both extremes (those that are too secure—and those that are insecure) are less

Figure 16-6. *Job Security Dropping*

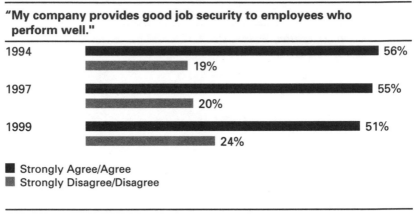

"My company provides good job security to employees who
  perform well."

1994 — 56% / 19%
1997 — 55% / 20%
1999 — 51% / 24%

■ Strongly Agree/Agree
■ Strongly Disagree/Disagree

WorkUSA® 2000

productive than companies that are able to find a balance. The European HCI research illustrates this point—many European organizations provide high levels of job security by statute; those organizations that provided even higher levels in the survey were shown to create less economic value. In other words, they have pushed job security beyond advisable levels and are actually causing value downturns.

What's Behind the Trends

Downsizing Seems Easier Than the Alternative

Providing job security does not mean sacrificing all else. What we mean by job security is that a company actively focuses on maintaining total employment. Jeffrey Pfeffer, in *The Human Equation,* writes, "Employment security means that employees are not quickly put on the street for things such as economic downturns or the strategic mistakes of senior management, over which they have no control. The policy focuses on maintaining total employment, not on protecting individuals from the consequences of their individual behavior on the job."[4]

Why Do Companies Downsize?

It is not the firing of poorly performing individual workers that threatens workers' perceptions of job security. And emergency lay-offs designed to stop the hemorrhaging at a financially desperate company are understandable even by many of those losing jobs. What is of concern—and threatening to employees' perception of job security—is the somewhat capricious downsizing that has swept industry after industry for more than a decade.

The reality is that cutting costs is much easier and faster than the longer-term solution of growing the market. When a CEO feels the pressure from stockholders to improve Return On Investment (ROI), there are only two choices: grow the numerator (net income) or reduce the denominator (net assets). The latter is the only safe bet in the near term, thus CEOs begin to cut.

Does Downsizing Work?

The ironic truth about downsizing is that it might not even work—or at least not for long. According to *Competing for the Future*, "Restructuring seldom results in fundamental improvement in the business. At best it buys time. One study of 16 large U.S. companies with at least three years of restructuring experience found that although restructuring usually did improve a firm's share price, the improvement was almost always temporary. Three years into restructuring, the share prices of the companies surveyed were, on average, lagging even farther behind index growth rates than they had been when the restructuring began."[5]

Why does downsizing fail to achieve its goals? Because its focus is backward, rather than forward. It is a response to the recent past, rather than a commitment to business opportunities in the future. That is why it may work for a little while, until it becomes clear that being smaller does not help a company to negotiate a new, foreign landscape. It only makes the company smaller.

It is really not surprising that downsizing usually fails to improve profitability. After all, there were reasons the organization was in trouble, and cutting staff has not addressed them. The products remain uninspired or less than top quality, the customer service remains poor, the leadership still lacks vision, and so on. Moreover, given that downsizing is so easy to do, it hardly gives a company a competitive advantage because the competition can easily jump to the same "solution."

The Costs of Downsizing Are High

There is a great deal of negative fallout from downsizing. It's important to look at the big picture when considering that route.

The Financial Costs

Layoffs are expensive. And the more careful the hiring process has been, the more expensive the letting go will turn out to have been. What's more, companies that continually expand and contract their workforce with the tide seemingly refuse to accept the most basic maxim: "Buy low, sell high." Many firms lay people off in cyclical downturns and then, when the entire industry is booming and staff is scarce, they engage in bidding contests to rehire the skills that they let walk out the door not long ago.

The Social Costs

Our *WorkUSA®* data shows that losing a job is a very big deal. Numerous other studies rank job loss up at the top with death and divorce as one of the most stressful events anyone can experience. Employees who experience a layoff may have to move to find employment, which can be distressing for the entire family. And continuing unemployment can cause financial, marital and other personal crises. Those effects, multiplied by thousands of layoffs in a small town, can impact family life, schools, and crime on an even larger scale.

The Hit to Employee Morale

One could argue that an organization is under no obligation to care about the psychological health of its ex-employees. Perhaps not. But it is in an organization's best self-interest to care about the message it sends to current employees. Watching the trauma experienced by those who were once coworkers contributes to plummeting employee morale, which often leads to lower productivity. Remaining employees are likely to feel stressed themselves, wondering who will be next, and probably resenting the fact that fewer workers are left doing more work. Topping it all off is less faith in management than ever. As the authors of *Competing for the Future* write, "Employees have a hard time squaring all the talk about the importance of human capital with seemingly indiscriminate cutting."[6]

The Loss of Employee Commitment

Managers often finds themselves in the unenviable position of notifying workers that they cannot expect security and then, in the next breath, requesting total commitment from them. Employees are then left wondering, "Why bother?"

The bottom line is that these are reciprocal relationships. The more commitment a company demonstrates to its workers, the more commitment employees are going to show the company.

How It Plays Out

How Successful Companies Treat Job Security

Treating Jobs as Careers

The best companies look at jobs as careers, and they train and promote from within. That is, obviously, inconsistent with a philosophy of casual downsizing.

According to *Fortune*'s "World's Most Admired Companies" research, the best firms invest more heavily not just in additional training, but also in leadership coaching, rotational assignments, and management accountability.[6]

- Intel spends 6 percent of its payroll on training and professional development.
- All entry-level employees at Procter & Gamble spend four days at "P&G College" with courses taught by senior managers.
- Managers at SmithKline are given a "2+2+2" orientation to career development, rotating through two businesses, two countries and two functions early in their careers.

In general, the study found that highly admired companies make it a point to compute their "investment per employee" and ensure that they are at the high end of the averages for their industry. They also turn much of their leadership's focus on career development. Executives in many of these companies are held personally accountable for successful development of top managers. These leaders are expected to take a primary role in transferring and expanding the organization's knowledge base, not only through formal instruction, but also through individual coaching and mentoring.

That sets the companies up to promote easily from within as openings occur, which is not only efficient, but contributes substantially to employee satisfaction.

Reciprocal Commitment

Implicit in the practices described above is a commitment to the employee. Some companies decide to make that arrangement more explicit. As Jeffrey Pfeffer detailed in *The Human Equation,* Berlin Packaging has developed a statement of mutual obligations between the company and its people.[7] Andrew Berlin, the president of this growing $120 million, privately owned company, was heading a change program to more closely align employees with the business. He came up with the following:

Mutual Obligations at Berlin Packaging

Berlin Owes the Employee	The Employee Owes Berlin
Rewards	Productivity
Chance to grow	Profitability
Job security	Loyalty
Collegiality	Teamwork
Leadership/coach	Work ethic
Training	Innovation

How to Avoid Layoffs

If successful firms approach each job hire as a career hire, and emphasize mutual commitment, what in fact do they do when circumstances (and shareholders) seem to cry out for a downsizing? There are, in fact, some viable alternatives that can be put into place.

1. **Spreading the pain.** Companies might consider opting for either proportionally reducing work hours or cutting wages for all employees. This sends a message that can unite a workforce: "We're all in this together. We're going through a tough time, as every business does, but if we all sacrifice now we'll make it together."

2. **Changing what people typically do.** If the company is thinking of cutting from one division and hiring in another, perhaps people could be retrained and shifted around. Work that is outsourced could be taken back in-house. Production or staff people could be put into sales to build demand. Or down time could be an opportunity for employees to concentrate on projects that were continually put on the back burner when the pace was faster.

3. **Altering hiring practices.** Obviously, putting a hold on hiring is a possibility. Thinking longer-term, some companies deliberately refuse to staff up when demand is at its highest, because it will inevitably lead to overemployment when things slow down.

Will these approaches always work? Certainly not. Are they worth investigating? For companies concerned about shareholder value, employee commitment, productivity, effective change management, and trust in senior management, the answer is yes.

Be Cautious About Developmental Training

"It is always with the best intentions that the worst work is done."
—Oscar Wilde

Throughout this book, we have emphasized that today's business climate demands a skilled, knowledgeable workforce. Common wisdom maintains that training is a critical component of that goal. It is—but there is a caveat: Training must be handled carefully if it is to boost shareholder value.

The right training, delivered at the right time, will not only make employees more productive, but will increase their commitment to the organization as well. That makes so much sense that U.S. corporations are spending unprecedented amounts—anywhere from $30 billion to $300 billion, depending on which study is cited—annually on internal training programs. The most common figure cited is about $60 billion.

Unfortunately, it is our belief that employers are getting a poor return on that investment—especially where developmental training (aimed at career advancement) is concerned. Why? Some of the training is simply of low quality. And in high-quality programs, many teach "interesting" skills and knowledge that employees will never apply on the job. And finally, some of the best training teaches employees how to walk right out the door by building skills for the next job—rather than the one they currently hold. If an organization providing top-notch developmental training does not have a higher-level position open for its newly skilled employee, the competition will.

Does that mean we discourage developmental training programs? Absolutely not. But in the face of the numbers that tell us training can actually be harmful to the bottom line, we have become healthy skeptics. All training is not equal. Companies must take a rigorous approach to the design of training programs in order to reap the benefits of increased productivity, employee commitment, and shareholder value.

What the Numbers Say

It's a Mixed Bag

It is no surprise to anyone in human resources that workers are very interested in developing their skills. A quick scan of our own research shows the following:

- A chance to use their skills on the job is one of the two biggest factors contributing to employee commitment. (*WorkUSA® 2000*)
- Top-performing employees cite the opportunity to develop skills as the third most important factor in attracting them to a new company. (*Strategic Rewards® 2001*)
- Top-performing professional/technical employees and top performers under 30 rate the opportunity to develop skills as the most important factor in attracting them to a new company. (*Strategic Rewards® 2001*)

Those statistics certainly seem to argue for instituting training programs to attract, motivate, and retain employees.

But our Human Capital Index is waving a cautionary flag. In our study, training is actually linked to lower shareholder value, with companies providing training being worth 5.6 percent less. Companies that maintained training programs even during less-than-favorable economic circumstances were worth 3.4 percent less. (See Figure 17-1.)

And although controversial, politically incorrect, and contrary to conventional human resources wisdom, we found a similar pattern of results both in 1999 and 2001.

We are not the only ones who were unable to detect a positive link between training and better financial performance. Lisa Lynch of the Fletcher School and Sandra Black of Harvard addressed the issue of training in their 1995 report "Beyond the Incidence of Training: Evidence from a National Employers Survey."[1] They did an exhaustive review of the research, looking for evidence of training effectiveness. They found nothing truly definitive. What they did find is that "the impact of employer-provided training differs according to the nature, timing, and location of the employer investments."

What is indisputable is that employer-provided training is on the rise. The American Society for Training and Development found that employer-provided training in the United States is rising in terms of both money spent and number of trainees. Leading firms (by ASTD's definition) currently spend 4.4 percent of payroll on training and over 85 percent of employees receive some type of training.[2]

Figure 17-1. *Links Between Training and Shareholder Value*

Practice	Impact on Market Value
Employees have access to training	-5.6%
Training programs are maintained even during less than favorable economic circumstances	-3.4%

Expected change associated with a significant (1SD) improvement in practice

Watson Wyatt's Human Capital Index®

Why It May Not Work

Employees or Competitors Capture Returns

We have now had two separate HCI surveys deliver the same clear results: Training decreases a company's market value. How can that possibly be true? Our hypothesis is twofold, and centers on the idea that employers are emphasizing training in skills for the next job, rather than teaching workers how to perform their current jobs more effectively. This developmental training is popular with employees, who are interested in becoming more marketable. But after the training, one of two things happens, neither of which will contribute positively to shareholder value:

1. *Employees, Rather than Companies, Capture the Returns from Developmental Training.* The employee demands a raise commensurate with the greater contribution she makes as a result of her new skills. The raise cancels out any increased productivity the company might otherwise have captured. Other Watson Wyatt research, "Training, Productivity and Shareholder Returns," says, "More training leads to higher productivity, but the employee reaps the benefits through higher pay and the firm is not creating any surplus value. A 10 percent increase in productivity leads to a 10 percent increase in pay. Training has no incremental benefit to the company."[3]

2. *Developmental Training without Proper Career Opportunity Increases Turnover.* The employee is eager to use the new skills after training, but the current job offers no opportunity to do so. She becomes frustrated as no new positions open up at the company. She sends out her newly impressive resume. A great new job materializes with the competition, which has just recouped the investment the first company made in training.

We think those are the critical factors behind the negative associations we are seeing between training and stock market performance.

However, there are other elements at work as well, as we will outline below.

Poaching, Particularly During Tough Times

Our numbers say that training during an economic downturn is particularly harmful to the financial picture. Some argue that a corporation should remain committed to training even during difficult financial periods, because that is when employees have more time. But our research shows they are incorrect. Successful companies cut discretionary costs when times are tough. Sticking with a training program when the competition has done away with theirs will usually mean newly educated workers get poached. That hurts the bottom line.

While forgoing training at times may be the smart individual business choice, it does present a public policy problem. If companies will not train, the result is an undertrained workforce. MIT economics professor Lester Thurow touched on this problem in his June 1999 *Atlantic* piece, "Building Wealth: The New Rules for Individuals, Companies and Nations." He noted that rather than training employees, it is advantageous for companies to hire people who already possess the necessary skills. (We obviously agree. See Chapter 2, "Hire People Who Will Hit the Ground Running.") Thurow goes on to bemoan the dynamic whereby companies who do train will be penalized through poaching. "When new knowledge makes old skills obsolete, firms want to employ workers who already have that knowledge. They don't want to pay for retraining…How does anyone rationally plan an educational investment? What skills will pay off? No one wants to waste investment funds on skills that will go unused… 'You train, I'll hire' is the American way."[4]

Poor Quality

Much of the time, the quality of the training is simply poor. Training programs are pulled together quickly, outside vendors are hired, workers are informed they must attend—all because everyone agrees that "training" is a good thing. And how many companies truly evaluate their programs afterward, going beyond the quick questionnaire at the door on the way out? It is difficult to track the impact training has on effectiveness, which is why most companies do not do it. The result? Training programs that remain poorly designed.

Not Targeted

Some training receives high ratings from participants, but what does that really mean? Typically, surveys ask participants if they found a session "interesting" or "enjoyable." The questionnaire might ask if the attendees "learned something." What these surveys typically do not ask is the one question our research suggests is important: Will this training help you to perform your current job?

If the trainee improves her current performance, the company will likely get a good return on its investment. The employee will become more productive and more committed to the company.

Environment Won't Support New Approach

Sometimes training fails because the environment doesn't allow trainees to put the principles to work. For example, training in innovating thinking does no good if the employees return to a work environment that discourages innovation.

How to Do It Right

Adopt a Rigorous Approach

Companies need to approach training the way they would approach any business initiative. They need to apply disciplined thinking. There must be a strategy for ROI. The organization must capitalize on the new skills.

Target Your Effort

Training is usually available for everyone, demonstrating the organization's interest in all employees' development. But training is never appropriate for everyone in the organization and can backfire when employees feel their time is being wasted. Instead, companies should take a very close look at employees' competencies and train specific individuals in specific job-related skills based on the organization's needs.

Do a Training Needs Analysis

Sometimes training doesn't work because managers are trying to train their way out of a deficiency that would best be solved through a new hire. A more thorough analysis of the company's needs will lead to better training decisions and more appropriate content. Companies should ask the following questions:

- What does the organization need to do to succeed in the future?
- What current organizational practices are perceived as "less than" compared to the competition?
- What is the gap? What competencies are needed for the future?
- How do we educate the employees on a just-in-time basis? If we are implementing a new performance measurement effort, do we educate on coaching that's six months away?
- How do we use training programs as a vehicle to begin knowledge transfer in the organization?

Employ the Right Method

Using ineffective methods is a major cause of disappointing returns on training investment dollars. All too often, organizations rely on lectures ("spray and pray"), inspirational speeches or videos, discussion groups, and simulation exercises. These methods may receive high marks from participants, but whether they change behavior on the job is debatable. Knowing something new doesn't necessarily give employees the ability to do something different. Old habits are hard to change.

A few ways an organization can improve the odds that workers will incorporate new skills into everyday job behavior include:

- Use training technologies that build how-to skills that are highly relevant and immediately applicable.
- Stay away from theoretical or inspirational training approaches where the "rubber meets the sky."
- Follow up on training sessions with on-the-job coaching and support from managers.
- Build training around organizational objectives and strategies.
- Use credible trainers; senior management involvement is critical.

Look at the System

Sometimes training fails to take hold even when careful consideration was given to who should be trained, how, and in what. The often-overlooked culprit is the organization's structure and its "way of doing work." Organizations must ensure that their culture and performance support their training efforts. Leading firms align their training with a number of innovative practices that include:

- High-performance work practices such as self-directed teams; easy access to business information and performance measurement programs aligned with the organization's strategy.
- Compensation practices rewarding the use of training, collaboration, and self-development.
- Mentoring or coaching programs, training information systems, and self-directed education.

Assess the Results

Most companies simply run their training programs over and over and over. They might ask if the sessions were "satisfactory," but tend to stop there. To build a training effort that helps their bottom line, companies need to measure efficacy. They need to ask participants if the programs helped them perform their jobs better, and how. They need to ask supervisors if the training helped achieve the unit's business goals.

If organizations adopt this kind of disciplined approach, then the resulting training will accomplish what everyone believes training should accomplish: Employees will be more productive, and, knowing that their company has invested in their growth and development, more committed as well.

PART

Open Up Communication between Management and Employees

CHAPTER

Make Communication Open and Candid

"All men by nature desire to know."
—Aristotle

"Don't use information to intimidate, control or manipulate people. Use it to teach people how to work together to achieve common goals and thereby gain control over their lives."
—Jack Stack, CEO of Springfield ReManufacturing Company (SRC)[1]

Any company still asking, "How much should we tell our employees, and when should we tell them?" is in trouble. Technology has rendered it pointless to attempt to withhold or manipulate information. Communication now takes place in real time. New content is being created at all levels, in very public forums. Companies that still approach employee communications with control rather than candor in mind will not only fail in their objective, but will keep the organization from achieving greater shareholder value.

New research shows that in today's environment, a policy of open, direct, and immediate communication increases:

- Trust in senior leadership
- Employee commitment
- Shareholder value

No company would willingly pass up those opportunities. Yet our studies show many organizations still have a ways to go in sharing important information in a timely, honest fashion, or at least they do in the eyes of their employees. Some organizations have more trouble than others letting go of the old style, where knowledge was power, and power was concentrated at the top.

But there's no ignoring the paradigm shift. The increasing pace of business and the rise of the knowledge economy have combined with new technology and a "net-centric" workforce to create an atmosphere where employees need, demand, and get immediate access to information. That does not mean the concept of a communications strategy is outdated. Quite the contrary. It simply means the question has changed. Companies now must ask: "How can we help employees understand and digest all of this information, so we can best harness their talents for our mutual success?"

What the Numbers Say

Candor Vital to Trust in Leadership and Employee Commitment

Our Human Capital Index shows that the more open companies are with their employees regarding business strategy and financial information and the more willing they are to listen to employees' ideas and suggestions, the more value they are able to create for shareholders. (See Figure 18-1.) Our data suggest that companies that practice a high degree of information sharing enjoy 1.8 percent higher shareholder value.

Open communication also plays a role in increasing employee commitment. As we discussed in Chapter 11, two of the seven largest drivers of employee commitment are related to a management style that emphasizes candid communication. (See Figure 18-2.)

What creates that trust? One of the top four drivers is "explaining reasons behind major decisions" according to our *WorkUSA® 2000* research. (See Figure 18.3.) Also factoring in are creating a culture that encourages employee involvement and management that actively gains support from employees for the business direction and acts on their suggestions. (For a full discussion on trust in senior leadership, see Chapter 14.) The key here is the presence of upward and downward communication. It's both ways now—all the time. It's about giving employees the straight story, letting them know how it affects them, and what they should do to contribute.

Not only do shareholder value, employee commitment, and trust in senior leadership decline when communications are less than open and candid, but change management is negatively

Figure 18-1. *Links Between Information Sharing and Value Creation*

Practice	Impact on Market Value
Company shares business plans and goals with employees	0.59%
Company shares financial information with employees	0.49%

Expected change associated with a significant (1SD) improvement in practice

Watson Wyatt's Human Capital Index®

Figure 18-2. *Key Drivers of Employee Commitment*

Factor	% Impact of Each Factor
Trust and confidence in senior leadership	14%
Honesty and integrity of company's business conduct	7%

WorkUSA® 2000

affected as well. Many of the top drivers of effective change management fall under the category of open communication. (See Figure 18-4.)

The research makes a solid case for adopting open and candid communications to maximize shareholder value—yet it also reveals

Figure 18-3. *Key Drivers of Trust in Senior Leadership*

Factor	% Impact of Each Factor
Motivating workforce to high performance	10%
Promoting the most qualified employees	10%
Gaining support for the business direction	10%
Explaining reasons behind major decisions	10%
Acting on employee suggestions	9%
Providing job security	9%
Encouraging employee involvement	8%
All other factors	34%

WorkUSA® 2000

Figure 18-4. *Drivers of Effective Change Management*

Factor	% Impact of Each Factor
Confidence in performance of senior management	12%
Employees support business direction	11%
Company provides good information about change	7%
Changes seen as necessary to compete effectively	5%

WorkUSA® 2000

that most companies have considerable room for improvement. Employees gave their employers less than impressive ratings in this area in our *WorkUSA® 2000* survey:

- Only 52 percent say information from management is credible
- Only 41 percent feel free to voice opinions
- Only 35 percent say trust between employees and management is good
- Only 37 percent see management decisions as good
- Only 32 percent see management decisions as timely
- Only 28 percent see management decisions as well-communicated
- Only 27 percent feel involved in management decisions

Why It Works

Informed Employees Are More Effective, More Engaged

In the beginning of this book, we argued that the increasing pace of business means the talent on the field has become the success differentiator—thus the importance of recruiting. But it makes no sense to hire the best people and then tie their hands by withholding information that could enhance their performance on the job. As Jeffrey Pfeffer says in *The Human Equation,* "Even motivated and trained people cannot contribute to enhancing organizational performance if they don't have information on important dimensions of [that] performance."[2] If employees are to respond quickly and act decisively, they need to have all relevant information as soon as possible.

Candid Communication Builds Trust

Many corporations still follow what seems to have been the old golden rule of employee communications, which is: Nothing Bad

Has Ever Happened. Whatever the topic, the spin is positive: The financial picture is rosy, the merger will be a win-win, and the new operations system will be up and running on Monday.

The upside to this approach is that management does not have to publicly address problems, since it claims there aren't any. The downside is that it creates new problems, which won't stay invisible for long. Employees are simply not fooled. And every new spin serves to distance employees from senior management, to chip away at trust and respect, and to make it clear to employees that they are in one group (not "in the know") and management is in another—regardless of any talk about being one big team.

In contrast, when complete, immediate information is offered, trust begins to build. Employees feel respected and entrusted with valuable information. And as they begin to understand all aspects of the situation, their respect for management's challenges increases.

They Will Find Out Anyway

There is one final reason to be open and candid: Technology has advanced to the point that there are no secrets anymore, at least not for long. By the time a carefully crafted message is delivered, the real story has been out for some time through the grapevine. The company looks foolish trying to twist the message—and that then becomes the story. Any efforts at damage control only make the situation worse, as the channels for information flow are buzzing with negative responses.

Today, anyone can set up a Web site on any topic, including disgruntled employees. In a very public forum, employees can gripe about anything from benefits to unethical business conduct. Anyone can air rumors about mergers, acquisitions, and finances. The only viable option for management is to be the first to release the truth, and do a lot of listening and responding.

How to Do It Right

From Control to Candor

To approach communications in a way that will maximize shareholder value, companies must believe three things:

1. Information is important to the bottom line.
2. Employees require information to be successful.
3. It is better to be timely, open, and honest than it is to control and overmanage information.

Senior management should no longer act as gatekeepers of information. They must instead be facilitators of information sharing. In spite of the evidence showing how important this transformation is, executives are reluctant to change their ways. Why? Jeffrey Pfeffer in *The Human Equation* notes: "If sharing information makes simple, common sense, you might wonder why sharing information about operations and financial performance is not more widespread. One reason is that information is power, and sharing information diffuses that power."[3] And yet the incentive for sharing is there, because those newly empowered employees can add tremendously to shareholder value.

In the journey from gatekeeper to facilitator, many structures and systems must be jettisoned. The channels created to review, edit, and approve a carefully crafted message now only serve to ensure the story is outdated by the time it hits its audience. Instead of spending time and resources wondering how employees will interpret various versions of the message, companies should shift their focus. They need to get all the information out fast, remain accessible, and send out additional information as required to make the message digestible. Then they need to concentrate on responding to follow-up questions and concerns.

For example:

- Companies used to simply announce a decision to move into a new segment of the market. Employees might have questioned the thought process at the water cooler, but that would have been the end of it. Not anymore. Now companies need to get employees on board. They need to communicate their rationale, outlining the business case and sharing the numbers they used to reach their conclusion. They need to explain why they rejected other options and why they chose this one. And they need to address concerns and objections. What's more, companies should rate this communication as a high priority, so that employees are not the last to know. In return for all this work, companies will earn the goodwill of employees.

■ Companies typically spend even less time worrying about how to inform employees about more mundane matters—such as a system conversion. The "Nothing Bad Ever Happened" approach would insist that a perfect new system will be up and running Monday morning. When the inevitable delays and problems surfaced, company management would take the hit. Employees would grumble about the company not knowing what it's doing, and complain that the leadership is unaware, uninvolved, and unconcerned about the employees' frustrations. The right approach would be to acknowledge that working through the kinks will be a challenge at first, but that the company will keep at it until it's working right. Furthermore, management will keep employees in the loop throughout the process.

■ We are seeing a return to more intimate modes of communication. The chat with the CEO (via video conference or the intranet) is on the upswing. Many companies are instituting "town hall meetings"—sometimes with real-time global participation. There is a growing emphasis on "management by walking around." And many companies have created hot lines where employees can get information about the most urgent issues.

It seems simple: Be honest; offer complete information; be realistic; ask for support. But doing it well requires a strategy—not a strategy to craft a message, but a strategy to get the right information accurately and quickly to the right audience.

How It Plays Out

Open Communications Approach Includes Web-Based Forum and In-House TV Network

Company:	*Motorola*
Revenues:	*$3 billion+*
Number of Employees:	*10,000*
Industry:	*Broadband Products*
Location of Headquarters:	*Horsham, PA*

Motorola has an open and candid communications philosophy. Its primary purpose is to acknowledge the value of the company's employees and the contribution they make to the company's success. Motorola's merger with General Instruments added another goal to the communication program: to unify the two cultures while maintaining a high quality of operations.

Forthright Answers Make Web Forum Credible

One part of the communications effort, initiated in 1998 by Motorola's Broadband Communications Sector (BCS), has been particularly well received by employees: a Web-based discussion forum conducted in real time on the company's intranet. Employees all over the world participate. Those who want to pose questions to management are encouraged to do so—anonymously, if they choose. Appropriate company officials are alerted when questions pertaining to their areas of responsibility are posted. Turnaround time has varied, with most questions being answered in a day or two.

Discussions on the Forum have ranged from major issues to topics that are merely interesting; from the cost of benefits to issues related to IT and facilities; and from general market conditions to the company's product offerings. Few topics (less than 1 percent) are deemed off limits or inappropriate. Questions related to specific personnel and proprietary information fall into this category. Replies from any of the 30 or so managers or functional heads of business units carry the implied force of policy; the corporate vice president of HR for BCS is directly responsible for supporting that intent.

The Forum has proved to be an invaluable, cohesive influence, keeping Motorola's global workforce apprised of key employee issues. Management's commitment to providing forthright answers to all but the most sensitive questions has made it a credible communication tool. Employees consider the Forum a positive and effective method for communicating with management and colleagues and for enabling them to provide input on the company's policies and practices.

TV Network, Newsletters, Intranet Work Together

The Forum is one of several successful communication programs the company supports. Others include biweekly and monthly newsletters that inform employees of events within the corporation and around the world; global emails; an intranet; and all-employee meetings conducted offsite in special venues.

Financial information is shared throughout the company in a quarterly letter from the BCS president. Since the company's incentive programs are tied to its financial performance, this communication is critical and eagerly received.

Available technology has played a major role in Motorola's employee communication strategy over the years, and especially since the merger. The company recently redesigned its intranet to be more responsive to employees' needs and easier to maintain. An in-house TV network conveys news, stock market information, and company announcements 24 hours a day. Monitors are installed in cafeterias, kitchens, and lobbies throughout its facilities.

The company periodically surveys its employees on issues ranging from their understanding of the company's vision to the effectiveness of senior management. Other surveys may ask employees about HR services or their supervisors, or gauge perceptions on how seriously the company regards its customers. The results are compiled and considered when planning new programs and are also shared with the workforce, a practice that has added to the reliability of the outcomes and increased participation over time.

Motorola Sought to Reduce Turnover

A strong desire for improved, real-time discussion of issues with employees prompted the company to rethink its internal communication processes in 1999. It focused on programs that would facilitate wider employee participation in dialogues with management and create clearer links between individual performance and the company's mission and ultimately help reduce employee turnover and recruitment costs.

Having employees participate in candid dialogues with management was a challenge at first. Guaranteed anonymity was crucial to surfacing deeply held concerns and questions, after which they could be dealt with constructively. It took three to four months before employees became comfortable with the new programs and accepted the process.

Soon, management and employees were discussing specific employee benefits and HR policies such as Motorola's smoking rules and targeted Web site blocking. Lively debates arose around the company's dress code and whether to install Microsoft 2000. Before the new communication initiatives, such concerns would have stayed hidden and likely harmed morale. They are now discussed openly and rationally, dealt with, and laid to rest.

Implementing the New Initiatives

The director of communications, employee communications manager, director of HR, and HR generalists shared responsibility for implementing the communications initiatives. The programs were pilot tested at the sector headquarters in Pennsylvania, then rolled out to Motorola's San Diego office, and from there, to the rest of the country. Although employees in the company's international offices, such as those in Taiwan and Mexico, enjoy communication vehicles similar to those of their U.S. colleagues, cultural considerations necessitate some variations.

All communication programs are reviewed annually. The communications department, HR and the sector president, who are also responsible for planning improvements and modifications, evaluate their effectiveness by inviting employees to provide input through surveys, e-mail, and postings to the Forum.

Positive Impact Beginning to Show

The Forum provides the primary mechanism for monitoring the effectiveness of Motorola's employee communication practices. The nature and content of employee postings, coming as they do from throughout the company in real time, provide valuable clues about workplace concerns and serve as early warning signals about issues that require attention from management. For issues requiring immediate responses, a pop-up window with specific questions can be activated on the Forum Web page.

Periodic employee surveys supplement the information gathered via the Forum.

In their second year, Motorola's communication initiatives enjoyed greater participation and acceptance from both employees and management. As their credibility has increased, so has their usefulness as feedback mechanisms for employee concerns. Their effect on morale and employee retention rates are correspondingly positive.

Communication activity in the Forum has never been more enthusiastic. By providing better access to the company's performance data and management's assessment of it, the Forum and other communication vehicles have helped employees gain a clearer understanding of the company's goals and objectives and how they can affect its bottom line.

CHAPTER

Enable Employees to Share Knowledge by Capitalizing on Technology

In this era of the knowledge worker, nothing differentiates a company more clearly than the amount and the rate at which its employees share their expertise. A company boasting a global workforce filled with top-notch talent has a competitive advantage. But if that company is not using cutting-edge communications technology to capture the knowledge held by that impressive employee base, it is failing to leverage its greatest investment.

Capitalizing on current technology enables employees to get answers, information, decisions, research, and opinions from each other at a speed that allows first-rate performance and customer service. Every effort by the organization reflects the experience and knowledge of a larger number of employees. Faster, higher-quality performance is the result.

But providing the tools that allow for the transfer of information is only the first step. Technology alone cannot create a true culture of exchange. Second, and arguably more difficult, senior management must establish an environment where sharing knowledge is recognized—and rewarded—as vitally important to the company's bottom line.

What the Numbers Say

Access to Technology Helps Bottom Line

Our Human Capital Index research shows that companies whose employees have easy access to technologies for communicating—such as e-mail and a user-friendly intranet —are worth an impressive 4.2 percent more in the market. (See Figure 19-1.)

Our research confirms what everyone in the workplace already knows: The Internet is now the preeminent method of communication. According to Watson Wyatt's 2000 survey, "The Net Effect," Web technology has become the predominant method for delivering HR-related services—including communication—to employees, outpacing interactive voice response and call center systems.[1] (See Figure 19-2.)

When it comes to giving employees access to documents, Web technology is used most often. (See Figure 19-3.) But far beyond access to documents and programs, Web technology provides—and is the number-one source for—the knowledge-sharing platform that companies need to support the collaboration

Figure 19-1. *Links Between Technology Access for Communication and Value Creation*

Practice	Impact on Market Value
Employees have easy access to technologies for communicating	4.2%

Expected change associated with a significant (1SD) improvement in practice

Watson Wyatt's Human Capital Index®

Figure 19-2. *Prevalence of Various Technologies*

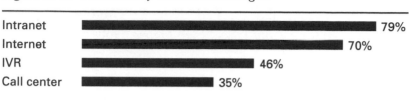

Intranet	79%
Internet	70%
IVR	46%
Call center	35%

The Net Effect: eHR™ and the Internet, 2000 Survey Report

Figure 19-3. *Functions Performed Using Various Technologies (When Technology Is in Use)*

	Access to documents	Access to personal data	HR transactions	Knowledge share
Intranet	77%	30%	42%	75%
Internet	53%	29%	33%	62%
IVR	19%	52%	77%	16%
Call Center	42%	71%	71%	33%

The Net Effect: eHR™ and the Internet, 2000 Survey Report

Figure 19-4. *Preferred Vehicle for Service Delivery*

	Intranet/ Internet	IVR	Call Center	Outsourcing
Corporate communications	■			
Benefits information	■			
Job postings	■			
Recruiting and staffing	■			
Retirement planning	■			
Benefits enrollment		■		
Performance appraisal	■			
Personal data changes	■			
Total compensation statements				■
New hire orientation	■			

The Net Effect: eHR™ and the Internet, 2000 Survey Report

and communication demands of today's workforce. In all likelihood, the Internet would be the most popular option for providing access to personal data and making HR transactions, but its use is limited because some employees do not have a computer.[2]

Again, when it comes to the preferred method of communicating, the Internet takes the lead, when we asked which vehicle was preferred for various tasks.[3] (See Figure 19-4.)

Why It Works

Technology Lets Employees Work More Powerfully, Efficiently for the Company

Recent technological advances have revolutionized the way the business world communicates. Companies that capitalize on that new technology are creating higher shareholder value. How? By enabling their employees to work much more quickly and powerfully, thereby advancing the organization's agenda.

Connecting People

Ten years ago e-mail was rare, but now it's hard to imagine a company trying to conduct business without it. It has become the primary mode of communication for most organizations. E-mail has been a significant factor behind the increasing pace of business—no more time spent finding letterhead, printing, putting a document in an envelope or fax machine, and waiting for delivery or receipt. Not only are decisions made faster, they often reflect more viewpoints, as it is easier to include more stakeholders and hold discussions via e-mail.

Along with mobile phones, pagers, personal digital assistants (PDAs), and ever-shrinking laptops, e-mail has enabled employees to be in conversation with the office anytime, from anywhere—which means companies that make use of these vehicles have access to an exponentially increased talent pool. This technology has made flexible work arrangements work, by enabling flexible workers to be just as productive and in-touch as those at the office during regular hours.

Then there are the technologies that gained popularity first with teenagers but, in the hands of enterprising employees, can become important business tools. For example, instant messaging is actually adding a new layer of communication to the corporate world. If five people are on a conference call, two of them can be simultaneously having a sidebar conversation via instant messaging on their computer screens, comparing notes and collaborating as they go. The same process can take place in a physical meeting, as two PDA owners can "beam" messages to each other.

Access to Information

In addition to allowing instantaneous connections between employees, technology has enabled employees to easily access information. When intranets first came on the scene, they were typically repositories for documents (for example, a policy manual). It was a convenient way for companies to send one message to a massive audience. But as Web browsers have improved, companies have been able to communicate with employees in a more targeted, personal way. People can search for exactly the information they need, tailored to their particular situations. The most recent phase of technological development has taken browsers into the transactional phase, where employees can interact online. For example, now employees can not only access information regarding their savings account balance, but also enroll in different programs and transfer funds from one account to another.

The implication? The shift from one-message-fits-all to personalized information increases productivity by saving time; it also moves a company toward a less hierarchical corporate culture by making employees more self-reliant and knowledgeable.

Sharing Knowledge

Perhaps the most far-reaching of the technological advances is in the area of knowledge management. Today's systems can, in a sense, give an employee immediate access to another employee's mind and experience. Companies can create databases of documents, research, presentations, and background information, as well as databases with information on skills and relationships with clients and vendors. That means:

- A Kansas City employee trying to pitch a client in a certain industry can now tap into the company's intranet and find a presentation created a month previously by a colleague in Tokyo. It has updated industry stats and growth projections and has identified industry-specific threats and opportunities.
- A team's technical expert is having emergency surgery, and a client needs an answer, fast. The team searches the database and a source in Chicago has used this system for the same kind of work, and can walk the team through the process.
- An opportunity exists to work with a Russian group on aerospace technology. But negotiations are getting bogged down with language issues. The database immediately reveals several employees (out of the company's 10,000) who are fluent in Russian and previously worked in the aerospace industry.

Companies have long promoted their "globalness," listing their areas of expertise and various locations in their marketing materials. With the new knowledge management systems, it takes on new, real meaning.

The Challenges Ahead

Lack of Participation, Information Overload

There are two main dangers that can keep a company's investment in communications technology from paying off. Historically, more than 75 percent of technology initiatives fail. The reason most often cited? Failure to address the organizational and people issues. For technology to live up to its potential, people have to be able to use it, and they have to have an incentive to use it.

Information Overload

The very success of e-mail could prove to be its undoing. In some firms, a typical employee receives hundreds of e-mails in a day, an overload that could obviously interfere with productivity. How do employees sift through all those messages, identifying those that require immediate attention? As e-mail has become more widely used, it is rapidly losing in effectiveness. In Watson Wyatt's 1999 Communications Study, 90 percent of participants rated e-mail as the most frequently used medium—but only 55 percent rated it as the most effective.[4]

This overload phenomenon does not pertain only to e-mail. Everyone who is online has access to an overwhelming array of information. Employees are overburdened with sources and may be spending too much time navigating their way through them, possibly even becoming less, rather than more, productive.

As we look at mounting frustration in the face of information and communication overload, a troubling question emerges: Have we already squeezed most of the productivity gain out of this technology? The corporate world has already capitalized on the technology to a great extent. There is a clear sense that things are beginning to fall through the cracks as a result of information overload.

The answers will come from two sources. First, there is a new role for communications experts. Rather than spending time crafting messages, these professionals will need to help bridge the gap between information and understanding, providing access rather than overload. They will need to make information more user friendly and relevant. They will have to shift their focus from giving more employees access to making access more effective.

At the same time, companies need to hire people who are simply better at prioritizing in the midst of the onslaught of messages. The skills of navigating effectively through information sources will no doubt become a key competency in the near future.

Only As Good As Participation Level

Knowledge management technology could essentially turn a corporation into one enormous storehouse of information featuring immediate yet varying degrees of access for all employees. But the rooms of that storehouse will be vacant if employees see no reason to share their information.

In some organizations, employees may be reluctant to participate because they simply lack the time. How can they devote the time needed to upload their presentations with a tough deadline staring them in the face? In other organizations, the disincentive is even stronger: Sharing their expertise makes them feel less valuable. Perhaps they have worked hard to develop their skills and a certain depth of experience and enjoy the associated financial rewards and enhanced status. Giving all colleagues (who can be viewed as competitors for those financial and psychic rewards) easy access to their expertise may feel like giving away the store.

The solution, for both problems, is the creative, public use of incentives. Employees need to receive visible rewards for sharing their knowledge. For example, performance appraisals might focus on how much knowledge a worker adds to the firm, with content contributed to the corporate database serving as a measurement. Many different rewards can be geared around knowledge sharing—spot bonuses for employees who work on the database at a certain random time or contribute a certain amount of meaningful content, for example. Incentives will get the ball rolling, and once a pattern of sharing is in place, the philosophy of contributing to the company's "library" will become more automatic. Employees will find satisfaction in seeing their work widely applied, finding that rather than diminishing status, sharing knowledge enhances it in a gratifying and visible manner.

How It Plays Out

High-Tech Company Builds Culture of Exchange Using Technology

Company:	*Network Appliance*
Revenues:	*$1 billion*
Number of Employees:	*1500*
Industry:	*High Technology*
Corporate Headquarters:	*Sunnyvale, California*

Network Appliance, Inc., is a leading provider of network-attached data access and content management solutions. A veteran in network file serving and caching, the company has been providing data access solutions since 1992, and is a member of both the S&P 500 and NASDAQ 100 index. Many major corporations and ISPs deploy NetApp solutions. NetApp Internet caching solutions (NetCache™ appliances) and file servers (filers) deliver fast, simple, reliable and cost-effective access to network-stored data and enable simultaneous shared file services for UNIX®, Windows NT® and the World Wide Web.

Network Appliance is expanding its global and domestic operations rapidly and relies on its internal communications efforts to keep employees aligned with corporate goals. The programs have the following key objectives:

- Educate employees about corporate values.
- Encourage employees to participate in building a dynamic company.
- Build cohesion in a corporate environment that is continually changing.

Network Appliance values direct and open communication and strives to keep the communications "Fast, Simple, and Reliable." A key component of its effort is the broad use of technology.

Employee Access to Technologies

As a technology industry leader, Network Appliance understands the importance of using technology to make employee communications easier and more effective. The following programs briefly highlight some of the tools used at this time.

- Webcast Employee Meetings—Network Appliance has begun using its own streaming media technology to Web-cast real-time employee meetings, called All Hands Meetings. The All Hands Meetings are broadcast to several domestic and European locations quarterly, with accommodations for employees who dial in from remote locations. The meetings are scheduled at times that allow most employees around the world to participate.

The CEO values these meetings as opportunities to directly interact with all employees and uses the forum to deliver corporate objectives and financial reports, as well as to recognize individual employee contributions.

- WAFL Talk Radio—The sales and marketing function produces informational CDs called WAFL Talk Radio, which gets its name from the acronym for a patented technology (Write Anywhere File-System Layout). The CDs are distributed to sales and marketing employees for educational purposes, using them to review specific business information that will help them do their jobs, with the option of listening to them in their spare time, such as driving to their next sales call.
- E-mail and Intranet—Like most companies, Network Appliance relies on e-mail and intranet postings for a major portion of employee communications.
- The Hitchhiker's Guide to Network Appliance Engineering—This online new-employee orientation tool is accessible to all employees. It includes critical information necessary to pass the technical certification as well

as more whimsical commentary on how to obtain supplies and get one's bearings in the company. It is also a prime example of how employees use the Internet for training and are called upon to keep the document updated. (There are online instructions as well as contact information in how to help with the effort.)

■ Pagers—Employees working in the field or often away from their desks receive pagers, ensuring that they can be reached at all times

Opportunities for Employee Input

The company values employee input and strives to create an environment with an open exchange of ideas.

■ All Hands Meeting Q&A—During question-and-answer sessions at the end of the quarterly employee meetings, employees can ask executives questions on any topic. This is a priority for Network Appliance, keeping the executive staff accessible and creating further opportunities for fast, simple, reliable communication. Employees appreciate having executives deliver immediate answers to their questions in front of a large audience.

■ Cross-functional teams—The company encourages collaboration by assigning cross-functional teams to complete a given task. Participation is based on the value that an individual adds, rather than on rank or title. Less experienced analysts often work side-by-side with senior directors to complete tasks, reinforcing the company's commitment to open communication.

■ T.O.A.S.T.—Senior management is serious about introducing new employees to the corporate culture at Network Appliance. Training On All Special Things (TOAST) is the monthly new-hire orientation training session for all employees, which is conducted within the first four to eight weeks of hire. Members of the executive staff

participate in the TOAST program by providing an
overview of business objectives, company history, and culture. After the presentation, executives have lunch with
the group and are available to address employee questions
in a question-and-answer session.

- Engineering Tech Talks Weekly—Engineering tech talks
  by either internal or external speakers help build knowledge and cross-functional understanding within the engineering community at NetApp. The educational portion
  of the meeting is often followed by a social event on Friday afternoons. This supports collaboration, group problem-solving, and social interaction for engineers. From
  time to time, engineering invites other departments to
  join them to build stronger relationships across the
  entire company.

- Clothing—Employees joke, "It's not just a job; it's a
  wardrobe." All employees are given shirts upon completion of TOAST; sales staff are given shirts at the end of
  sales training and annual sales kick-off meetings; and
  engineers are given shirts after they finish studying the
  Hitchhiker's Guide to Network Appliance and pass their
  certification exams. There is quiet pride in wearing logo-
  imprinted clothing that acknowledges a team's contributions to the success of the company.

Sharing Corporate Information

Network Appliance uses a variety of open communication methods to share important company information with employees.
Corporate objectives are linked to the front page of the intranet
and posted on bulletin boards as a way of making sure that individual and corporate objectives are on the same page.

The company also openly shares financial information with
employees. Since all employees are issued stock options when
they start work, they have a personal interest in the company's
financial performance and growth. Employees receive corporate

financial information at the quarterly All Hands Meetings, and also receive e-mail alerts immediately following press releases of earnings reports. Given the culture of mutual respect, other confidential information is also discretely shared with employees with the reminder they are to keep highly confidential information to themselves.

Cohesiveness Amid Change

Since the company has doubled its size for the past two years, there is a constant stream of new employees from a variety of different backgrounds, creating a culture that is constantly evolving. To remain cohesive and successful, Network Appliance has developed an effective communication programs that reinforces its corporate values and keeps employees targeted to corporate objectives while working in an environment characterized by explosive growth and acquisitions. For example, internal Web sites were developed as part of the news announcements of two recent acquisitions—complete with FAQ's and information explaining the strategic importance of the moves.

Metrics Show Success

Network Appliance is still in the process of creating and implementing metrics for gauging its communication program. Currently, the success of the Network Appliance communication programs is based on feedback gathered from employees through Web-based surveys, the polling of employees, and focus groups.

Employees often e-mail ideas and suggestions to management. The open communication style at Network Appliance encourages this type of unsolicited feedback, since employees know that their input is taken seriously.

The company is currently in the process of enhancing employee feedback mechanisms and will soon add an intranet template allowing employees to formally submit feedback to the Web page owner. Network Appliance is also conducting focus groups to discuss employee needs with regard to the Intranet. Additionally, the company plans to solicit employee feedback using a Web-based survey.

The rapid growth at Network Appliance has created challenges for the organization, but the high-tech communications efforts are proving up to the task.

CHAPTER

Be Careful in Implementing 360-Degree Feedback

"If a single e-mail can send the pulse racing, it's the one from human resources announcing that it's time for another round of 360-degree feedback."
—Maury A. Peirperl in the *Harvard Business Review*[1]

A hot trend in human capital management is asking people to give performance feedback on their peers and their managers. The premise is quite logical—the people who work most closely with an employee are far better judges of his performance than the manager, alone, since they see the employee's actual behavior from a variety of angles. And, as the theory goes, the broader and deeper a worker's understanding of his performance, the more likely he is to successfully achieve the desired performance profile.

The theory is very promising. The reality, on the other hand, can be problematic. When not handled well, 360-degree review can actually decrease shareholder value. It can interfere substantially with teamwork, and it can take up so much time that it negatively affects productivity. Companies interested in the enhanced performance that 360-degree review could provide must approach this practice with care.

What the Numbers Say

Majority of Companies Use It, but It's Harmful to Bottom Line

Feedback from multiple sources is a performance appraisal approach that relies on the input of a manager's supervisor, colleagues, subordinates, and sometimes the company's suppliers and customers about their perceptions of the manager's work. The majority of 360-degree feedback programs are focused on the manager level and above, especially for development of leadership skills.

This practice has become dramatically more popular in recent years. In fact, the majority of companies now use some kind of multisource feedback program, according to a study by William H. Mercer.[2] (See Figure 20-1.)

What is fueling the shift? Our theory, based on the available research and many client interviews, is that the primary driver is the move toward less hierarchical structures. Multisource review is more in keeping with a team-based philosophy. It is difficult to

Figure 20-1. *Number of Companies Using Multisource Feedback*

| 1995 | 40% |
| 2000 | 65% |

Source: William H. Mercer

make the argument that "we are all one big team" and then leave the most important personnel decisions up to one supervisor. In addition, breaking down the hierarchy has sometimes moved supervisors away from the managers they would normally review. As Maury Peirperl writes in the *Harvard Business Review,* "In flatter organizations with looser hierarchies, bosses may no longer have all the information they need to appraise subordinates."[3]

Multisource review is popular, but it may not be effective. In fact, the Human Capital Index research showed that companies using multisource feedback have lower market value. (See Figure 20-2.) Peer review is associated with a decrease in a company's value by 4.9 percent, and allowing employees to evaluate their managers is linked to an even more detrimental effect, lowering market value by 5.7 percent. Taken together, these practices are linked to a very serious 10.6 percent decrease.

To be fair, managers and employees rate most performance appraisal systems poorly in terms of their value and effect on the organization. Research shows that most systems do not encourage the necessary frankness, and that most people do not put in the time it would take to make the exercise worthwhile. (Lyle Spencer, a recognized expert in performance management and author of *Competence at Work: Models for Superior Performance,* has reviewed the literature and found that 50 to 75 percent of firms express some dissatisfaction with their systems.)[4] But while other systems tend to be largely viewed as ineffective, our numbers show that 360-degree review might actually be damaging.

Figure 20-1. *Links Between 360° Feedback and Value Creation*

Practice	Impact on Market Value
Employees have opportunity to evaluate managers	-5.7%
Employees have opportunity to evaluate peers	-4.9%

Expected change associated with a significant (1SD) improvement in practice

Watson Wyatt's Human Capital Index®

Why It Happens

Teamwork Interference, Time Wasting

The main risk in implementing 360-degree feedback is interfering with teamwork. The process of judging might encourage employees to view their peers more critically and offers an opportunity to act on any of the hostilities that typically arise on the job. The risk of hurting teamwork is even higher when companies ask employees to evaluate their managers. As Carol Hymowitz wrote in the *Wall Street Journal,* "Since most 360-degree reviews are done anonymously, staff members with an axe to grind can use the system to even scores."[5] The result? An increase in tensions among the very group that should be working together most harmoniously. While we suspect that is the most significant factor in the failure of 360-degree reviews to live up to their promise, there are many other potential trouble spots.

Takes Too Much Time

In attempting to capture every nuance of the worker's performance, many multisource feedback programs have become so complex that they require much more in time than they deliver in value. Many efforts require input from 8 to 12 people, each of whom must complete a form that may be pages and pages long for many different coworkers. Supervisors, then, must review volumes of paper.

High Stress and Questionable Results

Most people are "hard-wired" and socialized to avoid conflict. As a result, giving honest performance feedback—particularly of the critical variety—is something that many people avoid at all costs. While 360-feedback programs are typically supposed to be anonymous, many employees do not believe their responses will stay confidential for long. So, the more employees are pushed to be confrontational, the greater the anxiety levels surrounding the process. This makes the task of multisource feedback even more arduous and painstaking. People then avoid it and anguish over their responses, which makes the process take even longer.

Conflict aversion can also skew the results. Many people will opt for submitting a false evaluation rather than risk offending peers or managers. And in some cases an unwritten deal is made, with everyone being purposely gentle with each other, knowing the favor will be returned.

Lack of Role Models

People often become managers as a result of their technical skills, not their people management skills. A consequence is that most managers do not understand how to hold an effective performance conversation with their direct reports. When managers do not set an example, no one else learns how to hold effective performance conversations either, and a vicious cycle ensues. The more time spent in ineffective performance reviews, the less time is left over to create value. Multisource review will not cure systematic management problems.

No Consequences

Some data show that performance improves after multisource feedback[6] (Smither et al, 1995). But what we hear most often is that there is no follow-up after feedback, resulting in a lack of clarity among both reviewers and those reviewed about the results. When there are no consequences for poor performance, which is often the case, people do not take the feedback seriously; performance does not change, and the program has wasted valuable energy.

Lack of Commitment

Another problem that brings down many multisource feedback programs is lack of commitment. When management is not fully behind the program, participation varies by business unit and degree, with some parts of the company not participating at all. For 360-degree feedback to work, every business unit and level of the company should go through the same process.

HR-Driven, Not Line-Driven

Unless line management takes ownership for multisource feedback as a useful means of aligning employees with business strategy, the programs are not taken seriously by anyone else, either. Unfortunately, many multisource systems are HR-driven. Forcing people to engage in activities they believe are irrelevant does not lead to value creation. To achieve program goals, the supervisor must take all feedback seriously and hold the manager accountable for change.

Specificity of Behavior Change

Often, 360-degree feedback programs rely on abstract ratings of competencies—things like communication effectiveness or change facilitation—rather than outlining specific behavior change objectives. In order to fully realize the potential benefits of this type of feedback, the competencies need to be clearly identified to everyone involved and tracked or measured over time. Branching 360-degree feedback programs can help identify specific objectives (see Chapter 11), as can the use of intranets to capture specific comments.

How to Do It Right

Establish an Open Culture; Keep Process Simple; Train

Despite these drawbacks, there is a good reason that most companies use multisource feedback today. When handled correctly, it stands to dramatically deepen each employee's understanding of her own performance. It can help companies create value by better aligning job performance with business strategy. But the company has to be ready, and the program has to be implemented strategically.

Is the Company Ready?

Before implementing a 360-degree review process, there are several questions companies must ask themselves:

- **What is the trust level in the organization, work unit, or team?** If there is already a high degree of trust and communication, multisource feedback will be accepted naturally. If not, trying to impose a 360-degree program without making other adjustments first will be counterproductive. Asking managers to step back, forget the rigid hierarchy that governs all of their normal behavior at work, and speak freely about peers and supervisors is destined to fail. Even if managers speak freely, the culture will not support changes that come through this kind of out-of-sync channel.

- **Will the feedback process support ongoing business initiatives?** If the feedback the employees receive does not relate to current company goals, it will either be a distraction or will be ignored. Either way, the process will hurt company value. Instead, the feedback should help employees to prioritize, in an every-changing business environment, the skills they should work on first.

- **Do managers have the necessary feedback skills?** As noted above, it is somewhat unnatural and very difficult to offer or receive critical feedback. To do it well, and constructively, takes instruction, training, and practice. Companies that implement multisource feedback without first checking/developing managers' feedback skills risk serious damage to teamwork and morale. An emphasis should be placed on learning to give and receive very specific feedback in a nonthreatening manner. Again, branching technology (see Chapter 11) can be used very effectively here. For example, if the reviewers note that the "supervisor doesn't communicate well," branching technology can prompt them to explain whether that comment is related to stating goals or discussing performance.

Strategic Implementation

Multisource feedback programs look very different at different companies. Individual organizations must rely on their own culture to guide them in determining which and how many workers should participate, when the process should take place, and other factors. But some rules for success are common across all kinds of organizations. Here are the best practices to keep in mind when implementing 360-degree review:

1. Focus the performance feedback on business goals and strategy.
2. Make multisource feedback a regular developmental process, not an event for distributing pay.
3. Keep it short, simple, and to the point.
4. Give line employees a voice in designing and implementing the program to ensure relevance and ownership.
5. Make sure executives play a key, visible role—modeling the way from the very top of the company.
6. Develop people in the art of giving and receiving feedback.
7. Enforce consequences for continued nonperformance.
8. Make multisource feedback an opportunity to celebrate good performance.
9. Program must include the creation of an "action plan" for each employee based on the feedback.
10. Make coaching a clear expectation and responsibility of team leaders.
11. Make follow-up a part of the process.
12. Monitor implementation, ask for ideas for improvement, and make adjustments.

These practices will ensure that 360-degree feedback helps to focus and reinforce work behavior that is aligned with achieving desired business results.

Implementing a successful 360-degree feedback program is akin to managing your own investment portfolio—it's hard—but not impossible to make a profit. Given the fact that most firms fail, organizations undertaking this effort should simply proceed cautiously.

Physician, Heal Thyself: The Role of HR

"HR finds itself facing a crisis of confidence and credibility with line managers and business people as firms address the challenges of competition with dramatic changes to their strategies, structures and processes."
—from "Rethinking Human Resources," a report by The Conference Board

Most executives would insist passionately that the management of human capital is a chief priority for their organization. But many of the same executives maintain a narrow view of the human resources function and HR professionals themselves—regarding their own company's HR group as facilitators of administrative needs rather than as strategic partners in accomplishing the company's overall business goals.

These customers are interested in having HR fulfill the basics (i.e., getting the HRIS data accurate) before seeing them venture into the strategic realm. And there is good reason for this—many of HR's functions and its spending is inherently out of touch with line priorities.

But HR executives argue that this thinking is outdated—that the time has come for HR to claim its rightful seat at the head table. The landscape has changed, they say, and the critical role of people management in business success suggests that HR should play on the key decision-making team.

They have a point. On the other hand, an altered landscape alone does not mean HR is entitled to a role at the forefront of an organization. HR needs to earn that spot on its own merits. The HR group at every corporation has to battle against the perception—fair or not—that it is the land of administrative implementers. It has to raise its own profile and prove that it can add value.

That means moving beyond day-to-day operations. It means defining the organization's strategies and building programs to attract, retain, and support the right workforce. It means creating the processes and environments that enable workers to perform most productively. And it means linking the human capital strategies to the right technology solutions.

This is a critical juncture in the evolution of HR, where changes in the business climate have combined with demographics to offer HR a lead role. Only when it gets its own house in order will HR be able to claim that role.

The Negative Perception

There is no denying that a stereotype exists. Every HR professional has come across the perception that HR departments are bloated, staffed by legions of rule-followers insisting on handling things by the book. They have not kept pace with changes and do not rise to meet new challenges. They rarely provide solutions, and when they do, the solutions cost too much. In short, they satisfy no one. Thomas A. Stewart spoke for all those with this point of view in *Fortune*'s January 15th, 1996 issue:

> "Nestling warm and sleepy in your company, like the asp in Cleopatra's bosom, is a department whose

employees spend 80% of their time on routine administrative tasks. Nearly every function of this department can be performed more expertly for less by
others. Chances are its leaders are unable to describe
their contribution to value added except in trendy,
unquantifiable and wannabe terms…I am describing
your human resource department and have a modest
proposal: Why not blow it up?"[1]

It is a provocative passage. It makes many in HR angry. But here it
serves an important purpose. This book demonstrates how human
capital management can play a crucial and immense role in determining a company's financial success. However, before closing, we
feel compelled to note that an HR department that even hints of
the weaknesses outlined above will not be able to lead the charge.

Even an HR group that keeps up with changing times can
suffer from the impression that it is not providing as much value
as it thinks. Researchers at Cornell compared the perceptions of
line executives and HR executives regarding HR effectiveness. In
every category across the board, line executives rated HR effectiveness less highly than HR executives themselves did.

The study also examined how HR's effectiveness in different
roles was perceived. Again, the line executives rated HR less
highly in every category. (See Figure A-1.) Both groups agreed

Figure A-1. *Effectiveness of HR Roles*

Area	HR Mean	Line Mean
Providing HR services	7.3	6.1
Change consulting	6.2	4.7
Business partner	6.1	5.3
Development	6.5	5.2
Tailoring practices	6.8	5.3

Source: Comparing Line and HR Executives' Perceptions of HR Effectiveness: Services,
Roles and Contributions

that HR fulfilled its HR services role best and its "change consulting" role least effectively.

Finally, and most troubling, the Cornell researchers looked at how the two groups valued HR's overall contribution to the success of the firm. The HR executives gave themselves significantly higher ratings than the line executives. (See Figure A-2.)

The findings are not, perhaps, surprising. But—justified or not—they constitute a major hurdle. Perception is almost reality, and any HR department perceived as less than top quality will not be able to guide a company into the kind of human capital management that raises shareholder value.

Getting the House in Order

Organizations have to walk before they can run. And that means HR departments have to establish credibility through seamless performance of their basic operations before moving into more strategic areas. Line managers want to see that their staffing requirements are met. They want to see the HRIS system accurate and up to date. They want a compensation system that is easy to understand and lets them reward (and keep) their key talent. In short, they want to see the trains running on time. Only then will they be interested in HR's perspective on strategic change.

Figure A-2. *Effectiveness of HR Contributions*

Area	HR Mean	Line Mean
Performing the expected job	4.5	3.9
Responsive to customer needs	5.0	4.2
Enhancing competitiveness	5.0	3.8
Value-added contribution	5.0	4.1
Core competence	4.8	4.2

Source: Comparing Line and HR Executives' Perceptions of HR Effectiveness: Services, Roles and Contributions

The first step is for HR groups to assess their own effectiveness. That means taking stock, and asking the hard questions:

- What is the HR vision, strategy, and mission? How does it align with the overall company business plan?
- How is HR actually allocating its time and money?
- What functions are currently performed?
- What is the level of satisfaction for the customers HR serves (line executives and employees)?
- How does the organization compare to industry benchmarks in terms of cost and performance?
- Does the current structure still make sense?
- Is the right talent, with the necessary competencies, in place?

Conducting an HR audit can be very cathartic—in going through the process, line managers and HR managers often table their differences and find areas of agreement in terms of what needs "fixing." Successful organizations have figured out that transforming HR's function and processes requires in-depth analyses of current systems and the development of new HR business strategies that are in line with the company's business plan. HR must reduce costs and improve efficiencies by identifying existing problems, creating detailed solutions, and reinventing the HR structure. The following is one example of how investigating current processes can uncover hidden costs.

The $100,000 Form

A large airline recently discovered that a simple employee data change form was creating great confusion among its workers due to a design and communication error that, after multiple reviews, phone calls, and resubmissions of the form, was costing the company plenty of money.

Consider the following:

- 40,000 of the forms were received each year

- $15/hour employee takes five minutes to review, for a total cost of $50,000
- Wrong forms required a letter to be written; time + postage = $25,000
- 10 percent also required a phone call; time + phone expense = $2,500

By redesigning the form—or, even better, implementing technology to automate its employee data changes—the company had the potential to save as much as $100,000 annually. And that was just *one* form. The possibilities for increased efficiency and savings across the organization are huge.

Use Technology to Improve Service, Reduce Cost

HR technology—for example, online benefits enrollment, retirement planning, compensation and pension administration, and e-recruiting tools—can play a dramatic role in helping HR get its act together. But show caution with the intentions. Our Human Capital Index provides a fascinating group of statistics, showing that if the new technology is implemented with the fundamentals in mind—improving accuracy, service, and cost-effectiveness—it pays off in higher shareholder value (as much as 6.5 percent). But when HR groups use technology starting with less clear, less quantifiable goals—such as "enhancing communication" and "promoting culture"—implementing technology is actually linked to a whopping 14.3 percent decrease in market value. (See Figure A-3.)

The message? Stop fooling around. Stick with the basics. And get the HR house in order. Only then can organizations go about the very real business of maximizing shareholder value through superior human capital management.

Figure A-3. *Links Between HR Service Technology and Value Creation*

Practice	Impact on Market Value
Company uses HRSD technology to enhance communication	-7.7%
Company uses HRSD technology to promote culture	-6.6%
Company uses HRSD technology to improve transaction accuracy/integrity	+1.9%
Company uses HRSD technology to improve service	+2.3%
Company uses HRSD technology to reduce cost	+2.3%

Expected change associated with a significant (1SD) improvement in practice

Watson Wyatt's Human Capital Index®

About the Research

As noted in the Introduction, there are several key studies that form the backbone of this book. Below is a bit more information about this research.

The Human Capital Index™

In 1999, Watson Wyatt received responses to a structured questionnaire from human resources executives at more than 400 U.S.- and Canada-based publicly traded companies with at least three years of shareholder returns and a minimum of $100 million in revenue or market value. A wide range of questions was asked about how organizations carry out their human resources practices, including pay, developing people, communications, and staffing.

Responses were matched to objective financial measures including market value, three- and five-year total returns to shareholders (TRS) and Tobin's Q, an economist's ratio that measures an organization's ability to create value beyond its physical assets. Publicly available data from Hunt-Scanlon and Standard and Poor's Compustat databases was used to access the financial information needed.

To investigate the relationship between human capital practices and economic value creation, a series of regression analyses and cross-lagged panel correlation analyses was done, identifying a clear relationship between the effectiveness of a company's human capital and shareholder value creation. The relationship was so clear that a significant improvement in 30 key HR practices was associated with a 30 percent increase in market value. Using the regression equations and standard scoring conversion, total HCI scores were created for individual organization, so that results could be expressed on a scale of 0 to 100. An HCI score of 0 represents the poorest human capital management, while 100 is ideal—the summary score is the organization's Human Capital Index.

In 2000, a European HCI survey was conducted to gain a more global perspective on these issues. More than 250 responses from 16 countries were received. The survey included 200 questions, in six languages, and covered companies of all sizes and from all sectors of the economy—more than a third of participants are in the Euro 500 and more than a quarter are in the Global 500.

The European and North American HCI surveys used the same questions relating to finding, developing, supporting, and rewarding human capital. The European survey also included additional questions in these areas and on integration of HR policies across Europe, the effect of trade unions, and the degree of management hierarchy. The findings from the European study were similar to the North American results, with improvements in 19 key HR practices associated with a 26 percent increase in market value.

In early 2001, the HCI research was done again, this time including responses from more than 500 North American companies. In this most recent research, the participants reflected a broader view of business and included some larger, more prominent firms—80 were privately held firms, 61 companies had 10,000 or more employees and more than $5 billion in sales, and 34 companies had more than 50,000 employees. Fifty-one of these companies participated in both the 1999 and 2001 surveys.

The European and new North American data were then merged. The result was a complete respondent base of more than 750 companies in the United States, Canada, and Europe with at least three years of shareholder returns, 1000 or more employees, and a minimum of $100 million in revenues or market value.

Analysis began by identifying the key human capital constructs that drive firm performance. Although the survey questionnaire contained more than 130 items, most of these items were related to a few human capital areas identified in the researchers' experience and in previous research as key human capital drivers (e.g., rewards, communications, career development, culture, staffing). Note the following examples from the questionnaire (respondents were asked to indicate the degree to which they agree with the statement, on a five-point scale, from Strongly Disagree to Strongly Agree):

A. Among new job applicants, this company has an established reputation as a desirable place to work.
B. Professional new hires are usually already well equipped to perform their duties and do not require much, if any, additional training.
C. Hourly/clerical new hires are usually already well equipped to perform their duties and do not require much, if any, additional training.
D. It is usually fairly easy to find applicants who possess the skills this company most needs to remain competitive.
E. During the hiring process, job candidates are interviewed by a number of individuals, representing a cross-section of functional areas.
F. Recruiting efforts are specifically designed to support the company's business plan.
G. There is a formal recruiting strategy for filling critical skill positions (i.e., positions requiring special knowledge and competencies that are directly related to the company's ability).

Based on a prior assessment of the areas covered by each question, these items were combined into a single construct—recruiting and retention excellence—and Cronbach's alpha tests were performed to verify these as statistically valid constructs. Each construct developed was tested this way.

Many of the constructs that were formed by this method were strongly correlated with each other. In the next stage of the research, as many of the constructs as possible were combined into factors through factor analysis. In this method, constructs which had over one-third of their variation explained by the other constructs were combined using the optimal weighting scheme developed in the factor analysis, while others were included separately in the regressions. In this way, the potential effects of multicolinearity in the regressions were substantially reduced. The resulting regressions yielded the estimated effect of each factor or construct on firm performance. These estimated effects are the weights used to form the Human Capital Index raw score. These regressions were performed using both the European and North American databases along with important industry and financial control variables that would affect the firm's performance measure. Overall, these variables explained approximately 40 percent of the variation in firm performance. In addition, the human capital constructs were collectively significant at the 1 percent level. For purposes of exposition, the effects of individual questions have been disaggregated and are discussed in logical order.

The findings in the book report the expected change in market value associated with a significant improvement in a particular HCI practice. The 1999 HCI research found that improvements in 30 key HR practices were associated with an increase of 30 percent in market value. In 2001, the HCI research found that improvements in 53 key HR practices were associated with an increase of 47 percent in market value. To get an idea of the magnitude of this change, for the average firm in the sample, the standard deviation of their market value on a monthly basis over the last two years has been approximately 32 percent.

For example, the practice of having a formal recruiting strategy for filling critical skill positions received a score of 0.6 percent. If a company makes a significant improvement in that practice, the associated change in market value would be + 0.6 percent. What constitutes "significant?" It is a one standard deviation increase. And this standard deviation, of course, varies from item to item. Most answers to HCI questions are on a 1–5 scale, as a rule of thumb, so a one standard deviation change is a one-point movement from a 1 to a 2, 2 to a 3, and so on.

The majority of the combined findings from these surveys were consistent, making it a logical and useful tool from which to draw conclusions. It is important to point out, however, that there were notable differences in emphasis between the European and North American studies. For instance, certain questions about benefits and HR service delivery were included only in the North American survey. In addition, the database is weighted nearly 2 to 1 to North American companies, so the generalized findings should be considered with that in mind. Watson Wyatt will publish more about the similarities and differences between the studies in the future.

Some of the companies included in the global HCI research include American Express, BIC Corporation, Campbell Soup Company, DaimlerChrysler, General Motors Co., IBM, Kraft Foods, Liberty Mutual Group, and Siemens AG.

The Skeptic's Corner: Correlation or Causation?

Is there truly a causal relationship between human capital management and shareholder value? Or is it solely a correlation?

The debate has raged for years: How should we interpret the positive relationship between the quality of HR practices and economic outcomes? Do effective HR practices drive (cause) positive financial results or do positive financial results lead to better HR practices (i.e., successful business can afford higher quality HR programs).

We first addressed this in 1999 following the initial HCI research, which was the first to demonstrate correlation (a statistical relationship where two variables move together). It did not prove a direct cause and effect between the two variables (in this case good human capital management and high economic value creation), though we had evidence that it might. At that time we conceded that the relationship possibly runs in the opposite direction: Good financial performance gives organizations the resources and time to invest in human capital programs. Our hypothesis was, however, that the relationship moves both ways, creating a "virtuous cycle."

In addition—and important to note—the best-performing companies do not simply have more or more well-funded human capital programs. They have very *different* human capital portfolios compared with the lowest performing. High performers use certain programs (e.g., broad-based stock options) that others do not, and do not use, or use in a very different manner, some others (e.g., training for promotions). If it were true that good financial performance simply afforded rich companies the ability to implement elaborate HR programs, then one would expect them to apply these across the board. *The HCI results suggest that they do not.*

The HCI results are consistent with other studies that address these issues, and with the logical basis that organizations with better resources and processes should generally outperform inferior ones.

Further Watson Wyatt research on this causation issue has shown that the high HCI companies have outperformed in TRS compared with low HCI companies, demonstrating that the Human Capital Index thus far exhibits some predictive qualities.

But most importantly, the longitudinal relationship between financial outcomes and Human Capital Index scores over the last three years (over time) yields powerful new insights into answering the correlation versus causation question. (See Figure AP-1.)

- Correlation A is the correlation between 1999 HCI score and 2001 financial performance
- Correlation B is the correlation between 1999 financial performance and 2001 HCI score.

If financial performance drives HCI (i.e., more successful companies have the luxury of enhancing their human resources practices), then Correlation B should be larger than Correlation A.

If effective human capital practices drive financial performance, then Correlation A should be larger than Correlation B

As the cross-lag panel analysis below clearly shows, Correlation A is significantly larger than Correlation B—dramatic evidence that HR practices are not only associated with businesses outcomes but drive business outcomes. Moreover, a careful inspection of all the data in Figure AP-1 shows that for every available correlation calculated over time, the relationship between past HR practice and future financial performance is stronger than the relationship between past financial outcomes and future HR practices. We will be following this data prospectively in longitudinal studies, but for now the weight of the evidence clearly favors human capital practices as a *leading* rather than a *lagging* indicator of business success.

Figure AP-1. *Cross-Lag Panel Analysis of the Correlation Between Human Capital Index and Financial Outcomes*

Financial Outcome (Tobin's Q)	Human Capital Index 1999	Human Capital Index 2001
1997	.26	.26
1998	.29	.27
1999	.28	.19 (Correlation B)
2000	.41 (Correlation A)	.35

Watson Wyatt's Human Capital Index®

Positive Bias from HR Executives?

Could these results be biased because human resources executives have an overly rosy view of their human capital management practices?

We don't believe so, for two reasons. First, employee viewpoints corroborate many of the key HCI findings. It is possible that human resources executives view their own company's HR practices more favorably than do outside sources or their own employees. And the authors concede that their responses tend to be more alike than different—a tendency that causes a statistical phenomenon known as "restriction of range." For example, if we were trying to determine a relationship between height and weight, but the comparison range of heights spanned only one inch, it would be difficult to convey the relationship. For this study, the fact that strong statistical relationships between human capital management and shareholder value were found—in spite of this restriction of range—actually strengthens the findings.

WorkUSA® 2000

WorkUSA® 2000 identifies workplace perceptions and satisfaction and measures how well organizations are aligning employees with business strategies and goals. It answers questions like:

- What drives employee commitment?
- What are the organizational effects of these drivers?
- Which HR practices generate the highest commitment?
- What is the economic value of employee commitment?

The findings are based on the most recent research available. The *WorkUSA® 2000* database is the largest, most statistically representative and up-to-date survey in existence on the attitudes of American workers. It is not simply an aggregate of results from surveyed companies; instead, scientific sampling techniques were used to ensure the overall sampling error is less than ±1 percent.

The Employee Commitment Index (ECI) is a Watson Wyatt metric based on the *WorkUSA® 2000* research. It is derived from six key questions in the survey that when combined offer a reliable, robust measure of an employee's commitment to work—and to the company.

Employee commitment goes beyond old-fashioned loyalty; the Watson Wyatt ECI measures whether or not a company is an employer of choice. It measures the degree to which employees:

- Are satisfied with their job
- Are satisfied with their company
- Are proud to work for their company
- Would recommend the company to others
- Would remain with the company even if offered a comparable job elsewhere
- Would rate their company superior to others

Employee commitment is linked to the workforce's discretionary effort—an engaged, committed workforce will go the extra mile for the good of the organization. Employers that fail to inspire that level of commitment simply won't reap the same rewards.

In *WorkUSA® 2000,* the sixth such survey since 1987, Watson Wyatt surveyed 7500 U.S. workers at all levels of the full-time working U.S. population, representing various industries, including financial services, health care, high tech, manufacturing, retail trade, consumer products, and utilities about their attitudes toward their workplace and their employers. Questions addressed the key areas of:

- Leadership effectiveness
- Compensation and benefits
- Teamwork
- Work process effectiveness
- Communications
- Quality and customer service
- Adequacy of technology and other resources
- Physical work environment

- Decision making
- Diversity
- Supervision
- Flexible workplace
- Work-life balance
- Performance management
- Career development and training
- Job content and satisfaction

Strategic Rewards®

In the most recent (2000/2001) annual *Strategic Rewards®* survey, Watson Wyatt surveyed 410 U.S. and Canada employers, employing nearly 3 million full- and part-time employees. While nearly one-quarter (24 percent) of the respondents were information-based companies, all major industry sectors were represented.

In select instances, data was drawn from Watson Wyatt's *Supplemental Survey of Top-Performing Employees.* In that study, over 3600 employees—identified as top performers by their organizations—gave their opinions on how companies can successfully attract and retain top talent.

The Fortune Research

In 1997, while managing director of the Hay Group's research practice, Bruce Pfau led a team to conduct a follow-up study on the human capital practices of *Fortune* magazine's 1997 list of the "World's Most Admired Companies." The initial Fortune/Hay Group study began by identifying the 500 largest public companies in the world, as listed in the FORTUNE Global 500. These companies were then divided into 19 global industry groupings, and a questionnaire was developed for each of the groupings. The questionnaire listed companies in that particular industry that were either represented on the FORTUNE Global 500 list or had scored highly on previous surveys of most admired firms.

The questionnaire asked that each listed company be rated in each of nine performance dimensions. The questionnaires were sent to industry-specific lists of 5000 senior executives, outside boards of directors, and financial analysts with relevant expertise. Returns were tabulated to calculate an overall "reputation score" for each company using an average respondents' rating.

The research team then set out to identify business practices that helped these companies to attain their status. The research revealed that, of nine dimensions studied, the one with the strongest correlation to a company's overall "reputation score" was the ability to attract, retain, and develop talented people.

The team then conducted in-depth interviews with the chief executives, chief operations officers, and human resources officers at 18 highly rated companies. Interviewees included several organizations that had earned the top rating in their industry grouping, along with others that scored highly in an industry grouping or in other rankings of highly admired firms. Interviews focused on key questions in critical management areas, including attraction and recruitment, retention, training and development, motivation, rewards and recognition, aligning business and HR strategies, and globalization. Several key themes emerged from the research—namely, that highly admired and successful companies take their HR responsibilities more seriously than their competitors.

Companies included Bayer, Bertlesmann, Citibank, Daimler-Benz, Dai Nippon, Disney, General Electric, Gillette, Federal Express, Intel, L'Oreal, Nestle, Nucor, Procter & Gamble, Roche Holdings, SBC Communications, Smith Kline Beecham, and Sony.

Other Watson Wyatt Research Studies Cited in the Book:

Executive Pay in 2001: The Land of Opportunity
Executive Pay in 2000: Superior Pay for Superior Performance

1999 Communications Study: Linking Communications
  with Strategy to Achieve Business Goals
Strategic Rewards®: The New Employment Deals.
  1999/2000.
Maximizing the Potential of Your 401(k) Plan. 2000.

NOTES

Introduction

1. Detailed descriptions of our research methodologies can be found in the Appendix.
2. *Watson Wyatt's Human Capital Index™, 2001Research,* Watson Wyatt Worldwide, 2001
3. *WorkUSA® 2000 Employee Commitment and the Bottom Line, Study of Employee Attitudes and Opinions,* Watson Wyatt Worldwide, 2000.
4. The generally higher TRS figures presented in the WorkUSA® and Strategic Rewards® findings are due to the significant differences in overall stock market performance in recent years. WorkUSA® and Strategic Rewards® data were compiled in 1996–1998. Watson Wyatt's Human Capital™ data were collected 1996–2000.
5. *Playing to Win: Strategic Rewards® in the War for Talent, Fifth Annual Survey Report 2000/2001,* Watson Wyatt Worldwide, 2001.
6. Peter G. Peterson, "Will America Grow Up Before It Grows Old?" *The Atlantic Monthly,* May, 1996.
7. Rebecca Gardyn, "Who's the Boss?," *American Demographics,* September, 2000, 53–58.

Chapter 1

1. Bradford D. Smart, PhD., *Topgrading: How Leading Companies Win By Hiring, Coaching and Keeping the Best People* (Paramus, New Jersey: Prentice Hall Press, 1999), 5, 45–55.
2. *Watson Wyatt's Human Capital Index™, 2001 Research,* Watson Wyatt Worldwide, 2001.
3. Ibid.
4. "Recruiting Industry Will Hit $15 Billion Mark By 2005 According to Hunt-Scanlon Advisors," press release, Hunt-Scanlon, September 19, 2000.
5. Bruce N. Pfau, *Human Resources Lessons from the World's Most Admired Companies: A Hay Group White Paper,* Hay Group, 1997, 14.
6. Ibid.
7. Ibid.

8. Society for Human Resource Management/Employee Management Association 2000 Cost Per Hire and Staffing Metrics Survey, Summary of Findings, 2000, 3.
9. "Online Recruiting Industry Will Hit $8 Billion Mark By 2005 According to Hunt-Scanlon Advisors," press release, Hunt-Scanlon, September 14, 2000.
10. Recruiters Network, The Association for Internet Recruiting, Internet Recruiting Poll, July 9, 1999.
11. Society for Human Resource Management/Employee Management Association 2000 Cost Per hire and Staffing Metrics Survey, 2000, 3.
12. Wetfeet.com, "Recruitment Marketing Strategies: Building an Employer Brand that Attracts Talent" Volume 1, 2000, 5.
13. Wetfeet.com, "WebRecruiting 2000," 2000, 2.

Chapter 2

1. Bruce N. Pfau, *Human Resources Lessons from the World's Most Admired Companies: A Hay Group White Paper,* Hay Group, 1997.

Chapter 3

1. WetFeet.com, "Recruitment Marketing Strategies: Building an Employer Brand that Attracts Talent," Volume 1, 2000, 4.
2. Ibid.
3. Bruce N. Pfau, *Human Resources Lessons from the World's Most Admired Companies: A Hay Group White Paper,* Hay Group, 1997.
4. David Dell, Nathan Ainspan, et al., The Conference Board, "Engaging Employees Through Your Brand: Preliminary Findings," April 19, 2001.
5. Mary Jo Hatch, Mogens Holten Larsen, and Majken Schultz, *The Expressive Organization: Linking Identity, Reputation and the Corporate Brand* (Oxford: Oxford University Press, 2000), 1.
6. Wetfeet.com, "Recruitment Marketing Strategies: Building an Employer Brand That Attracts Talent," Volume 1, 2000, 4.
7. Ibid., 5.
8. Ibid., 30.
9. Ibid., 31.
10. David Dell, Nathan Ainspan, et al., The Conference Board, "Engaging Employees Through Your Brand: Preliminary Findings," April 19, 2001.

Chapter 4

1. *Watson Wyatt's Human Capital Index™, 2001Research,* Watson Wyatt Worldwide, 2001.

2. Potter, Edward E., and Yi K. Ngan, "Estimating the Potential Productivity and Real Wage Effects of Employee Involvement." Washington: Employment Policy Foundation, 1996.
3. John Parkington, "Employee Involvement in the Hiring Process," Watson Wyatt, 2000, 1.
4. Ibid.
5. Potter, Edward E., and Yi K. Ngan, "Estimating the Potential Productivity and Real Wage Effects of Employee Involvement." Washington: Employment Policy Foundation, 1996.

Chapter 5

1. *What do Employees Really Want? The Perception vs. The Reality,* Korn/Ferry International.
2. "Know Future," *The Economist,* December 23, 2000, 2 (Web version).

Chapter 6

1. Elizabeth G. Chambers, Mark Foulon, Helen Handfield-Jones, Steven M. Hankin, and Edward G. Michaels III, "The War for Talent," *The McKinsey Quarterly,* no. 3 (1998): 44–57.
2. Alfie Kohn, *Punished by Rewards: the trouble with gold stars, incentive plans, A's, praise, and other bribes* (New York: Houghton Mifflin Co., 1993).

Chapter 7

1. *Executive Pay in 2001: The Land of Opportunity,* Watson Wyatt Worldwide, 2001.
2. Ibid.
3. ECS Geographic Report on Top Management Compensation, Volume 2, Watson Wyatt Data Services, 2000/2001, 1235.
4. *Executive Pay in 2001: The Land of Opportunity,* Watson Wyatt Worldwide, 2001, 13.
5. Ibid.
6. Robert Holthausen and David Larcker, "Performance Consequences of Requiring Target Stock Ownership Levels," working paper, December 1999.
7. Ira T. Kay, *CEO Pay and Shareholder Value: Helping the U.S. Win the Global Economic War* (Boca Raton: St. Lucie Press, 1998), xiii.
8. *Stock Option Overhang: Shareholder Boon or Shareholder Burden?,* The 2001 Study, Watson Wyatt Worldwide, 2001.
9. *Executive Pay in 2001: The Land of Opportunity,* Watson Wyatt Worldwide, 2001.

10. Ira T. Kay and Steven E. Rushbrook, "The U.S. Executive Pay Model," *World-at-Work Journal* 10, no. 1 (first quarter 2001).
11. Ira T. Kay, *CEO Pay and Shareholder Value: Helping the U.S. Win the Global Economic War,* (Boca Raton: St. Lucie Press, 1998), 3–4.
12. Ibid.
13. The Black-Scholes stock option pricing methodology uses a sophisticated mathematical formula to put a present value or economic value on a stock option. This method, or related methods, are used by professional option traders to determine whether they should buy or sell an option. It has been adopted by compensation professionals to estimate the value of employee (underline employee) stock options. It allows them to add the value of the stock option grant to salary and bonus to yield Total Direct Compensation.

   The Black-Scholes value tends to be 20 percent to 70 percent of the grant value (number of options 3 exercise price). The value for any specific company depends upon stock price volatility, dividends, time period, and so on. For example, if the Black-Scholes percentage was 50, then 1000 options granted at a $20 exercise price (with a market price of $20) would have a present value of $10,000 (50% 3 $20 3 1000).

Chapter 8

1. Joseph Glasi, Douglas Kruse, James Sesil, Maya Kroumova, Ed Carberry, "Stock Options, Corporate Performance and Organizational Change," The National Center for Employee Ownership, 3.
2. Ibid., 14.
3. Ibid., 12.
4. Ibid.
5. Ibid., 14.
6. Ibid.
7. Ibid., 17.
8. Ibid., 21.
9. Ibid., 3.
10. Stock Option Overhang: Shareholder Boon or Shareholder Burden?, The 2001 Study. Watson Wyatt Worldwide, 2001, 5.
11. Ibid.
12. Ibid.
13. Ibid.
14. Ibid.
15. Ibid.
16. Ibid.

Chapter 9

1. Edward E. Lawler III, *Strategic Pay: Aligning Organizational Strategies and Pay Systems* (San Francisco: Jossey-Bass, Inc. 1990), 61.
2. Patrick Kelly, "Bank One Axes Senior Retirement Plan," *American Banker,* March 19, 2001.
3. Ira T. Kay, *CEO Pay and Shareholder Value: Helping the U.S. Win the Global Economic War,* (Boca Raton: St. Lucie Press, 1998), 93.
4. Ibid., 14.
5. James K. Galbraith, *Created Unequal: The Crisis in American Pay* (New York: Free Press, 1998).
6. Ira T. Kay, CEO Pay and Shareholder Value: Helping the U.S. Win the Global Economic War, (Boca Raton: St. Lucie Press, 1998).
7. Edward E. Lawler III, *Strategic Pay: Aligning Organizational Strategies and Pay Systems* (San Francisco: Jossey-Bass, Inc. 1990), 71.

Chapter 11

1. Kevin Freiberg and Jackie Freiberg, *Nuts: Southwest Airlines' Crazy Recipe for Business and Personal Success* (Austin: Bard Press, 1996), 274.
2. James L. Heskett, Thomas O. Jones, Gary W. Loveman, W. Earl Sasser, Jr., and Leonard A Schlesinger, "Putting the Service-Profit Chain to Work," *Harvard Business Review,* March 1994, 164–174.
3. Marcus Buckingham and Curt Coffman, *First, Break All the Rules: What the World's Greatest Managers Do Differently* (New York: Simon & Schuster, 1999), 32.
4. Ibid., 33.
5. James L. Heskett, Thomas O. Jones, Gary W. Loveman, W. Earl Sasser, Jr., and Leonard A Schlesinger, "Putting the Service-Profit Chain to Work," *Harvard Business Review,* March 1994, 164.
6. Ibid.
7. Ibid., 165.
8. Ibid., 166.
9. Anthony J. Rucci, Steven P. Kirn, and Richard T. Quinn, "The Employee-Customer Profit Chain at Sears," *Harvard Business Review,* January–February 1998, 84.

Chapter 12

1. Tom Peters, *Thriving on Chaos* (New York: Knopf, 1987), 382.
2. Linda Moran and Jack D. Orsburn, *The New Self-Directed Work Teams: Mastering the Challenge* (New York: McGraw-Hill, 1990), 90.

3. Gary Hamel and C.K. Prahalad, *Competing for the Future* (Boston: Harvard Business School Press, 1994).
4. "Intel Is…Intel Isn't…"
   <http://www.intel.com/jobs/workplace/working.htm>

Chapter 13

1. "100 Best Companies to Work for in America," *Fortune,* January 10, 2000, 90.
2. Ibid.
3. 2001 Society for Human Resources Management Benefits Survey, 2000, 4.
4. www.workfamily.com/open/studies.htm
5. Ibid.
6. Ibid.
7. "Holding a Job, Having a Life: Strategies for Change," Executive Summary, Work in America Institute, 2000, v.
8. Sarah Fister Gale, "Formalized Flextime: The Perk That Brings Productivity," *Workforce,* February, 2001, 40.
9. *Work/Life Today,* National Institute of Business Management, September, 1997.
10. Sarah Fister Gale, "Formalized Flextime: The Perk That Brings Productivity," *Workforce,* February, 2001, 40.

Chapter 14

1. John P. Kotter, "John P. Kotter on What Leaders Really Do," (Boston: *Harvard Business Review,* 1999), 51.
2. *Leadership in the Global Economy,* Watson Wyatt Worldwide, 1997.
3. John P. Kotter, "John P. Kotter on What Leaders Really Do," (Boston: *Harvard Business Review,* 1999), 1.
4. Ibid., 10.
5. *Leadership in the Global Economy,* Watson Wyatt Worldwide, 1997.
6. Ibid.
7. Bruce N. Pfau, *Human Resources Lessons from the World's Most Admired Companies: A Hay Group White Paper*, Hay Group, 1997.

Chapter 15

1. Bruce N. Pfau, *Human Resources Lessons from the World's Most Admired Companies: A Hay Group White Paper,* Hay Group, 1997, 24–27.
2. Ibid., 24.
3. Ibid., 25.

4. James A. Belasco, *Teaching the Elephant to Dance* (New York: Crown, 1990), 13.
5. John P. Kotter, "John P. Kotter on What Leaders Really Do," (Boston: *Harvard Business Review,* 1999), 74–92.
6. Ibid.

Chapter 16

1. Gary Hamel and C.K. Prahalad, *Competing for the Future* (Boston: Harvard Business School Press, 1994), 11.
2. *2000 SHRM Retention Practices Survey,* Society for Human Resources Management, 2000, 8.
3. Sanford M Jacoby, "Are Career Jobs Headed for Extinction?" *California Management Review* (1 October 1999).
4. Jeffrey Pfeffer, *The Human Equation* (Boston: Harvard Business School Press, 1998), 69.
5. Gary Hamel and C. K. Prahalad, *Competing for the Future* (Boston: Harvard Business School Press, 1994), 11.
6. Ibid.
7. Bruce N. Pfau, *Human Resources Lessons from the World's Most Admired Companies: A Hay Group White Paper,* Hay Group, 1997, 15.
8. Jeffrey Pfeffer, *The Human Equation* (Boston: Harvard Business School Press, 1998), 182.

Chapter 17

1. Lisa M. Lynch and Sandra E. Black, "Beyond the Incidence of Training: Evidence from a National Employers Survey," National Bureau of Economic Research, Working Paper Series, (August 1995).
2. Laurie J. Bassi and Mark E. Van Buren, "Sharpening the Leading Edge," *1999 American Society for Training and Development's State of the Industry Report.*
3. Richard Luss, *Training, Productivity and Shareholder Returns,* Watson Wyatt Worldwide working paper, 1999.
4. Lester Thurow, "Building Wealth: The New Rules for Individuals, Companies and Nations." *Atlantic* (June 1999).

Chapter 18

1. Jeffrey Pfeffer, *The Human Equation* (Boston: Harvard Business School Press, 1998), 94.
2. Ibid.
3. Ibid., 95.

Chapter 19

1. *The Net Effect: eHR and the Internet,* Watson Wyatt Worldwide, 2000.
2. Ibid.
3. Ibid.
4. *Communications Study,* Watson Wyatt Worldwide, 1999.

Chapter 20

1. Maury A. Peiperl, "Getting 360 Degree Feedback Right," *Harvard Business Review,* January 2001, 142.
2. Carol Hymowitz, "Do '360' Job Reviews By Colleagues Promote Honesty or Insults?" *Wall Street Journal,* 12 December 2000, B1.
3. Maury A. Peiperl, "Getting 360 Degree Feedback Right," *Harvard Business Review,* January 2001, 142.
4. Lyle Spencer and Signe Spencer, *Competence at Work: Models for Superior Performance,* (John Wiley & Sons, 1993).
5. Carol Hymowitz, "Do '360' Job Reviews By Colleagues Promote Honesty or Insults?" *Wall Street Journal,* 12 December 2000, B1.
6. Smither J. W., London M., Vasilopoulos N. I., Reilly R. R., Millsap R. E., Salvemini N., "An examination of the effects of an upward feedback program over time." *Personnel Psychology,* 48. 1–34

Afterword

1. Thomas A. Steward, "Taking on the Last Bureaucracy," *Fortune* (15 January 1996): 105.

Appendix

1. Bruce N. Pfau, *Human Resources Lessons from the World's Most Admired Companies: A Hay Group White Paper,* Hay Group, 1997, 14.

INDEX

ABOUT THE AUTHORS

Bruce N. Pfau, Ph.D., is National Practice Director of Organization Effectiveness at Watson Wyatt Worldwide and has over two decades of experience in helping clients build high-performance organizations. Dr. Pfau is an internationally recognized expert in employee motivation, corporate culture, and organization management, and is a pioneer on the subject of aligning human resources practices and business performance.

Ira T. Kay, Ph.D., is director of the U.S. compensation practice at Watson Wyatt. An influential writer and speaker on strategic and executive compensation issues, Dr. Kay is the author of *Value at the Top* and *CEO Pay and Shareholder Value*.